A Text Book of

ENTERPRISE RESOURCE PLANNING

FOR
MCA : (MANAGEMENT) : SEMESTER – II
SUBJECT CODE : IT24

AS PER NEW REVISED SYLLABUS OF PUNE UNIVERSITY FOR
MCA (PART II) FROM ACADEMIC YEAR 2012-2013

JYOTINDRA ZAVERI
Computer Engineering (Germany)
I.T. Professional Since 1975
Formerly with IBM

N1199

ENTERPRISE RESOURCE PLANNING　　　　　　　　　　　ISBN 978-93-82448-90-7
First Edition : January 2013
© : Author

The text of this publication, or any part thereof, should not be reproduced or transmitted in any form or stored in any computer storage system or device for distribution including photocopy, recording, taping or information retrieval system or reproduced on any disc, tape, perforated media or other information storage device etc., without the written permission of Author with whom the rights are reserved. Breach of this condition is liable for legal action.

Every effort has been made to avoid errors or omissions in this publication. In spite of this, errors may have crept in. Any mistake, error or discrepancy so noted and shall be brought to our notice shall be taken care of in the next edition. It is notified that neither the publisher nor the author or seller shall be responsible for any damage or loss of action to any one, of any kind, in any manner, therefrom.

Published By :	Printed By :
NIRALI PRAKASHAN Abhyudaya Pragati, 1312, Shivaji Nagar, Off J.M. Road, PUNE – 411005 Tel - (020) 25512336/37/39, Fax - (020) 25511379 Email : niralipune@pragationline.com	Repro Knowledgecast Limited, Thane

DISTRIBUTION CENTRES

PUNE
Nirali Prakashan
119, Budhwar Peth, Jogeshwari Mandir Lane
Pune 411002, Maharashtra
Tel : (020) 2445 2044, 66022708
Fax : (020) 2445 1538
Email : bookorder@pragationline.com

MUMBAI
Nirali Prakashan
385, S.V.P. Road, Rasdhara Co-op. Hsg. Society Ltd.,
Girgaum, Mumbai 400004, Maharashtra
Tel : (022) 2385 6339 / 2386 9976,
Fax : (022) 2386 9976
Email : niralimumbai@pragationline.com

DISTRIBUTION BRANCHES

NAGPUR
Pratibha Book Distributors
Above Maratha Mandir, Shop No. 3, First Floor,
Rani Jhanshi Square, Sitabuldi, Nagpur 440012,
Maharashtra, Tel : (0712) 254 7129

BENGALURU
Pragati Book House
House No. 1,Sanjeevappa Lane, Avenue Road Cross,
Opp. Rice Church, Bengaluru – 560002.
Tel : (080) 64513344, 64513355,
Mob : 9880582331, 9845021552
Email:bharatsavla@yahoo.com

JALGAON
Nirali Prakashan
34, V. V. Golani Market, Navi Peth, Jalgaon 425001,
Maharashtra, Tel : (0257) 222 0395
Mob : 9423491860

KOLHAPUR
Nirali Prakashan
New Mahadvar Road,
Kedar Plaza, 1st Floor Opp. IDBI Bank
Kolhapur 416 012, Maharashtra. Mob : 9855046155

CHENNAI
Pragati Books
9/1, Montieth Road, Behind Taas Mahal, Egmore,
Chennai 600008 Tamil Nadu, Tel : (044) 6518 3535,
Mob : 94440 01782 / 98450 21552 / 98805 82331
Email : bharatsavla@yahoo.com

RETAIL OUTLETS
PUNE

Pragati Book Centre
157, Budhwar Peth, Opp. Ratan Talkies,
Pune 411002, Maharashtra
Tel : (020) 2445 8887 / 6602 2707, Fax : (020) 2445 8887

Pragati Book Centre
Amber Chamber, 28/A, Budhwar Peth,
Appa Balwant Chowk, Pune : 411002, Maharashtra,
Tel : (020) 20240335 / 66281669
Email : pbcpune@pragationline.com

Pragati Book Centre
676/B, Budhwar Peth, Opp. Jogeshwari Mandir,
Pune 411002, Maharashtra
Tel : (020) 6601 7784 / 6602 0855

PBC Book Sellers & Stationers
152, Budhwar Peth, Pune 411002, Maharashtra
Tel : (020) 2445 2254 / 6609 2463

MUMBAI
Pragati Book Corner
Indira Niwas, 111 - A, Bhavani Shankar Road, Dadar (W), Mumbai 400028, Maharashtra
Tel : (022) 2422 3526 / 6662 5254
Email : pbcmumbai@pragationline.com

www.pragationline.com　　　　　　　　　　　　　　　　　　　　info@pragationline.com

ABOUT THE AUTHOR

Prof. Jyotindra Zaveri (aka Jyoti) is an IT consultant and trainer and has done his engineering in the field of Computer Science from Germany.

- IT professional since 1975.
- Specialist in ERP and Digital Marketing.
- Sought after visiting faculty and speaker at seminars.
- Designed and developed ERP Software for several SMEs.
- He has been working with innovative technologies in IT to build a digital ecosystem, to empower users. He has mastered fifteen digital platforms and specialises in topics such as Social Media, ERP, CRM, and e-Commerce.
- He is passionate about Business Process Re-engineering (BPR) and challenging the legacy methods. He enjoys working with motivated and inspiring people providing creative solutions to business needs.
- He specialises in digital platforms with a passion for tapping the power of the social media and related technologies and applying them for business development.
- Travelled extensively around the world: Bahrain, France, Germany, Italy, Japan, Malaysia, Netherland, Singapore, Switzerland, Thailand, UAE, UK, and USA.
- IT consultant with knowledge of computer hardware, software and Internet technologies; which is rather a unique combination.
- After completing studies, his first job was in IBM (1975). He completed his training in Leipzig, Germany.
- He has written seven books to date.
- He has over 36 years of experience in IT, combined with academic credentials in Electronics and Electrical Engineering from VJTI, Mumbai, India.
- See month-by-month and year-by-year track-record since …1975 at http://www.dnserp.com/track_record.htm

PREFACE

I had an opportunity to design and develop Enterprise Resource Planning (ERP) software for small and medium size enterprises in India and overseas. My ERP Package is being used by several SMEs in India for over a decade. This has given me invaluable experience in the field of designing, developing and implementation of ERP. While implementing ERP systems in these organisations I observed lack of comprehension as far as the basic concept of ERP is concerned. I am therefore delighted that this important subject has been included in the syllabus of post-graduate students. The inclusion of this subject is the first significant step towards becoming a confident manager in the field of business using ERP software system.

Here I would like to caution students that although ERP is basically a software, this book is not focusing on computer programming per se, but is focusing on understanding the basic procedures such as sales, purchase, accounts, etc., from the management point of view. Like medicine there is an expiry date attached to Information Technology and ERP software is no exception.

Technology and management styles change rapidly and thus to keep abreast of all changes I have added key on-line resources at the end of each chapter. I strongly recommend all readers to follow these sites and gain knowledge of the latest in the field, and get involved in discussions with your peers. These websites and links will also help you to get in touch with experts easily.

My sincere request to the faculty, who will be teaching this subject, is to carry out the exercises/activities given at the end of each chapter to get a better understanding of the ERP subject. At the same time I strongly advise students to seriously follow and do the same to appreciate the subject from a practical point of view.

An outstanding team of dedicated professionals at Nirali Prakashan made the creation of this book a pleasure. Teams led by Mr. Jignesh Furia, MD and enthusiastically backed by Ms. Nirja Sharma played a large role in shaping the book and then publishing it.

I thus take this opportunity to thank the publisher Nirali Prakashan, the team consisting of Mr. Malik Shaikh, Mr. Prasad R. Chintakindi, Ms. Sarita Bansal, Ms. Sarika, Ms. Neha Deshpande and all others involved in the publishing of this book especially prescribed for University students. I am grateful to Mr. Jignesh Furia, in commanding his team to compile this book and print for your benefit. Last but not the least I must thank Ms. Nirja Sharma who meticulously edited and patiently followed up with me right from start to finish.

Finally, I am indebted to my two daughters Preksha, an IT professional and Amrapali, who has undertaken research in Bioinformatics, for trying to surpass me, and therefore compelling me to keep up with the state-of-the-art technology.

I hope this book would not only be interesting for the students but also be a source of inspiration for them to undertake further specialisation in ERP.

Any comments (positive or negative), feedback, corrections and suggestions from the readers will be highly appreciated.

Please communicate by email to j.zaveri@dnserp.com

Jyotindra Zaveri, Pune, India.
Website www.dnserp.com

SYLLABUS

1. **Enterprise Resource Planning**
   1.1 Introduction
   1.2 What Is ERP?
   1.3 Need of ERP
   1.4 Advantage of ERP
   1.5 Growth of ERP
2. **ERP and related technologies**
   2.1 Business Process Re-Engineering (BPR)
   2.2 Management Information System (MIS)
   2.3 Decision Support System (DSS)
   2.4 Executive Support System (ESS)
   2.5 Data Warehousing, Data Mining
   2.6 On-Line Analytical Processing (OLAP)
   2.7 Supply Chain Management
   2.8 Customer Relationship Management
3. **ERP Modules and Vendors**
   3.1 Finance
   3.2 Production Planning, Control and Management
   3.3 Sales and Distribution
   3.4 Human Resource Management
   3.5 Inventory Control System
   3.6 Quality Management
   3.7 ERP market, Comparison of Current ERP Packages and Vendors, like; SAP, Oracle, PeopleSoft, BAAN etc.
   3.8 Disadvantages of Non-ERP sys. Importance of ERP vice versa In-house Applications
   3.9 Benefits of Integration
   3.10 Standardisation of Data Code
4. **ERP Implementation Life Cycle**
   4.1 Evaluation and Selection of ERP Package
   4.2 Project planning, Implementation,
   4.3 Team Training and Testing
   4.4 End User Training and Going Live
   4.5 Post Evaluation and Maintenance
   4.6 Role of Organisation Management and Vendor
5. **ERP Case Studies**
   5.1 Post Implementation Review of ERP Packages
   5.2 Case Studies in Manufacturing, Services and Others Organisations
   5.3 Customisation of ERP for Different Types of Industries

CONTENTS

1. Enterprise Resource Planning   1.1 - 1.6

    1.1 Introduction   1.1

    1.2 The Definition of ERP   1.2

    1.3 What Is ERP?   1.2

    1.4 Need for ERP   1.2

    1.5 Advantages of ERP   1.3

    1.6 Growth of ERP   1.4

    1.7 Global Scenario   1.4

    • Practice Questions   1.6

    • Activity   1.6

2. ERP Related Technologies   2.1 - 2.24

    2.1 Introduction   2.1

    2.2 Business Process Re-Engineering (BPR)   2.3

    2.3 Management Information System (MIS)   2.7

    2.4 Decision Support System (DSS)   2.9

    2.5 Executive Support System (ESS)   2.11

    2.6 Data Warehousing, Data Mining   2.13

    2.7 On-Line Analytical Processing (OLAP)   2.16

    2.8 Supply Chain Management   2.17

    2.9 Customer Relationship Management (CRM)   2.21

    • Practice Questions   2.24

    • Activity   2.24

3. ERP Modules and Vendors 3.1 - 3.92
    3.1 Finance 3.2
    3.2 Production Planning, Control and Management 3.4
    3.3 Sales and Distribution 3.22
    3.4 Quality Management 3.30
    3.5 Human Resource Management 3.34
    3.6 Inventory Control System 3.39
    3.7 ERP market, Comparison of Current ERP Packages and Vendors like SAP, Oracle, PeopleSoft, BAAN etc. 3.41
    3.8 Disadvantages of non-ERP Systems Importance of ERP vice-versa In-house Applications 3.58
    3.9 Benefits of Integration 3.59
    3.10 Standardisation of data Code 3.64
    3.11 Example: ERP modules complete list with details of master, transactions, and Reports 3.67
- Practice Questions 3.92
- Activity 3.92

4. ERP Implementation Life Cycle 4.1 - 4.36
    4.1 Evaluation and Selection of ERP Package 4.4
    4.2 Project Planning and Implementation 4.14
    4.3 Team Training and Testing 4.27
    4.4 End User Training and Going Live 4.30
    4.5 Post Evaluation and Maintenance 4.32
    4.6 Role of Organisation Management and Vendor 4.33
- Practice Questions 4.36
- Activity 4.36

5. ERP Case Studies 5.1 - 5.56
    5.1 Post Implementation Review of ERP Packages 5.1
    5.2 In Manufacturing, Services and Other Organisations 5.9
    5.3 Customisation of ERP for Different Types of Industries 5.46
- Practice Questions 5.56
- Activity 5.56

***

Chapter 1...

ENTERPRISE RESOURCE PLANNING

1.1 Introduction

1.2 The Definition of ERP

1.3 What Is ERP?

1.4 Need for ERP

1.5 Advantages of ERP

1.6 Growth of ERP

1.7 Global Scenario

- Practice Questions
- Activity

Learning Objectives

After going through this unit, you will be able to:

- Discuss what ERP is?
- Explain the need for ERP.
- Examine the advantages of ERP.
- Describe and discuss the growth of ERP.

1.1 Introduction

If you visit a company and ask a question: "How many computers do you have in your company"? Typically, the answer would be: "Oh! We have fifty computers" or "We have computers / laptops for all our top managers," and so on. However, the problem arises when the CEO or the top brass of an organisation do not get the information they require. On enquiring, they typically get these answers; "Sir, the person concerned is not available presently" or "I have the file ready but I'm unable to submit it as there is a virus in my PC."

In other words, in spite of having so many computers the top management does not get instant reports. So how do we solve the problem? Well, the solution is to install one Server computer and a single software. Such software is called ERP.

1.2 The Definition of ERP

Enterprise Resource Planning (ERP) systems integrate internal and external management information across an entire organisation, embracing finance / accounting, manufacturing, sales and service, customer relationship management, purchase, etc. ERP systems automate this activity with an integrated software application. The purpose of ERP is to facilitate the flow of information between all business functions within the perimeter of the organisation and manage the connections with external stakeholders.

Author's definition

Enterprise Resource Planning system is a business management system that links all business activities automatically to provide all the required information and data to the decision-makers of the organisation.

1.3 What is ERP?

ERP is an acronym for Enterprise Resource Planning. This software is used by and for the entire organisation; hence the word Enterprise in the acronym. For example, in a manufacturing company, the term *resources* refer to Man, Money, Material, and Machine. The last word in the acronym *Planning*, refers to planning of these resources. That is, monitoring and reporting the status of man, money, material, and machine.

ERP is thus the software to manage and plan the resources of an organisation.

1.4 Need for ERP

Traditionally, a few experienced people within the organisation managed most businesses. However, it was realised that depending on some people may not be a good approach as the concerned person(s) may not always be available when required, either due to absence or they being pre-occupied with other tasks. The top management would then be compelled to wait for the person concerned to be available to perform the task at hand. It was circumstances like these, which necessitated defining a business process to eliminate the dependency on a person.

For instance, receiving an order is a business process. Making payment is a business process. Assembling a product is a business process. Now, let us define these processes, make a list and state their inter-relationships. This would become the business logic, which in turn would be translated into computer program logic. Such a program or software package is called ERP software.

With the help of ERP software, business can be managed without depending on people as the entire business process is built-in within the computer program.

1.5 Advantages of ERP

There are many advantages of a ERP Software package. For the top management, the advantages are as follows:

(a) The management can act confidently based on real time factual inputs.

(b) The operational efficiency is improved.

(c) It gives the enterprise the edge it needs to succeed.

(d) Even small and medium business (SMB) units can use ERP software to achieve a competitive advantage.

(e) It introduces organised and disciplined approach in the staff, as it does not accept any shortcuts.

(f) It reduces manual work.

(g) It eliminates the inefficient paper-based business processes. It makes the organisation less paper-dependent thus becoming more efficient.

(h) It can provide real-time and online MIS (Management Information System) for the management to know the exact status of the business at a click of the mouse and enables it to take timely business decisions.

(i) It allows cost control and cost reduction at every stage and improvement in profitability.

(j) It enables organisations to closely integrate their business processes with those of their trading partners.

(k) It enables increase in sales and faster processing of sale orders in turn means faster money.

(l) It allows better tracking of inventory.

(m) It provides better after sales-service to customers.

(n) It improves financial practices.

1.6 Growth of ERP

It is a well-known fact that Information Technology is developing rapidly. Like all other softwares, ERP software is also changing rapidly. The growth of ERP has been exponential, which means; a lot of improvisations and modifications are achieved in a short span of time leading to exponential growth in demand.

Presently, there is short supply of ERP professionals, which means companies are willing to pay higher salaries to employees proficient in ERP.

1.7 Global Scenario

ERP grew steadily at a much faster rate from 1985 to 2005. However, in last few years, the growth has not been significant due to many setbacks that have made companies adopt a cautious approach to implementing ERP. ERP is sold by 'per user license', meaning the user organisation pays the ERP vendor (supplier) for each user. So, if the numbers of employees are growing by say 20%, then the number of licenses sold also proportionately increases by 20%. This is the natural growth path of ERP companies.

Information Technology is changing at an exponential rate. New technology makes the old one obsolete. In other words, most IT companies change the software by offering better and faster versions. This process is called upgradation. This is not new. As we know Microsoft is always in the process of upgrading its Windows Operating System. In last fifteen years, many versions and upgrades have been sold, such as Windows 95 to Windows 98, Windows XP, Windows 7, Windows 8 and so on. Similarly, most ERP companies offer upgrades and make lots of money in the process. The end-user organisation thus does not have a choice but to upgrade the newer version. In this way, the ERP companies keep on upgrading and billing the end-user enterprise.

Some news articles which highlight the emerging growth of ERP are mentioned in this section. The first one is a news extract about the computer company DELL joining hands with Indian ERP Company Ramco Systems.

[**Source:** *Times of India, 10 September 2012*]

Today, Dell announced its strategic alliance with Ramco Systems to deliver Ramco's ERP as a service on the cloud to help mid-market businesses execute cost and operational efficiencies and accelerate revenue growth. The new offering strengthens Dell's growing portfolio of Software-as-a-Service (SaaS) solutions.

Ramco's ERP on cloud supports businesses with wide functionalities across various industry segments, including production planning, asset management and analytics, along with regular corporate functionalities of HR, Supply Chain Management (SCM), Customer Relationship Management (CRM), and Financial Management.

Below is a news item from The Times of India dated 14 March, 2012 regarding a large Paint Company investing in computer hardware and software. Indian corporates are sometime also referred as India Inc.

India Inc. is preparing to open its purse strings and spend more on IT in 2012 as it goes global and takes on rivals with more sophisticated IT systems and also caters to local growth and demand.

Asian Paints, for instance, plans to spend more on IT systems as it sets up its largest manufacturing plant this year and invest in equipping its sales force with tablets and integrating those devices with its sales force automation software.

We can therefore conclude that there will be a steady growth for ERP in India. IT Giants such as Dell joining hands with Ramco ERP indicate a bright future for ERP professionals in India.

Practice Questions

1. How Server Computer can solve problem of people dependency?
2. List benefits of Enterprise Resource Planning System.
3. Explain need of ERP software.
4. Define ERP.

Activity

1. Who is using ERP?
   (a) Make a list of Companies that you can contact.
   (b) Dived them into two groups: (1) SME Companies with turnover less than One Hundred Crore and (2) Large corporates with turnover more than One Hundred Crore.
   (c) Now find out which Companies are using ERP and if yes, which ERP they are using.

2. Additional online study material:
   (a) Study the Blog http://dnserp.wordpress.com/
   (b) Subscribe this Blog to get automatic updates about ERP.

***

Chapter 2...

ERP AND RELATED TECHNOLOGIES

2.1 Introduction
2.2 Business Process Re-Engineering (BPR)
2.3 Management Information System (MIS)
2.4 Decision Support System (DSS)
2.5 Executive Support System (ESS)
2.6 Data Warehousing, Data Mining
2.7 On-Line Analytical Processing (OLAP)
2.8 Supply Chain Management
2.9 Customer Relationship Management (CRM)
- Practice Questions
- Activity

Learning Objectives

After going through this unit, you will be able to:
- Understand the concept of Business Processing Re-engineering.
- Discuss Management Information, Decision Support, and Executive Support Systems.
- Examine Data Warehousing and Data Mining.
- Describe On-line Analytical Processing, Supply Chain and Customer Relationship Management.

2.1 Introduction

ERP is a wide concept and involves certain related technologies. Before a detailed discussion on ERP, it would be worthwhile to understand the concept of ERP modules. ERP is utilised for managing various departments or functions of an enterprise. For example, ERP is used to manage sales, purchase, production and accounts which are common functional areas covered in an ERP system. In many ERP Systems these are known as and are grouped together as ERP modules. Given below is a generic list of ERP modules. This list is not an exhaustive list and many more modules could be created/required based on type and content of business:

1. Accounts module – General Ledger Accounts.
2. After sales service module (spares management, warranty / AMC).
3. BOM – Bill of Materials module.
4. Cost sheet module – preparing estimate.
5. CRM module (Customer Relationship Management) and pre-sales module.
6. Distribution module for standard products, sold through channel partners.
7. e-Business.
8. Email alerts module.
9. Excise module.
10. Export sales module.
11. Helpdesk module (tracking calls, without spares management).
12. Import purchase module.
13. Inventory Management module.
14. ISO 9000 – Quality check module.
15. Machine scheduling module.
16. MRP - Material Requirement Planning module / Supply Chain Management (SCM).
17. Order Fulfillment module – Sales Accounting - (Shipping).
18. Payroll and HR module.
19. Plant maintenance module.
20. PPC – Production Planning and Control module.
21. Production module (Assembly Production and Process Production).
22. Project tracking module (Project based manufacturing).
23. Purchase and Pre-purchase module.
24. Security module.
25. Subcontractor IN module – Customer's material received for processing.
26. Sub-contractor OUT module.
27. VAT / Sales Tax module.

We will discuss some of these modules in detail later in this book.

2.2 Business Process Re-Engineering (BPR)

Every business needs to survive competition as well as remain cost effective in an ever changing dynamic environment. Businesses need to adapt themselves to the market forces, changing supply chain imperatives, developing management techniques and improving production processes. Change therefore is a business imperative. While these developments may be external to the business itself, it must introduce changes within to mitigate the effects of ever changing external forces. Such internal changes and adaptations or rather improvements are brought about through what is termed as Business Process Re-engineering. To sustain, businesses must keep in mind the following tenets.

2.2.1 Change Fast

"When change within a business is slower than that without, the organisation may be in trouble. You cannot predict the future but we can learn to react a lot faster than our competitor." Says Mr. Jack Welch, former CEO, General Electric.

In short, if an organisation does not change with the technology, another competitor company that has adapted to change will overtake it. Take the recent example of Nokia, which did not quickly change and Samsung mobile overtook Nokia in sales volumes by adapting the more popular Android Operating System.

2.2.2 Change is Necessary

Managers can unleash the real 'power' and great capabilities of computers by challenging old and traditional methods of working. The noteworthy aspect about change management is to use computers to not just automate but also help re-design existing business processes. First, managers need to have a re-look at one's existing business functions and practices. Then identify 'Gaps and Opportunity for Improvements (OFI)'. Last but not the least; align the new business practices to modern-day 'Best Practices'. This is called Business Process Re-engineering (BPR). ERP brings the best practices because the ERP software logic has matured and tested in hundreds of similar companies. Unfortunately, managers often think that whatever they are doing is the best and therefore ask for changes in the software specifications. This software change is called 'customisation'. ERP customisation is not only expensive but also time-consuming. Another important reason for undertaking BPR is that the upgrades are neither impossible nor very expensive.

2.2.3 BPR Cycle

The BPR cycle involves the following steps:

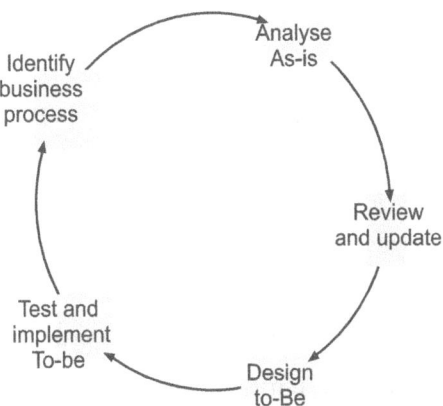

Fig. 2.1: BPR Cycle

A BPR implementation method involves the following steps:
1. Identify a business process.
2. Analyse As-Is: How user is doing today.
3. Review and update: Improve.
4. Design To-Be: Document new method of business process.
5. Test and implement: To-be.
6. The BPR cycle continues periodically, say every six months or every year.

One must remember that BPR and ERP are highly interlinked. In fact ERP must involve BPR as the first essential step to be beneficial. The following case study and discussions highlight this inter-relationship.

Case Study

Let us take example of the Ford Motor Company in USA. Ford is the pioneer in automobile manufacturing. Over a period of time, Ford became complacent; assuming that they do not have any competition and continued doing business without changes; whereas automobile companies in Japan started to adapt new ways of managing business by deploying ERP software. For instance, they started using purchase module that has vendor payment logic in the accounts payable section even though very few managers could successfully utilise it, whereas Ford had to keep hundred managers to do a similar task. Later on, Ford realised the mistake and engaged in BPR. ERP and BPR are closely linked to each other. Companies must try to implement BPR in the beginning, i.e. during the pilot run or the test run itself, because it is difficult to implement BPR after the project rollout.

> The BPR activity needs to be properly documented in the form of an S.O.P. - Standard Operating Procedures. This manual would eventually form the 'Foundation' of the 'New way of doing businesses'.

(i) It is time to 'stop paving the cow-paths'

Instead of embedding outdated business processes in ERP software, managers should get rid of them and start all over again. 'Out-of-The Box' thinking and innovation will give quick 'pay-back' results. BPR is used to standardise business activities, which not only simplifies the task but also makes the same independent of people.

(ii) Companies implement BPR to achieve dramatic improvements in performance

Note the word dramatic; implying not small, incremental improvements like 10% or 15% but of larger scale i.e. 300% or 400% improvement. For instance, think how we can use 'RFID' for better Inventory Control instead of Bar Code. RFID stands for Radio Frequency Identification technology that makes bar codes obsolete. Conventionally, the legacy (or traditional) system that organisations use today, captures only transactional data like 'what is bought', at what price and when. The RFID tag enables capturing the event data through wireless sensor (RFID reader) on each item and communicates to the ERP server on a 'Real-Time' basis. This gives a more accurate and fast information for efficient decision-making. Enterprises should "re-engineer" their businesses and harness the power of IT to radically re-design old business processes.

(iii) Think Big

Smaller companies doing business manually will find it increasingly difficult to compete with large companies, because of the economies of scale. The number game is important. In other words, large companies use ERP to manage very large quantities as compared to smaller quantities managed by traditional business person(s). Re-engineering while implementing ERP triggers changes of many kinds, not just of the business process itself, job profile, organisational structures, management systems, and most importantly 'Attitude' changes. Anything associated with the business process must be re-fashioned in an integrated way, which is why ERP is necessary. If done manually, people may again fall back to old methods. In other words, business process re-engineering is a tremendous effort that mandates change in many areas of the organisation.

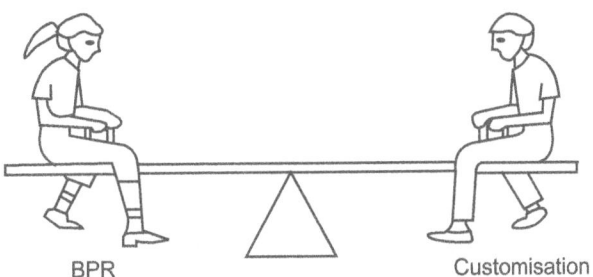

Fig. 2.2: Learn to Balance

Learn the balancing act. Like a see-saw, user must balance between BPR and customisation. On one end, the ERP vendor changes the software to suit current business processes, known as customisation. On the other end, user is ready to change the current business processes and adopts BPR. The logical way is to strike a balance somewhere in-between.

(iv) How to manage change

There is a golden rule named as "20-60-20." Once there is a change, 20% agree to it and accept it without difficulty; 60% might sway between positive or negative to the change depending on the approach and the last 20% would be opposed to the changes. Unfortunately, senior managers mainly fall in this group.

(v) BPR Method

As ERP projects involve all levels in an organisation; we should have a method to pay attention to all of them.
   (a) Awareness of the need for change.
   (b) Desire to participate in the change.
   (c) Knowledge about how to change.
   (d) Ability to implement the change.
   (e) Reinforcement to sustain the change.

For you to easily remember let us call it ADKAR method. That is the first letter of above five points.

(vi) Concept

The concept of re-engineering is concerned about outdated rules. BPR challenges a large number of fundamental assumptions and many of the presently accepted business rules in order to replace them with radically new ideas.

(vii) What is a business process?

A business process can be considered as a set of activities that when taken together produce a result which is of value to the end-customer. For example, preparing a Purchase order (PO) is a business process in the purchase department. Customer order execution is a business process in the sales department. When a customer order is being executed, it involves several activities cutting across different functions within organisation such as Sales, Stores (materials manager), Shipping/Logistics, and Accounts.

(viii) BPR is all about changing the business rule

For instance: **The old rule was:** Information is available within the organisation, but scattered across different locations, departments, or sections. One has to search and collect the required information. Time and effort was needed to be spent to achieve this. **The new business rule:** Information is made available at anywhere, irrespective of physical location at which it is generated. This is achieved by installing one database on the Server Computer. Information is available without significant efforts or time being spent.

(ix) Benefits of BPR

Companies using these techniques have reported significant bottom-line results, better customer relations, reductions in cycle time to market, increased productivity, fewer defects/errors, increased profitability, just to name a few.

(x) Return on Investment (ROI) on BPR is guaranteed

BPR uses proven techniques for improving business results and questions the effectiveness of the traditional organisational structure. Defining, measuring, analysing and re-engineering work processes to improve customer satisfaction pays off in many different ways.

(xi) Action plan

The action plan of a BPR starts with finding out the old business rules and replacing them with new business rules. Thereafter one needs to incorporate the new business rule in the ERP software. Remember that BPR and ERP implementation go hand in hand.

2.3 Management Information System (MIS)

Management Information System is a general name for the academic discipline covering the application of people, technologies, and procedures – collectively called information systems – to solve business problems.

Academically, the term is commonly used to refer to the group of information management methods tied to the automation or support of human decision-making, e.g. Decision Support Systems, Expert systems, and Executive information systems.

The MIS advantage: Through collaborative solutions for planning, reporting, and analysis, MIS empowers companies to drive performance in tomorrow's dynamic market places.

Modern approaches to MIS: Information is a strategic resource that gives managers the competitive advantage. The following two case studies will bring out how MIS enables information to become a strategic resource for educated decision making and bring benefits to businesses.

Case Study I - Honda Motor Company

Each quarter, Honda Motor Europe updates its pricing and profitability-forecasting system, which breaks down the factory-to-showroom prices and costs for its 14 different models. The old system was based on 182 linked Excel spreadsheets, with each of the thirteen countries requiring separate files listing the details of each model, exchange rates, and other key variables. A new system was designed and developed called 'Decisionware'. This is a multi-dimensional analytical engine with seamless integration into MS Excel. Now the spreadsheets are created automatically by the ERP system in matter of few minutes. During the first two days, the project team discussed and optimised the structure of the database before embarking on the detailed development work. At the end of ten days, the model was up and running and fully documented. Now the company gets MIS using the Decisionware ERP software system.

Case Study II - BAYER Case Study

The Bayer Group had approximately 1,08,600 employees worldwide (2008). Bayer's growth was mainly due to acquisitions and expansion in the BRIC countries - Brazil, Russia, India, China and other growth markets. Due to Bayer's substantial global presence, enterprise planning and control presented a significant challenge. Enterprise reporting, for example, must account for heterogeneous system environments, multiple languages, currencies, and even time zones. Bayer, therefore, decided to replace its technologically obsolete reporting system with a state-of-the-art ERP system with client-server architecture and a graphical user-interface. Bayer thus created 'BayInfo', a customised MIS (management information system) built using various components of MIS, Excel Integration as the flexible front end and centralised data storage. The CIO (Chief Information Officer) took on the task to implement a system that all affiliate companies could use for reporting to the Group's headquarters in Germany.

2.4 Decision Support System (DSS)

Decision making is an everyday challenge faced by any manager. For making a decision it is imperative to have all the required inputs in terms of information and the choices of decisions available. Finally the manager must also be able to perceive as to what effect will his choice of decision have on all the input variables as well as the final output. The first part regarding information can be taken care of through MIS, however, most managers would rely on mental abilities, mental calculations and experience to first develop a list of choices of decision and the final selected decision. We all do it in our day to day life. For example which motorcycle to buy? Information about price, mileage, features etc., is available through brochures, friends and showroom agents. Based on this a decision can be taken. Some of us will just take a impulsive decision whereas the more methodical ones may make a list of desirables, give a degree of importance to each of these desirables and then come to a calculated decision. While making such weighted lists may be alright for a motorcycle purchase, managers in big businesses, need to process a very large amount of information, rely on their innovative thought to evolve a list of choices and then take a decision. In brief, at such levels, decision making is a highly complex task. Today, technology is coming to the aid of these managers so that they do not miss out any aspect, are presented all suitable choices and finally get some calculated decisions. Following discussion points bring about this aspect as a technology related to decision making:

- Decision making is the developing of a concept leading to the selection of a course of action among variations. Every decision making process produces a final choice. Due to the large number of considerations involved in many decisions, computer-based decision support systems (DSS) have been developed to assist decision makers. DSS could be an action or an opinion. It begins when we need to do something but we do not know what. For example, decision to locate an item in the warehouse, and find a shortest distance to pick that item and give to the packers.

- Artificial intelligence (commonly abbreviated as AI) was defined as "The science of making machines to do things that would require intelligence, if done by humans. With artificial intelligence, programmers don't just set up computers to make decisions in response to certain inputs. They attempt to enable the systems to *learn from decisions*, and adapt. An expert system, also known as a knowledge-based system, is a computer program that contains some of the subject-specific knowledge, and contains the knowledge and analytical skills of one or more human experts.

- Hedge funds are turning more and more to the science of artificial intelligence to choose the best investment play. While traders sometimes repeat the same mistakes, these computers are trained to learn from errors and adapt so as not to make the same error in the future, thus improving its strategy.
- The concept of artificial intelligence was inspired by *ant colonies*. Consider case study of an AI system that can deliver to packers at the rate of one **every 6 seconds**. Ants are small but intelligent. Robots use Artificial Intelligence to manage warehouses. For example, GAP, Staples, Office Depot. For E-commerce websites, smart software focuses on solving the supply chain issues of retail merchandisers using complex AI computer programs. AI is used for efficient supply chain management, but it does not mimic human brain. The AI system gives instructions to robots to effectively do the job that would be difficult for humans given the millions of items stacked in the warehouse. Artificial Intelligence system applies the concepts of distributed intelligence to order fulfillment and inventory management using new material handling systems and order fulfillment software. Scientists learnt from ant colonies which are capable of performing large and complex tasks with limited central control, where the system allows inventory to organise itself, adapting to conditions as they change. The resulting solution combines store, move, and sort functions into one simple system that can deliver any item to any operator at any time.
- Automated warehouse system uses expert systems, where it involves hundreds of mobile robots, all of which move shelving around inside warehouses, making the entire pick-and-pack process easier, faster, and more accurate. Whether the challenge is picking same-day orders or delivering boxes of products to retail stores, Information Technology (IT) can help improve the distribution process. The entire operation is performed by robots. Each robot communicates wirelessly with the ERP server computer network in a warehouse to get directions when needed, but, for the most part, these little, *'orange metal men'* are on their own. No humans actually have to remember where the item is located. But such 'robots' are expensive. Investment could be in the range of two to twenty million dollars.
- Traditional stores are static and managed by humans. The robotic system is faster because the entire warehouse can adapt, in real time, to changes in demand. Software moves shelves with popular items closer to the workers, where the shelves can be quickly retrieved. Items that aren't selling are gradually moved farther away.

Robots rearrange the shelves to keep the fast-selling items at the perimeter, close to packing stations.

- **Are there any limitations in the expert system?** Yes, there are some limitations. The computer program may be intelligent but lacks human approach required in making some decisions. Human experts can respond to unusual circumstances with creative responses. Machines get confused if the circumstances were not defined. Another problem is that the domain experts are not always able to explain their logic and reasoning to the computer programmers. Automating complex processes is a challenge. Machines lack flexibility and ability to adapt to changing environments as programs are standard and cannot be changed.

Advantages and Uses of Expert System

In spite the above mentioned limitations, an expert system or artificial intelligence has many benefits as stated below:

1. Provide consistent answers for repetitive decisions, processes and tasks.
2. Hold and maintain significant levels of information (may be in Terabytes).
3. Review transactions that human experts may overlook.
4. Google is a giant IT company in America. Google has developed AI car. That is, a car that runs without a driver. It has video cameras that work like eyes and computer program that helps the car turn, stop at red signal, and apply brakes when required.
5. Credit card companies are using AI to track frauds.
6. Netflix is an online movie subscription company that shows films on Internet-enabled TV. Netflix uses AI to recommend movies to subscribers, based on their past choice, etc.

In short, computers are gaining more control in our world. Well it was our world. Not anymore. You will see intelligent and smart machines are taking over the control.

2.5 Executive Support System (ESS)

Executives need to take quick decisions at their workplace for which they require ESS. Therefore, executive support system is a specialised DSS, which combines computer hardware, software with data about economic conditions and complex planning models to help top managers develop and evaluate major new organisational initiatives.

Example of Executive Decision Making Levels is shown below.

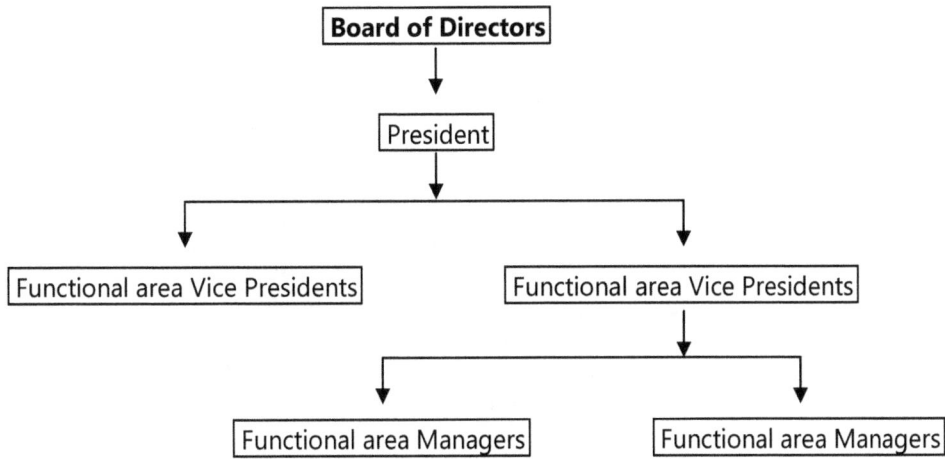

The following points are to be borne in mind by the executives behind every level while taking decisions:

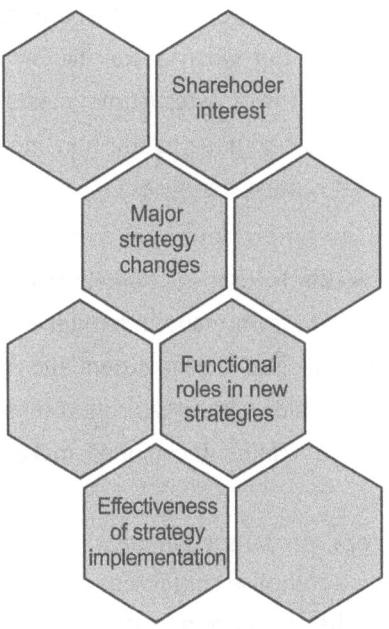

Fig. 2.3

2.6 Data Warehousing, Data Mining

The problem with data is that it is found everywhere, for instance in ERP database, emails, websites, blogs, and so on but when a specific report is required it is humanly impossible to manually analyse millions of bytes (sometimes even terabytes) of data as it is scattered all over the network. This brings us to the new idea of mining the data and for mining data you need a mine that is the warehouse.

Data Warehousing (DW), in simple terms, is a process of transforming data into information and making it available to user in a timely manner to make a difference. For organisational learning, to take data from many heterogeneous (different kinds of) sources must be gathered together and organised in a consistent and useful way, hence, we need the Data Warehousing technique. DW allows an organisation (enterprise) to remember what it has noticed about its data. *Data Mining* techniques make use of the data in a Data Warehouse.

A data warehouse is a copy of transaction data specifically structured for querying, analysis and reporting. The data warehouse contains a copy of the transactions which are not updated or changed later by the transaction system (unlike ERP). This data is specially structured, and may have been transformed or changed when it was copied into the data warehouse. Data Warehouse Architecture: A Data Mart is a smaller, more focused Data Warehouse. Let us call it a mini-warehouse.

Let us now define **Data Warehouse:**

Data Warehouse is a single, complete and consistent store of data obtained from a variety of different sources made available to end users in what they can understand and use in a business context.

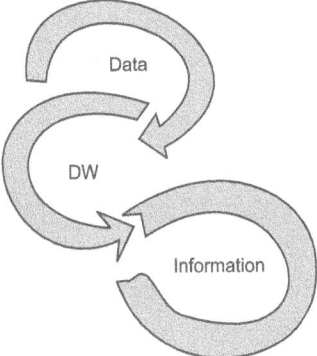

Fig. 2.3: Data to Information

Data Warehousing is necessary for management decision support. This is useful to manage and control business. Data Warehouse system is historical or it is a point-in-time, which is optimised for inquiry rather than update. Data Warehouse system is loosely defined and can be ad-hoc, not sequential. It is used by managers and end-users to understand the business and draw conclusions and arrive at decisions.

DW should be integrated across the enterprise and not just partially implemented. It is the summarised data that has a real value to the organisation. This historical data holds the key to understanding data over time. DW is very useful when 'What-if' capabilities are required. Data Warehousing is a process. It is a technique for assembling and managing data from various sources for the purpose of answering business questions. Thus, enabling in making decisions that were not previously possible with traditional ERP system.

Depot of data or Godown of data is data warehouse.

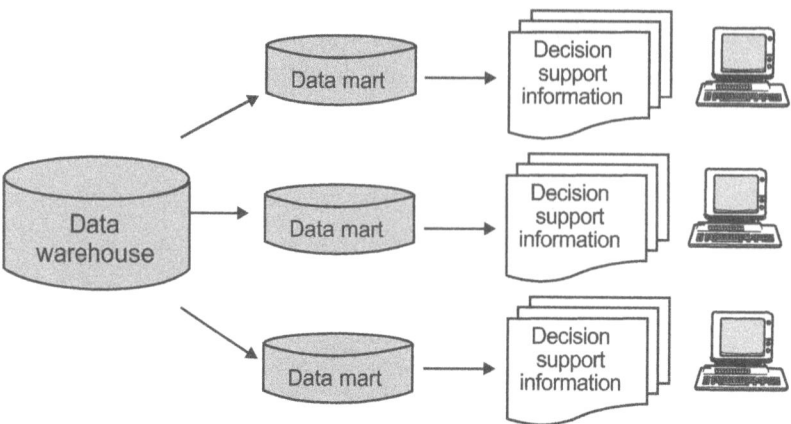

Fig. 2.4: Data Warehouse Concept Diagrams

DW is a decision support database maintained separately from the organisation's operational database. Traditional RDBMS (Relational Database Management System) uses OLTP (Online Transactional Processing).

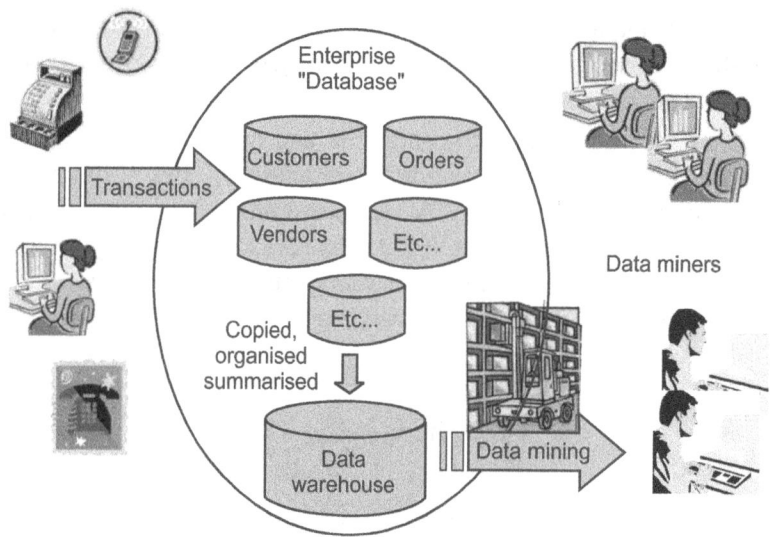

Fig. 2.5: Data Warehousing

Operational Database systems are traditionally used for OLTP or day-to-day transaction processing. For example, sale invoice is a transaction. OLTP data processing system do the clerical data processing tasks. This data gives a lot of details and is always up to date. This is a structured and repetitive task. This may read or update a few records. In such a system, recovery and integrity are critical.

Let us compare the OLTP and DW.

OLTP	DW
Application Oriented	Subject Oriented
Used to run business	Used to analyse business
Clerical User	Manager/Analyst
Detailed data	Summarised and refined
Current up to date	Snapshot data
Isolated Data	Integrated Data
Repetitive access by small transactions	Ad-hoc access using large queries
Read/Update access	Mostly read access (batch update)

2.7 On-Line Analytical Processing (OLAP)

"Business Intelligence Projects are not Mission Critical, but they are Business Critical".

On-Line Analytical Processing or OLAP allows business users to cut data or slice data whenever required. Normally, data in an enterprise is distributed in multiple data sources and are often incompatible with each other.

For instance, Point-of-sales (POS) data and sales made via the call-center or the website are stored in different location and formats. Now let us say, a top executive wants to know "What are the most popular products purchased by customers between the ages 15 to 30"? Due to different kind of format of data in POS, or call-center, or website, it is very difficult to get the answer by conventional methods. This is where OLAP techniques come in the picture. OLAP helps to get answer of such questions in minutes.

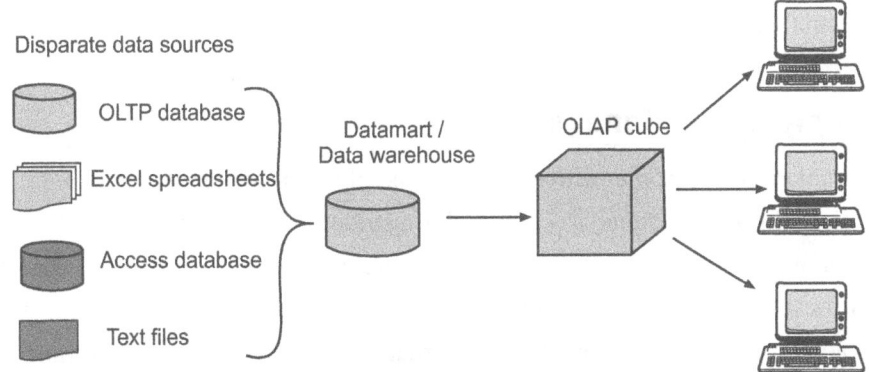

Fig. 2.6: Online Analytical Processing

The salient features and benefits of OLAP are as follows:

Managers have direct access to information

- Provides information to the managers.
- Eliminates the need for a complicated report utility.
- Allows users to ask questions to the database.

High Return on Investment

- Easier to maintain than most relational systems.
- Relatively easy to build and develop.
- Quick development cycle.

OLAP has become the analytical standard

- Lower costs have increased usage of OLAP products.
- Most RDBMS systems now include an OLAP tool.

A multidimensional cube can combine data from disparate data sources and store the information in a fashion that is logical for business users.

Some of the major OLAP companies are Hyperion, Cognos, Business Objects, and MicroStrategy, just to name a few. The cost per seat was in the range of Rs.7,500 to Rs.25,000 per year. The setting up of the environment to perform OLAP analysis would also require substantial investments in time and monetary resources.

Major database vendors have started to incorporate OLAP modules within their database offering. E.g. Microsoft SQL Server 2000 with Analysis Services, Oracle with Express, Darwin, and IBM with DB2.

2.8 Supply Chain Management

The market has become extremely dynamic due to the advancement of Internet technologies. The manufacturer as well as the distributor should now know the changing preferences of buyers. For example, if Nokia launches a mobile phone with a built-in camera, Samsung must also put similar or better product in the market very soon. The race is on between automobile manufacturers to ensure that they give what customers want. In other words, companies must know the pulse of the market quickly and react to it rapidly. This is possible by efficiently managing the supply chain.

There are two areas of managing the supply chain:

(a) Inbound Supply Chain Management.

(b) Outbound Supply Chain Management.

The following concepts are applicable to both the areas of managing supply chain.

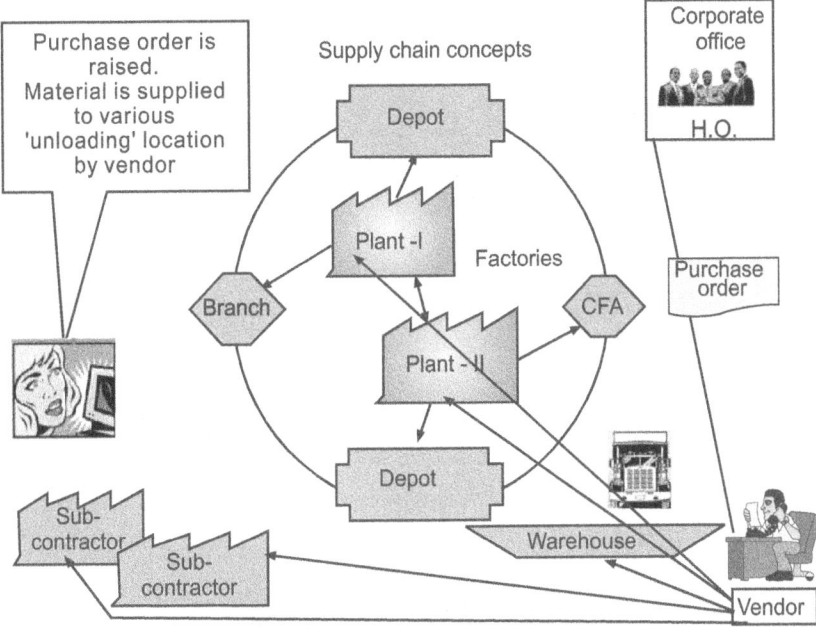

Fig. 2.7: Supply Chain Concepts

There may be multiple plants or number of factories in different cities (locations) and the head office may be in another city. The top executives in the head office would like to know what is going on in various factories. This is where ERP software helps to manage the entire supply chain. The Purchase Order (PO) is raised on the supplier (vendor) with clear written instructions that supply these raw materials to these locations, viz., warehouse or factory 1 or factory 2 or directly to the sub-contractor (outsourcing) and so on. The raw material that is received is then used to manufacture the product (finished goods) and distributed via the channel partners, depot, CFA (Carrying and Forwarding Agents), or branches, right up to the POS (Point of Sale) in the mall.

Bar Code and RFID

By this time reader must be aware about the bar codes. A barcode is an optical machine-readable representation of an alphanumeric data relating to the item to which it is attached. A picture of a typical Barcode is given below.

Fig. 2.8: Barcode

Barcodes originally were scanned by special optical scanners called barcode readers; later, scanners and interpretive software became available on devices including desktop printers and smartphones. But now a new technology known as RFID is replacing Bar codes in many applications.

Let us understand how the inventory management and asset tracking is done using RFID system.

RFID chip or tag is shown in the below figure.

Fig. 2.9: RFID Chip or Tag

RFID stands for Radio Frequency Identification. In the RFID, basically there is an electronic microchip attached to the item. The main difference is the method by which the data is read. In bar coding, the reading device scans a printed label with optical laser or imaging technology and in RFID the reading device scans a tag by using radio frequency signals. The main advantage is that in case of bar code you have to scan each item, one at a time where as in case of RFID you can scan many items simultaneously. Disadvantage of bar code is that you have to hold the scanner exactly in front of the bar code, whereas for reading the RFID tag it is not necessary to hold the device exactly in front of the tag.

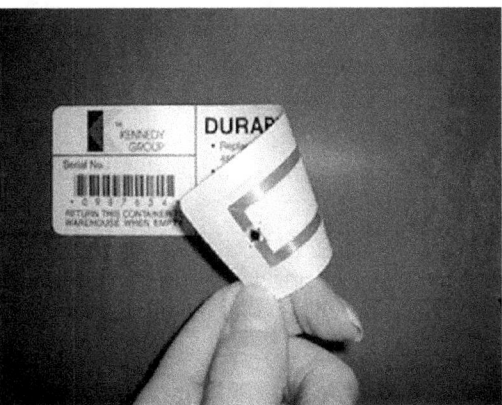

Fig. 2.10: RFID for Supply Chain Management - SCM

The most popular and widespread RFID application area in SCM is inventory management and tracking RFID is initially used to manage and track the identification of *large lots* of goods at the unit pallet, case, and carton levels. It is not necessary to open cartons or boxes. RFID facilities unit-level tagging of various items and will be the backbone until retailers switch completely to automated checkouts. Companies such as Wal-Mart have already started using the RFID to manage the inventory instead of Bar code.

RFID tags have unique serial identifier information that associates each lot with a corresponding document sent from the originator. Because RFID readers can scan tags many times during a one-second period, the serial identifier prevents the applicator making the data request from getting multiple counts of the same items, accurate information about inventory availability and high speed of transportation also adds to supply chain performance. RFID technology enables supplies to accurately determine the location of a pallet or a box, to track its journey through the supply chain.

One study estimates that the US retail sector loses over $70 billion annually due to lack of visibility and efficiency in the SCM. RFID – enabled inventory management would reduce this to a great extent. It would be possible to reduce counterfeiting and also track goods that are difficult to track like medicine. A company called TrenStar has developed a system, for this using RFID. Procter & Gamble estimates a cost saving of up to $200 million in inventory carrying costs with its RFID implementation. Logistics and supply chain services providers could track their containers in transit by maintaining a log or history of the containers. RFID tags and readers can be deployed in containers, yards, factories, godown, stores, etc.

Vendor Managed Inventory (VMI)

The promise of Vendor Managed Inventory (VMI) could be fully realised using RFID. Retailers can reduce their out-of-stocks, reduce Labour, and warehouse costs. The supplier has total control with access to point of sale and inventory information of the retailer. Inventory management can thereby be properly regulated at the supplier end. This would reduce inventory carrying cost, reduce out-of-stocks, and subsequent loss of sales. Overall reduction in working capital is possible due to RFID based inventory module of ERP. There would be reliable data for demand planning using RFID. This would include raw material stock, work-in-progress (WIP) and finished goods (FG) inventory. Information obtained from RFID can eliminate inaccuracies in data due to human error or absence of data. Timely data at the item level about the market demand for any product / service would help to develop more successful strategies in production, marketing and distribution.

2.9 Customer Relationship Management (CRM)

The idea of customer relationship is not new. Traditionally, companies used to appoint a senior manager for maintaining good relationship with customers. Such a position is called 'Public Relations Officer' or PRO. However, now the same task can be handled better by using the CRM Module of the ERP software. For closer relation with customer, the PRO should look upon customers as an asset. It is necessary to nurture this relationship, much like a gardener continuously takes care of the plants.

The main points to remember for CRM software are as follows:
(a) Keeping and improving relations with current customers rather than on acquiring new customers.
(b) Customers become long term partners using CRM module on the website, anywhere, anytime.
(c) Make commitments to maintain those relationships with quality, service and innovation.
(d) When CRM is done using the Internet it is called e-CRM.

The goals of e-CRM are as follows:
(a) Enhancing customer relations.
(b) Retaining customers.
(c) Satisfying customers.
(d) Getting new customers based on the word of mouth, that is reference business.

Customer relationship management (CRM) using RFID system helps business in the following way.

Retailers are able to reduce their out-of-stocks using RFID. Consumer behaviour studies have shown us the adverse impact on retail establishments not having adequate stocks. Both supplier and retailer are synchronised at all times with regard to the dynamics of demand and supply.

Customer order fulfilment can be realised in a better fashion as the chances of sending orders to wrong destinations is minimised due to the RFID usage. Such process changes will reduce the cost of operations and lead to reduced labour.

Suppliers are able lead to handle product recalls and return of faulty and defective items in an effective manner using RFID. For example, recently Toyota Company recalled cars due to some defective part. The relationship of a product to a particular sale or return is logged automatically in the ERP system. This is done by RFID technology. Retailers can also offer better after-sales service. Manufacturers are also shielded in case both the supplier and retailers are enhanced due to the RFID tagging of the items in the logistics.

CRM not only benefits sellers but also buyers. There are many benefits for customers too. Customers will use the product readily if CRM is properly implemented. Feeling of trust in the product or service provider gives positive feedback and references. CRM reduces anxiety. For example, let us consider the case of a courier company, as it is now possible to track a parcel on the Internet. Therefore now, for example, a mother who has sent a parcel to USA and is anxious of its status can track the same on the Company's website reducing anxiety and feeling comfortable in the knowledge of what to expect. When customer maintains a relationship with supplier of product or service, they free-up time for their other priorities. Many e-Commerce websites send an SMS to inform the buyer about the delivery status automatically. Customer does not have to waste time dialing telephone numbers to enquire about the delivery status.

Due to the CRM software, a customer feels that they are getting special service and personal touch. Intelligent websites are created with a CRM module that remembers customer's preferences. The CRM software gives benefits for the e-commerce enabled business organisation. The emotional attachment to a particular company makes it less likely that user will switch to another competition product or service, even if they learn about a competitor that might have better quality or a lower price. For example, airlines offer Frequent Flyer Programs. The passenger gets reward points by flying with the same airline frequently and thus will not go to another competition airline even if he or she will get discount.

Relationship is the basis for customer loyalty. Using ERP software, companies can capture demographic details like birth date/ anniversary date of customer or even employees. The server computer system knows 'today's' date' and will find the birth date / anniversary date and send greetings email to the person. The recipient will be very happy and will certainly remember the sender organisation.

Case Study

Hospitality industry: Let us see how a luxury hotel uses ERP to maintain relations with guests and increases business. The Ritz-Carlton hotel company is one of the leading hotels. In the hotel business, the customer is called 'Guest'. Hotel ERP can store personalised information about guests that can be accessed from anywhere in the world by the authorised managers. This guest's information empowers service provider to serve better. Hotel targets its services to business executives such as travelling sales managers. Ritz-Carlton has the database of 2,40,000 repeat guests (customers) with their likes and dislikes. The hotel guests get highly individual service automatically without asking.

Case Study

CRM software in TATA motors brings dealers closer. Tata Motors is India's largest integrated automaker, and market shares approaching 20 per cent of India's passenger car market. Tata motors implemented customer relationship management (CRM) software. It involves working with ~250 dealer organisations and more than ~1,600 locations staffed by more than ~10,000 salespeople across India.

This has delivered significant benefits across the extended organisation:
(a) Improved customer satisfaction.
(b) Increased revenue.
(c) Increased productivity.
(d) Reduction in operating costs.

There are many levels of relationship strategies:
- Financial bonds.
- Discounts to retain customers.
  - *Airline offering frequent flyer programs.*
  - *E.g. Lufthansa Airlines.*
- Social bonds
  - Binds customers through personal relationship.
  - *E.g. Lawyer, accountant, teachers, doctors, etc.*
- Customisation bonds
  - Satisfying specific needs of individual customers – one-to-one solutions. E.g. Tailored jeans.
- Structural bonds
  - Technology based service
  - *E.g., Ups or federal express giving web based tracking of parcel or via SMS on mobile, etc.*

80 / 20 Customer Pyramid

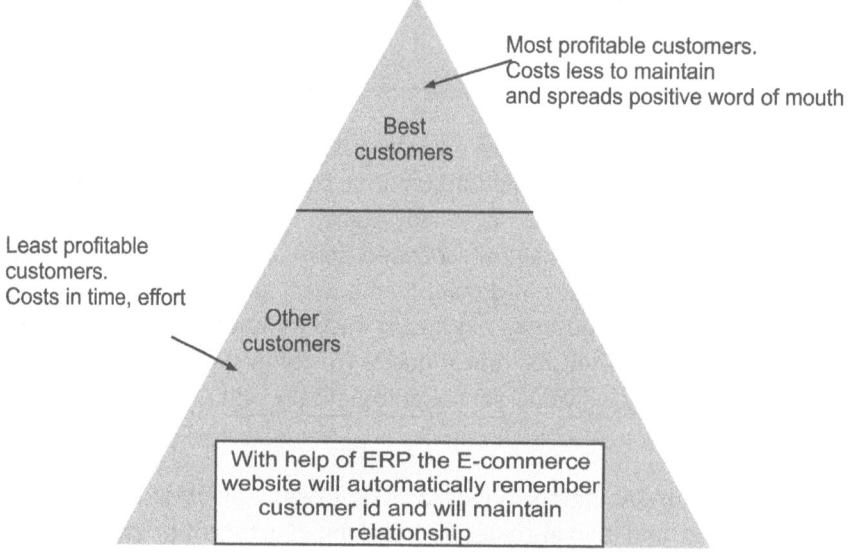

Fig. 2.11: 80/20 Customer Pyramid

Market Segmentation and Targeting

Market segments are formed by grouping customers who share common characteristics that are in some way meaningful to the design, delivery, promotion, or pricing or the service. CRM software endeavors to study the profiles of resulting segments and ensure that the target segments are compatible. For example, in the context of a hotel, families who are attracted by the discounted prices and college students on their Diwali holidays. So the CRM logic segments these two kinds of guests and allocates rooms accordingly.

Practice Questions

1. List ERP Modules.
2. Why management change is necessary?
3. Why BPR is necessary before implementing ERP?
4. Compare Online Transaction Processing and Data Warehouse.

Activity

1. List ERP companies that you have studied.
   (a) Study their websites to get insights of their customers.
   (b) Compare any two ERP companies.

2. Additional online study material:
   (a) Register with Twitter.com
   (b) Follow http://twitter.com/follow ERP to get automatic updates about ERP.

***

Chapter 3...

ERP MODULES AND VENDORS

3.1 Finance

3.2 Production Planning, Control and Management

3.3 Sales and Distribution

3.4 Human Resource Management

3.5 Inventory Control System

3.6 Quality Management

3.7 ERP market, Comparison of Current ERP Packages and Vendors like SAP, Oracle, PeopleSoft, BAAN etc.

3.8 Disadvantages of non-ERP System; Importance of ERP vice versa In-house Applications

3.9 Benefits of Integration

3.10 Standardisation of Data Code

- Practice Questions
- Activity

Learning Objectives

After going through this unit, you will be able to:

- Assess and compare current ERP packages and vendors.
- Explain how PPC module is applicable in an industry.
- Explain the finance module.
- Discuss the disadvantages of non-ERP system.

Most organisations have departments, which are responsible for specific functions. Usually each department has one person who is in-charge of his or her department. For instance, Sales department, Purchase department, Accounts department and so on. ERP software system is deployed to manage all these departments. The procedures followed in each department or function can be grouped as 'Module'. Therefore, in ERP we have sales module, purchase module, accounts module and so on. It is important to note that 'Once ERP is installed the department wall vanishes'. To understand this statement, let us consider one most common transaction called "sales invoice". Can you tell me which department owns the sales invoice? Usual answer is 'Sales department'. However, what about accounts department? Oh, yes it also belongs to accounts department. Similarly, you will find it also is required by the Sales tax and Excise department, and Material Manager (Finished Goods Stored). In other words one transaction can belong to many departments. Traditionally companies used to make number of copies. In turn same document will exist in many files. Now, when ERP is installed, no more copies are required. Any user who is authorised will access the same document (electronic copy) on his or her computer instantly. No more department wall exists. Even a junior manager if authorised can access any transaction without bothering to go to other department or ask on phone. ERP system brings transparency and thus we can say removes wall between departments.

Some of the key ERP modules are described below.

3.1 Finance

Let us consider the Finance module ERP. Generally, this comprises accounts-related information. The Finance Module in the ERP is one of the most important modules, because this gives instant information related to Assets and Liability, Income and Expenses.

The scope of these modules can be divided into three parts: Master, Transaction, and the MIS (reports) as shown in the diagram below.

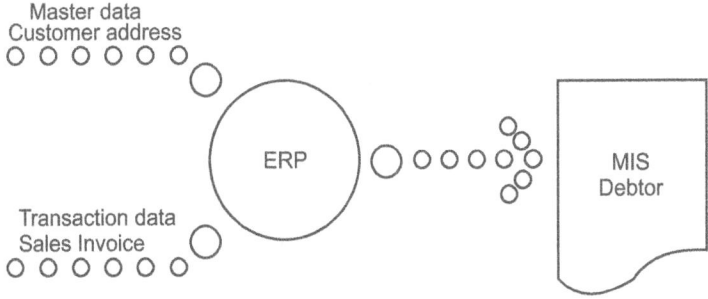

Fig. 3.1: Basic Concept Diagram for all ERP Modules

What is the difference between Master data and Transaction data?

Master data is the data that *usually* does not change, whereas the Transaction data changes. For example, name and address of a customer does not usually change, therefore it is master data. Sale invoice for the same customer will be changing every time, hence the transaction data. Example of reports is the sales ledger (debtor ledger) where customer name and address of customer is printed and the invoice number, date etc. are posted as the debit entry.

ERP **Finance Module** encompasses all the following procedures:

1. **Masters data**
   (i) Account Group Master.
   (ii) Subgroup Master.
   (iii) General Ledger Account Head Master with Tax, Bank, and Cash bifurcation.
   (iv) Detail Account Master.
   (v) Narration Master.
   (vi) TDS (Tax Deducted at Source) and % fields in the supplier / address (TP) masters.

2. **Transactions**
   (i) Bank and Cash receipt voucher.
   (ii) Bank and Cash payment voucher.
   (iii) Journal Voucher.
   (iv) Contra-entry voucher.
   (v) Credit Note and Debit Note.

3. **Key reports (output)**
   (i) Customer and Supplier (Sub-ledger) trial balance.
   (ii) Cash Book and Bank Book.
   (iii) Expense voucher register.
   (iv) General Ledger.
   (v) Credit note register.
   (vi) Debit note register.
   (vii) Fixed Asset register.
   (viii) Trial Balance.
   (ix) Balance Sheet and Profit and Loss account.
   (x) Bank reconciliation statement.

In case of Finance module, the Asset Life Cycle Management is one of the important activities and is described as follows:

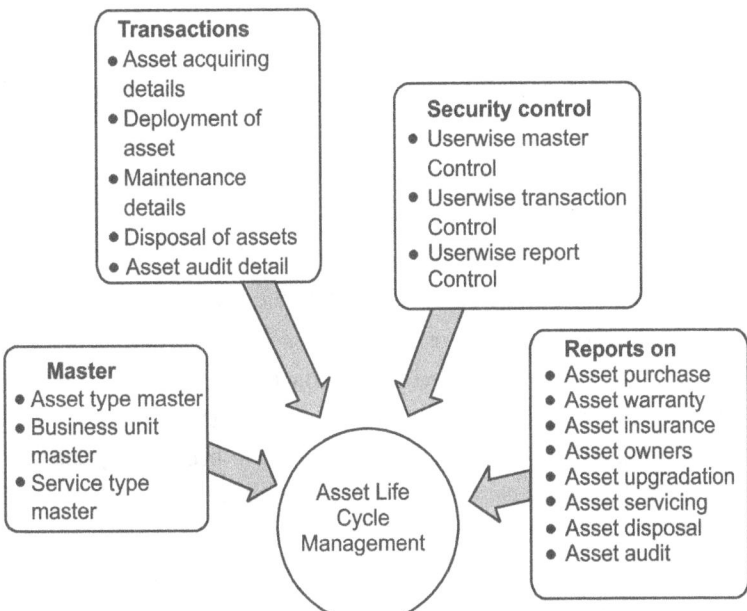

Fig. 3.2: Asset Life Cycle Management

- Asset Life Cycle Management includes Tagging, tracking, and managing fixed, mobile, and virtual assets in organisations.

In conclusion, the Enterprise Resource Planning (ERP) - Finance module is that part of the ERP package, which gathers financial data and generates reports such as ledgers, trail balance, overall balance sheets, and periodic financial reports.

3.2 Production Planning, Control and Management

In ERP parlance, "Production Planning, Control, and Management" is referred to as the PPC Module. The PPC Module is mostly applicable to a manufacturing enterprise.

3.2.1 Scope of PPC Module

The scope of PPC Module is as follows:

ERP captures both kinds of manufacturing:

1. Process production
2. Assembly production.

PPC Master File data stores information pertaining to the specific machine, number of shifts, operator names, and processes. There are three important transactions pertaining to the Production related activities: Work Order or Job Order, Production Entry, and Quality Check related readings.

The production manager uses the following outputs available from the ERP system to manage the manufacturing processes efficiently.

1. Work Order Register that also shows pending work order status.
2. Productions register.
3. Work Order type – In-house or sub-contractor or all.
4. Shift-wise, machine-wise, operator-wise production reports.

The prerequisite of the production module is the BOM master. It is necessary to first create the 'Bill-of-Materials' of the item being manufactured. Please note that here the word 'Bill' is confusing. Here Bill means List. BOM is actually list of material. Remember, if a discussion is about the BOM, it has nothing to do with the accounting Bill. The BOM or the recipe master tells the ERP what raw material is required to produce a given product. The raw material is called the child item and the item made is called the father item. For instance, to manufacture a Mobile phone (the father item), the production manager may need (child items), some electronic items, IC, PCB, keys, speaker, display, camera, and so on.

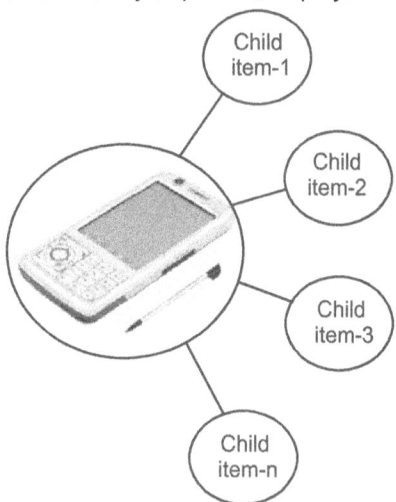

Fig. 3.3: Example of BOM Master

Store issues the child items to the shop floor as per the BOM Master. Consider a case where 10,000 mobiles are to be produced. The work order quantity would be 10,000 numbers. This will also show the required number of child items. Based on such a work order the stores will issue the material, no more, no less. This helps in controlling wastage. After receiving, the required quantity of child items (raw material) the plant will produce the father item (in this case, mobile phone). The production manager will inform ERP the item produced by using the production entry. Thus, the work order is the parent document for the production entry.

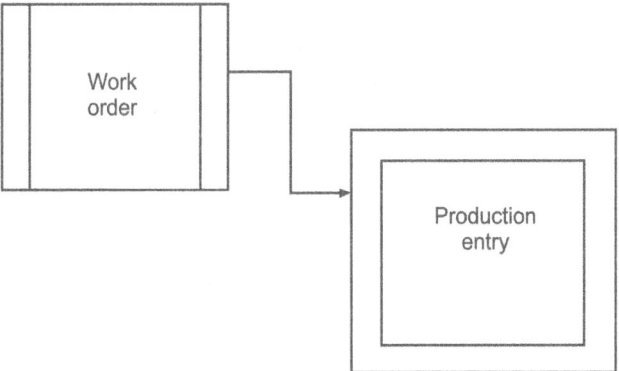

Fig. 3.4: Work order is a Parent Transaction for the Production Entry

Prerequisites: Before any production related transactions are entered, it is necessary to have correct item master and BOM master.

Sometimes during production some waste is produced, for example the 'End=Piece'. The end piece cannot be used anymore and has to be thrown or scrapped. Nevertheless, such item also can be sold (on weight basis) in the open market. The scrap material is transferred to the scrap location by entering a stock transfer note in ERP, and ultimately sold by using the scrap invoice transaction. In short, even the scrap can be monitored, and minimised as much as possible in ERP, saving lots of money.

Production Indent transaction is generated based on the sales order and finished goods stock position. If the item is available in the FG store, it is not necessary to produce. The production manager uses the 'Production indent' after combining (sum) all the sales order quantities to make a work order. In some case, the production indent may be generated based on internal order, based estimated demand, or forecasting. It is like, the planner says: "You make two thousand, I don't know who is actual customer" based on the past trend. This is referred as internal order, in any case now ERP ensures the production process and planning process is linked tightly.

Quality checks are done during every stage of production i.e. the quality is checked. The quality inspector accepts or rejects the item as per the quality data sheets. The reason for rejection is also recorded in the ERP system. The rejection report analysis helps the organisation to reduce rejection and increase the productivity.

(a) Process Production

In this kind of production, typically the main raw material undergoes number of processes. The finished goods are produced at the end of a *continuous* production run, which cannot be interrupted. Let us consider a case study of a chemical manufacturing company, producing pigments. The raw material is certain chemicals that are loaded in a special machine called the reactors. After few days of the *process production*, the FG is produced, in this case a Blue colour pigment. This pigment is sold to another company that will use it as a raw material and further produce the blue colour for plastic or blue colour for clothes, or blue colour ink and so on.

Another example of a process manufacturing company is petrol or oil refinery. Where crude oil is the main raw material that undergoes series of processes and the 'Petrol' is produced.

ERP Software is used to achieve operational excellence. The process manufacturers must be able to keep control over cost structures while meeting customer expectations. The factory must improve performance and increase profitability with integrated, comprehensive solutions that protect the people, process and assets, while reducing cost and improving productivity.

Some chemical manufacturers produce and sell consumer products such as detergent, and cosmetics, most chemical products are used as intermediate products for other goods, that are to the Original Equipment Manufacturers (OEM) customers. Factories may be located in different geographical locations. For instance, a pharmaceutical company has head office in Mumbai, and three plants are located in three different cities, Mandideep in Bhopal, Aurangabad in Maharashtra and Ankleshwar in Gujarat. You can imagine, the challenges and issues arise due to multi-locations. The head office gets all the reports in Mumbai automatically because of the ERP system. For instance, the purchase officer is raising a PO (Purchase Order) and asking the vendor to supply the raw material in various plants. When the material is received, say in Aurangabad, the stores will enter in ERP, so the accounts section, in Mumbai, will know and can make the payment to the vendor. In case of chemical industry the tolerance and the percentage of purity is very important, which is captured in the ERP database at every stage of the process production.

The following ERP modules may be used by process manufacturing company to meet the business challenges:

1. Security module - Log in id and the secret password.
2. Accounts module – General Ledger Accounts
3. VAT / Sales Tax module – statutory requirements.
4. Excise module - statutory requirements.
5. Material Management module – inventory.
6. Purchase and Pre-purchase module – procurement.
7. MRP module - Material Requirement Planning to generate indents.
8. BOM – Bill of Materials module.

9. Internet remote access – to manage multiple locations.
10. Sales module – Sales accounting.
11. Automatic email / SMS Alerts module that sends automatic messages to managers.
12. Payroll and HR module – salary slips.
13. Cost sheet module – preparing estimate.
14. CRM Module – Customer Relationship Management.

(b) Assembly Production

In this kind of production usually several parts are added progressively to make a finished product and is measured in numbers. This is also called discrete manufacturing. The FG is usually measure in numbers. For example, TATA Motors manufacturing vehicles.

3.2.2 Complete ERP Case study of Electro Stampings Limited (ESL)

To understand about ERP modules thoroughly; let us study a plant that is manufacturing an item that is called 'Stampings'. Stampings are used in turn to make the Electric Motors. ESL manufactures the Stampings as per exact specification given by the Motor manufacturing company and sells these to Motor manufacturing company as per its order. Therefore, it is called OEM customer.

Fig. 3.5: Automatic Stamping Machine

First, let us identify various types of vendors and make a 'Vendor type master'. This will help the purchase officer to group all vendors and get the vendor type wise reports. Example of types of vendor (or supplier) can be as follows:

1. Consumables
2. Die Steel
3. Export Services
4. Furniture and Fixtures
5. Gauges
6. General Vendor
7. Hardware
8. I. T.
9. Imported Steel
10. Indigenous Steel
11. Legal Advisor
12. Lubricant
13. Machine Maintenance
14. Machine Parts
15. Packing Material
16. Plant and Machinery
17. Printing and Stationary
18. Raw Material General
19. Service Provider
20. Tools
21. Transport Service

Next, we have to create the vendor master. The purpose is to enter vendor details such as name, address etc. This is used while preparing purchase related transactions such as PO (purchase order), etc. Some of the major fields to be entered are:

1. Organisation name
2. Vendor type (one of the types as explained above)
3. Contact person name
4. Telephone number
5. Email id
6. Address
7. City
8. State
9. Country

In India, all manufacturing companies must pay tax to the Government called Excise duty. So in ERP, the user must enter the ECC number, Excise Range, Division, State Sales Tax (SST) number, Central Sales Tax Number (CST), of the vendor in the vendor master.

One of the important transactions of the purchase department is the Purchase Order (PO). This transaction is used to ask vendor to supply the material. PO is given to an approved vendor only. Information such as vendor name, item to be procured, item quantity, rate, etc. is entered in the PO. The PO is used to procure Raw material, packing material, bought out items, etc.

The material is received in the store based on the PO. Stores manager cannot receive material if PO is not raised. Stores manager does not have authority to enter item or rate. PO is a parent document against which the Stores GRN and the Purchase Voucher is made. PO neither is posted in inventory nor accounts ledger therefore it is a passive document. PO does not affect the inventory or accounts. For example, PO is raised on the vendor 'Thyssenkrupp Electrical Steel, Nashik for CRNGO Parent Coil, for say 3 metric ton for a given rate. ERP also prints name of the person who has login to prepare the transaction, and prints date on the PO. All relevant additional amount is entered such as Discount, Excise, Cess, Sales tax, Insurance, etc.

In ERP, it is necessary to know who wanted the material. The manager who is asking is called the indenter. Indent By menu appears as follows: User selects name of the indenter from the Indent By drop down box. This is the name of the person who wanted the material. It is also called the purchase requisition.

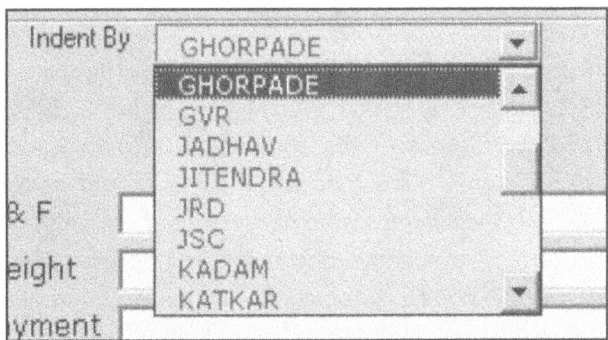

Fig. 3.6: Drop Down Menu to Select Indenter

In case customer is giving the material, it is necessary to enter as 'Customer Material IN' transaction. When customer is paying authority, user will tick the 'Labour Purchase Order' box as shown.

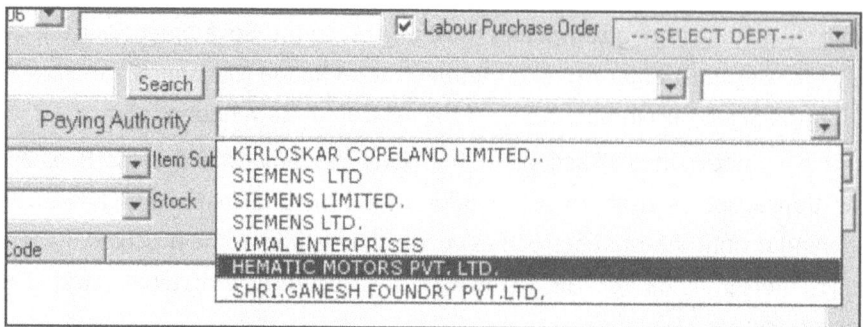

Fig. 3.7: Paying Authority Drop Down Menu

Purpose: When the material is received from vendor, a purchase voucher (PV) is prepared. However, if the material is received from customer (payment to vendor will be made by customer), then user will tick Labour PO. It is important that the customer type is 'Labour Bill'. The customer name should be in Address master, if the same is also third Party, (e.g. Kirloskar Copeland Ltd.), user will select customer type as 'Labour Bill'. The customer name should be in customer master, if the same is also normal customer but also paying authority, (e.g. Hematic Motors.), user will select customer type as 'Labour Bill'.

It is necessary to give document number to each transaction entered in ERP unlike in Telly accounting software. The idea is once the document number is given, the transaction cannot be changed or deleted. For each kind of transaction, there is a separate series of document number.

In India, the accounting year starts from 1st April and the year-end is 31st March. Whereas in rest of the world, the accounting year starts from 1st January and the year-end is 31st December. In each new accounting year the document number in each series is reset to 001.

Now let us consider that the item is received in the stores. The store's manager will enter a transaction in ERP called the Purchase Voucher or PV and GIIR Goods Receipt cum inspection transaction. The purpose of this transaction is to inform ERP software when material is received in the stores. PO is a parent document to make a PV. User will select vendor name. All pending PO will *default* automatically. User will enter Quantity information and save the PV. This document is active document. In ERP, user does not have to enter documents twice. PV will be posted automatically in the accounts ledger and inventory ledger. Traditionally this transaction is known as Stores Memo.

Purchase Voucher cum Goods Inward transactions does the following:
(1) PV will add material into stock (Hold location or material under inspection location).
(2) Credit the vendor (supplier) in the books of accounts.
(3) QC inspector or the Quality Assurance (QA) user can reopen PV and enter accepted quantity, this will automatically add item into main stores, and if item is rejected, it will add into Rejection Location.

(4) Prepares short quantity debit note based on Challan quantity and received quantity. In case the supplier quantity and the actual received, quantity does not match.

This PV and GIIR option can be seen under the Inventory menu in the Inventory menu → Inventory Transaction sub menu. The PV is a unique transaction that is integrated with purchase, inventory as well as creditor account.

Suppose the item is rejected by the QA then the same has to be sent back to vendor or sometimes scrapped. The goods are returned to vendor using RTV (Return-To-Vendor) (if not excisable). If excisable goods are to be returned, user will prepare sales invoice.

Let us have a look at some of the main Purchase section related Reports (MIS): User can select various *filters*; drop down list, to select a particular vendor or a particular item to get the transaction details. User can double-click on the raw to see the actual transaction. All reports (Registers) in ERP provide document level list (the first view by default) and also item level view. Drilldown button gives item wise details.

Vendor Master Printout: This is basically a list of vendors for the purchase department. Vendor's details such as Name, Address, Phone number, etc. are printed in alphabetical order. Care should be taken to enter name directly without M/s or Messer. Otherwise it will be listed under M and will be difficult to search.

Additional ERP reports are available to the authorised user as follows:

1. **PV Register:** List of Purchase Voucher or the Goods inward transactions. Material received in stores. This menu will be under inventory module.
2. **Expense Voucher Register:** List of Expense Vouchers (EV) or the service provider transactions. This may appear under the account module.
3. **PO Register:** List of Purchase Orders raised during a given period.

Material management

Let us meet the material manager to see various features of ERP system.

The most important master is the 'Inventory Master'. Major raw material and semi-finished goods and FG relation is established while making the Bill of Materials master (BOM). For example, the relation of Parent Coil and the Slitted Coil. Other items are defined in the item master of this company making 'Stampings':

1. Lamination
2. Loose lamination
3. Stack Lamination
4. Auto stack
5. Welded
6. Riveted
7. Stack
8. Finished Goods

Item Master

The item master data is the Master database containing information about all kinds of material: Raw material, factory made items and the Finished Goods. Everyone in the organization must call any material (item) by the same name (nomenclature). Proper classification or categorization of material is very important in the ERP. This discipline helps in getting useful MIS (Management Information System) reports. It is necessary to control the access to ERP data by locking with the login id and password. The secret password to prepare the item master should be restricted to authorised, technically qualified manger only. This will ensure correct grouping of items. All masters must be made on the main computer server only. No item is allowed to be created in the local computer hard drive. In other words, in ERP system user has one single database on the server hard disk or in the cloud. Cloud meaning on the internet server.

In ERP, it is not necessary to give alphanumerical item code to every item. Item code once given cannot be changed. Item code is nothing but a short name of the item. Item description is long name of an item. Item description can be edited later, but NOT the item code. User should select the main category of the item carefully. It is advisable to restrict number of category of items. This is one time database setting, and should be restricted to experienced person only.

It is necessary to identify each plant and location within each plant by a code. For example; Plant A or Plant B. Stores location in Plant A or stores location in Plant B, and so on. Therefore, we have the 'Main Location Master' and the 'Sub-Location master'.

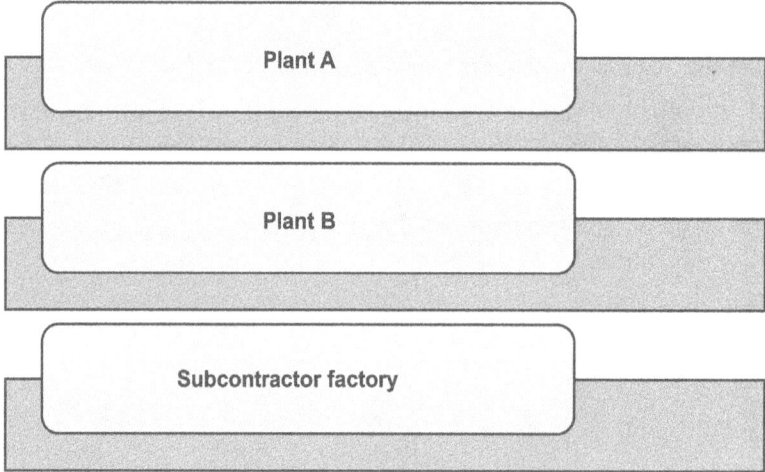

Fig. 3.8: Multiple Locations

Location code	Sub-location description
1. Plant A	Scrap
2. Plant A	Store
3. Plant A	WIP
4. Plant A	Rejection
5. Plant A	FG
6. Plant A	Hold
7. Plant B	Scrap
8. Plant B	Store
9. Plant B	WIP
10. Plant B	Rejection

Material is given to subcontractor for processing. It is necessary to define the location of the subcontractor factory, called Third Party.

11. Third Party S Enterprises
12. Third Party K Copeland Ltd. Unit II
13. Third Party G Engineering Works

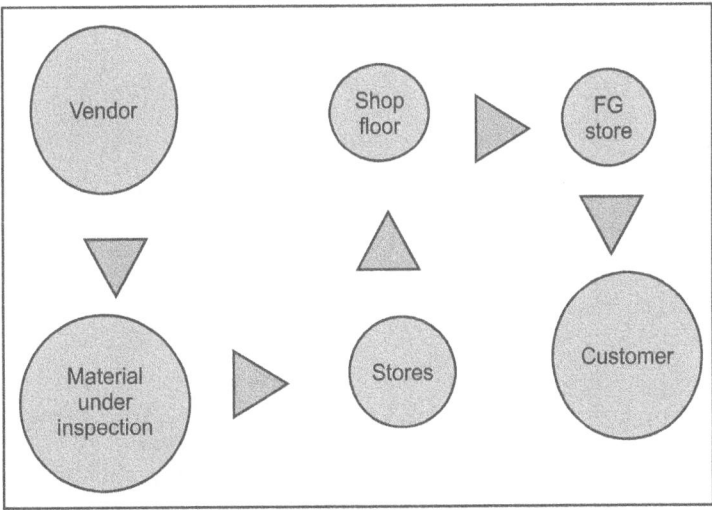

Fig. 3.9: Material Tracking

It is important to note that any material movement, in ERP, is always with respect to an inventory *location* that is predefined in the location and sub-location master database. This will ensure that the material manager will get Location wise inventory reports.

Material manager has identified the main category and item subcategory as follows:

Item Main Category	Subcategory
Capital Goods	
Components	
	Ms Rivet
Die Steel	
	Seamless Pipes
	Hchc D2 Round Bars
	Hss M2 Round Bars
	Hss M2 Plates
	Hchc D2 Plates
	Ohns Plates
	En 31 Round Bars
	Ohns Square Bar
	Hitachi Sld Round Bar
	Hitachi Yxm-1 Round Bar
Factory Made Item	
	Rotor Lamination Loose
	Stator Lamination Loose
	Trans (Without Decarb)
	Crngo Slitted Coil
	CRCA Slitted Coil
Fg Core Pack	
	Varroc Engg.
Fg Rotor Auto Stack	
	Varroc
	Ksb Pumps
	Motor Industries
	Lothian Electric
Fg Rotor Lamination	
	Ksb Sinnar
	Hematic Motors Pvt. Ltd.
	Ksb Pumps Ltd., Coimbatore
	Varroc, Plant III
	Varroc, Plant Iv
	Hematic
Fg Rotor Packet	
	Ksb Pump
	Kbl Shirwal
	Ksb Pumps Ltd Sinnar

Item Main Category	Subcategory
Fg Shunt Steel	
Fg Size 43	
	Wilo
Fg Size 52	
	Wilo Ag
Fg Size 53	
	Wilo Ag, Germany
Fg Size 63	
	Wilo - Ag
Fg Stator Auto Stack	
	Wilo Gmbh
Fg Stator Lamination	
	Pmp Components
	Ksb
	Ksb Sinnar
	Hematic Motors
	Ksb Pumps
	Pmp Components Ltd
Fg Stator Packet	
	Ksb Pumps
	Kbl Shirwals
	Ksb Pumps Sinnar
	Ksb - Sinnar
	Motor Industries
	Kirloskar Shirwal
	Kirloskar, Shirwal
	Kirloskar, Shirwal
	Kirloskar, Shirwal
	Kirloskar, Shirwal
	Kirloskar, Shirwal
	Hematic Motors Pvt Ltd
Fg Stator Riveted Stack	
	Motor Industries

Item Main Category	Subcategory
Fg Transformer	Venture
Fg Transformer Lamination	Venture Power Systems
Free Sample	
Gauges	
Packing Material	Corrugated Box Wooden Pallet Packing Material
Rm Aluminum	Aluminum
Rm Steel Parent Coil	Rm Crngo Parent Coil Rm CRCA Parent Coil
Scrap	Trimming End Strip Production Scrap
Services	Services
Sku (Shipping Unit)	Venture
Stores and Spares	Lubricant Gas Cylinder Binding Wire Consumable Grinding Wheels Polish Paper

Item Main Category	Subcategory
	S.S. Drills
	Ts Drills
	Files
	Cutting Tools
	Slot Cutters
	Mounted Point Wheels
	Diamond Dresser
	Oil Stone
	Filler Gauge Strips

When a senior executive askes: "How many?" The stores clerk says: "Five". This is incomplete answer. Five what? five kg, five numbers, five sets? To avoid such confusion it is necessary to define the UOM in the ERP master database as follows:

Accounting Unit or the Unit of Measurement or UOM Master: It displays various units of measurement, which are regularly used. E.g. Kg, each, pair, set, etc. This is 'accounting unit' required while creating item master.

KG
NO
MTR
LTR
MT
SQFT
DAY
BUNDLE
SET
PAIR

The Stampings are made from special quality steel. To identify the quality of the steel, Steel Grade identification is given. The Grade Master is created to ensure correct steel is used as follows:

User will create 'Grade ID' depending on the supplier to the item. Grade master is the prerequisite for the item master. That means grade id is required before making the item master.

GRADE DESCRIPTION	GRADE ID
35C250C3Y	EFH
35H300	NSB
450-50PPC6W	EFF
50C350APC6W	EFA
50C530C6W	EFC
50C700C6W	EFG
50C800C6W	EFB
50H1000	NLA
50H1300	NLB

As explained earlier the Purchases Voucher is an active transaction that affects both accounts and inventory.

PV [or the Goods Inward Note] does the following:

1. PV will add material into stock.
2. Credit the vendor (supplier). Automatic posting in creditor ledger ensures that both ledgers – item and account – are updated instantly after the material is accepted. QC inspector / Quality Assurance will enter accepted quantity – this will automatically add item into main stores and if item is rejected, add into Rejection Location. User may click on 'Labour bill material' radio button, ERP will ask user to select the paying authority.

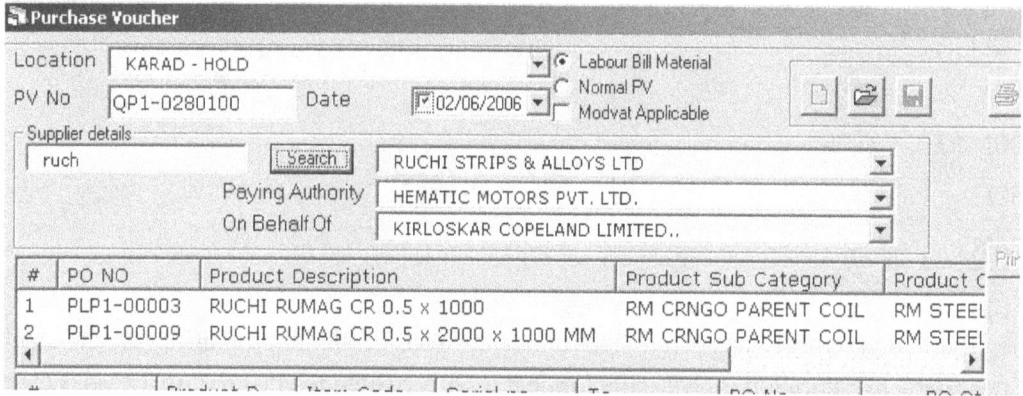

Fig. 3.10: Purchase Bill Data Entry Screen

Stock Transfer Challan (STC): STC is used to transfer material from one location to another. This does not consume material. User will select 'from' location and 'to' location. For CRNGO Steel raw material, ERP will capture the serial number and excise link is provided. Whereas for other material (e.g. bearing) it will be a normal STC for internal stock transfer from, say stores to shop floor, no serial number or excise is required. Since the material does not leave the factory premises.

Goods Delivery Note (GDN): To send material out for processing to third party. ERP will allow GDN entry only when there is sufficient stock in the selected (from) location. This will do the following:

(a) Reduce the stock of the selected location.

(b) Add the same at the selected TP (Job Worker's) location.

When GDN is prepared, Excise Challan IV under notification no. 214/86 (earlier 57 F4) is prepared automatically, as per the Excise rule.

Subsidiary Challan: This is used to transfer the material from Plant A to Plant B. This challan is made against main challan reference. Subsidiary challan will match stock transferred through main challan and will show the balance, if any.

Purchase return sales invoice: User will prepare Excise invoice when material is returned back to vendor. For non-excisable material user can prepare RTV or Return-To-Vendor. Reference of PV is required.

Sales Return or Return Goods Note (RGN): This is entered when material is received back from customer. (E.g. rejected by customer). To prepare RGN the reference of the original invoice is required, which is to be defaulted in ERP.

Goods Inward Note (GIN): This transaction is entered when material is received back from the third party. GIN is similar to purchase voucher. When GIN is prepared, ERP will create a production entry automatically, at the third party location, for that much quantity. The effect of GIN is as under:

(a) Semi-finished item received will be added to the shop floor location.

(b) Credits in the creditor account ledger.

(c) Parent document like job order (labour PO) is a must.

(d) Production entry will consume the corresponding child items from the TP location. (linked with the BOM).

Material Issue Note: MIN is used to consume material from a given location. For example, when an item 'ball bearing' is issued to shop floor, for repairs, an STC is made. When the spare is consumed, MIN is prepared. This is mostly used for item other than main raw material.

Stock Adjustment Note: SAN is used to add or remove item from the stock, for a given location. Access to SAN is given to authorised person only. This is useful to correct the stock balance in case of difference in the ERP stock and physical stock.

Store Memo Challan Making: Stores memo challan making is used when the Excise material (RM Parent coil) is transferred from Plant A hold to Plant B coil store. The PV or Stores memo is linked. User will select the store memo number from the dropdown. STC from A to B is prepared with 57 F4 excise challan. Challan number is auto generated, but user can change. Usually coil is sent to A for slitting. However, in case a slitted coil is purchased directly, the same needs to go to A. User may select required button 'Make Challan' or 'Keep in B' as shown in the following screen dump. Modvat is modified value added tax, now called CENVAT, used to indicate excise transaction.

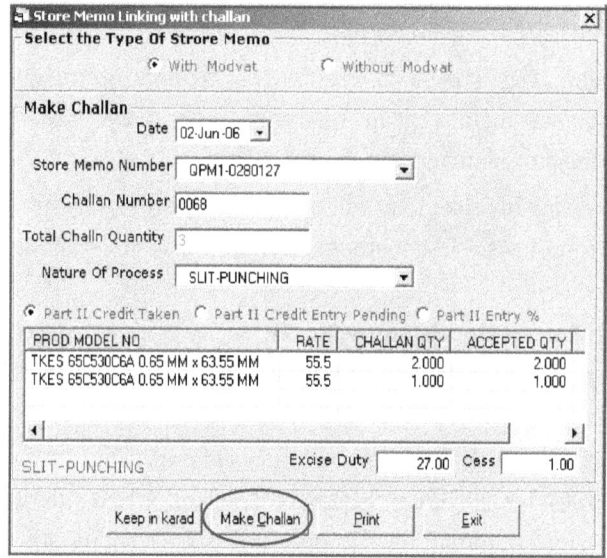

Fig. 3.11: Stores Data Entry Screen for Challan

Main challan can be generated to keep the material in B Coil store when direct slitted coil is purchased.

Closing Balance: One time exercise of entering inventory stock closing balance as on given date. From that date onwards, ERP will do the necessary arithmetic to give accurate closing stock, for a given location. This needs to be done once but requires lot of care and understanding of the concept.

3.3 Sales and Distribution

The sales and distribution module in ERP encompasses various procedures pertaining to the marketing of goods and services. The sales cycle starts with the lead generation activities followed by enquiry. Every enquiry received is captured in the ERP system with details such as name of the customer, item, etc. To keep track of each enquiry, a unique document number and date, is automatically generated by the system. The concerned sales person will then send the quotation for each enquiry.

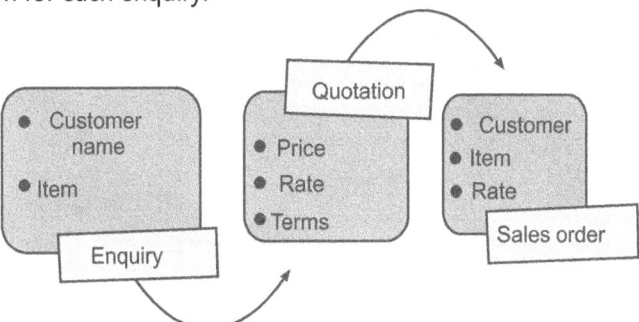

Fig. 3.12: Pre-sales Cycle

Pre-sales cycle: The ERP system will now link the quotation with the enquiry and 'close' it. Management will get an important MIS of 'Open Enquiry'. This report will clearly tell how many enquiries were received in a given period, and how many are still 'Open'. Senior person can follow-up with those sales man and ensure that the proposal is given as soon as possible. In short, ERP helps the management to ensure that no business opportunity is lost.

After some negotiation and follow up when customer places the order and the same is entered as 'Sales Order' transaction (SO), by linking the corresponding quotation. The SO will close the quotation. ERP will help top management to get an instant report of 'Open Quotation'. The Director in-charge of the sales department will know who gave how many quotations, how many orders is received, and so on. Important point to note is that all this information is available *without* asking any sales staff, or depending on their e-mail reports. If at all for some reason the order is lost, salesman will have to make an entry citing the reason.

Sales Cycle: After the order is received, (SO) the company will supply the Goods (FG) along with the sales invoice. In India, for all manufacturing companies the sales invoice must show clearly the Excise duty charges and the sales tax or VAT (Value Added Tax) component with relevant Excise registration number, sales tax number, etc. ERP system ensures there is no error in the invoice and is linked to the Sales Order, so that no mistake in quantity, rate or discount is made by the shipping section.

Let us visit a company, manufacturing Special Purpose Machines (SPM), to understand above procedures in more details as follows:

SPM is specialising in metal finishing machines. This company is engaged in manufacturing of Vibratory Finishing Machines and Centrifugal Finishing Machines under the brand name **"VIBRO-FIN & SUPER-FIN."** **SPM** also makes relevant accessories and consumables. SUPER-FIN enjoys unbeatable leadership in the market.

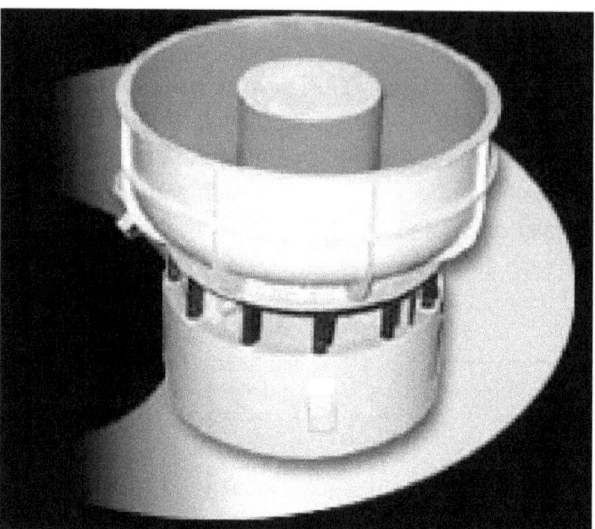

Fig. 3.13: VIBRO-FIN machine with Electrical Panel

Vibro – Fin machines are used deburring, descaling, edge radiusing, surface smoothing, polishing, pre-plating finish, and mirror polishing, etc.

SUPER-FIN range of centrifugal finishing systems are high energy, the most powerful machines meant for precision. Deburring to buff like polishing of metal / plastic parts.

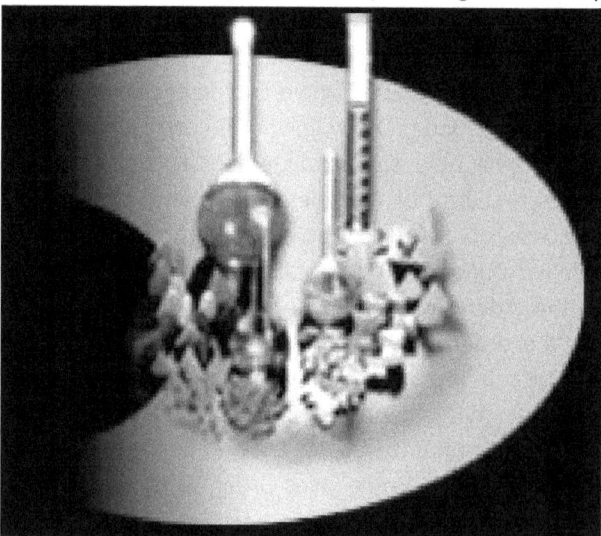

Fig. 3.14: Finished Goods

MEDIA: A scientifically designed, an extensive range of ceramic media, plastic media, steel media, corncobs and finishing compounds are provided with machine.

The Bill of Material example shows the relation of the child items to father item.

```
BOM Master Lis As on   24-08-07  12:50:00 PM Created By ASHOK

VIBROFIN SMA500 PU WITH STANDARD ACCESSORIES (VIBRO FIN Rate : 0 UOM : NO RNo : 1 DATE : 20-Mar-2007  TIME : 0)
            TERMINAL BOX  ALUMINIUM ( Quantity 1: 1 Quantity 2: 0 Rate : 96.56 UOM : NOS Time : )
            BASE WEDMENT FOR SM300 SMA500(SUB   ASSEMBLY( ) Quantity 1: 1 Quantity 2: 0 Rate : 0 UOM : NOS RNo : 1 Time : )
               FLAT RING FOR BASE SM300(SUB   ASSEMBLY( ) Quantity 1: 2 Quantity 2: 0 Rate : 0 UOM : NOS RNo : 1 Time : )
                    M.S.FLAT 40x10MM ( Quantity 1: 9.8 Quantity 2: 0 Rate : 0 UOM : KGS Time : )

            M.S.PLATE 5MM ( Quantity 1: 45.8 Quantity 2: 0 Rate : 36 UOM : KGS Time : )
            SPRING GUIDE SMALL(SUB   ASSEMBLY( ) Quantity 1: 25 Quantity 2: 0 Rate : 20 UOM : NOS RNo : 1 Time : )
                 M.S.ROUND 40MM ( Net Wt.: 0.396 Wastage Per.: 0 Rate : 38.5 UOM : KG Time : )


            BOWL MS DIA 4.3 FT UNLOADER  PU(SUB   ASSEMBLY( ) Quantity 1: 1 Quantity 2: 0 Rate : 0 UOM : NO RNo : 1 Time : )
               BOWL MS DIA 4.3 FT UNLOADER(SUB   ASSEMBLY( ) Quantity 1: 1 Quantity 2: 0 Rate : 0 UOM : NO RNo : 1 Time : )
                    0200 BRR ( Quantity 1: 1 Quantity 2: 0 Rate : 1220 UOM : NO Time : )
                    0200 TSR ( Quantity 1: 1 Quantity 2: 0 Rate : 1420 UOM : NO Time : )
                    DRAIN  PLATE 160 X 160 ( Quantity 1: 1 Quantity 2: 0 Rate : 225 UOM : NO Time : )
                    DISH SM300 DIA 1248(SUB   ASSEMBLY( ) Quantity 1: 1 Quantity 2: 0 Rate : 0 UOM : NOS RNo : 1 Time : )
                         M.S.PLATE 5MM ( Quantity 1: 81.3 Quantity 2: 0 Rate : 36 UOM : KGS Time : )

                    M.S.FLAT 32x10MM ( Quantity 1: 13.6 Quantity 2: 0 Rate : 34.2 UOM : KGS Time : )
                    M.S.PLATE 5MM ( Quantity 1: 130 Quantity 2: 0 Rate : 36 UOM : KGS Time : )
                    SPRING GUIDE SMALL(SUB   ASSEMBLY( ) Quantity 1: 25 Quantity 2: 0 Rate : 20 UOM : NOS RNo : 1 Time : )
                         M.S.ROUND 40MM ( Net Wt.: 0.396 Wastage Per.: 0 Rate : 38.5 UOM : KG Time : )


            Brass Links-BSL links for 3/6T ( Quantity 1: 3 Quantity 2: 0 Rate : 2.1 UOM : NOS Time : )
            H T HEX BOLT M20X180 ( Quantity 1: 3 Quantity 2: 0 Rate :  UOM : NO Time : )
            0300 VIBRO MOTOR FLANGE ASSLY(VIBRO MOTOR COMPLETE( ) Quantity 1: 1 Quantity 2: 0 Rate : 0 UOM : NOS RNo : 1 Time : )
               0300 VIBRO MOTOR FLANG(VIBRO   MOTORS( ) Quantity 1: 1 Quantity 2: 0 Rate : 0 UOM : NO RNo : 1 Time : )
                  0300 VM FL MACHINED PARTS(VIBRO   MOTORS( ) Quantity 1: 1 Quantity 2: 0 Rate :  UOM : SET RNo : 1 Time : )
                       0200 BBH ( Quantity 1: 1 Quantity 2: 0 Rate : 1330 UOM : NO Time : )
                       0200 BBIC ( Quantity 1: 1 Quantity 2: 0 Rate : 190 UOM : NO Time : )
```

Fig. 3.15: Bill of Materials (BOM)

The BOM Module in ERP shows all the Electrical sub-assemblies (Relation between the bought out items (child) and the Factory made items (Father) in above figure)

Items like plate need to be added in BOM as Bought out items (child) and the factory made items will be the small pieces made out of that big plate.

The layout drawing will be made to show how many smaller pieces will be made from one sheet. This will be outside DNS.

```
S.M.SYSTEMS PVT. LTD.
BOM Listing for item name : VIBRATORY FINISHING MACHINE MODEL SF 30 RNo : 1RDt: 01-17-2007 00:00:00'As On10-Apr-07 12:19:55 PMCreated ByDHIRAJ
VIBRATORY FINISHING MACHINE MODEL SF 30, SF 30, , 0, 0, VIBRO FIN, Rate : 5000, UOM : NO, RNo : 1, DATE : 17-Jan-07)
         UNUSED 5 / 7.5 HP MOTORS (OTHER.... Quantity 1: 1 Quantity 2: 0 Rate : 4810 UOM : NO RNo : 1)
         0014 VM FL MACHINED PARTS (VIBRO   MOTORS Quantity 1: 1 Quantity 2: 0 Rate : 0 UOM : SET RNo : 1)
              0014 BBH (CASTINGSS Gross Quantity : 1 Rate : 310 UOM : NO)
              0014 BBIC (CASTINGSS Gross Quantity : 1 Rate : 93 UOM : NO)
              0014 BBOC (CASTINGSS Gross Quantity : 1 Rate : 93 UOM : NO)
              0014 PIPE (VIBRO   MOTORS Gross Quantity : 1 Rate : 720 UOM : NOS)
              0014 TBH (CASTINGSS Gross Quantity : 1 Rate : 330 UOM : NO)
              0014 TBIC (CASTINGSS Gross Quantity : 1 Rate : 87 UOM : NO)
              0014 TBOC (CASTINGSS Gross Quantity : 1 Rate : 87 UOM : NO)
              CABLE PLATE TOP FOR ELECTRIC MOTORS (VIBRO   MOTORS Quantity 1: 1 Quantity 2: 0 Rate :  UOM : NO RNo : 1)
                   M.S.BRIGHT 50X10 (ROUND/SECTIONS Gross Wt. : 0.25 Rate : 44 UOM : KG)
              EN 8 DIA 40AA (EN SERIES Gross Wt. : 6.5 Rate : 40 UOM : KG)
              SOC HEAD CAP SCREW M10X50 (HARDWARES Gross Quantity : 12 Rate : 12.24 UOM : NO)
              SOC HEAD CAP SCREW M6X16 (HARDWARES Gross Quantity : 16 Rate : 4.49 UOM : NO)
         BEARING  6305ZZ (BEARINGSSS Gross Quantity : 1 Rate : 0 UOM : NO)
         BEARING  NU 306EJP1C3  FAG (BEARINGSSS Gross Quantity : 1 Rate : 0 UOM : NO)
         CENTER SHAFT (SUB   ASSEMBLY Quantity 1: 1 Quantity 2: 0 Rate : 0 UOM : NO RNo : 1)
              EN 8 DIA 40 X 860 (EN SERIES Gross Quantity : 1 Rate : 0 UOM : NO)
```

Fig. 3.16: BOM shows Father-Child Relation

Process Master shows the standard production processes to be carried out by the production department. There are different types of processes carried out at third party.

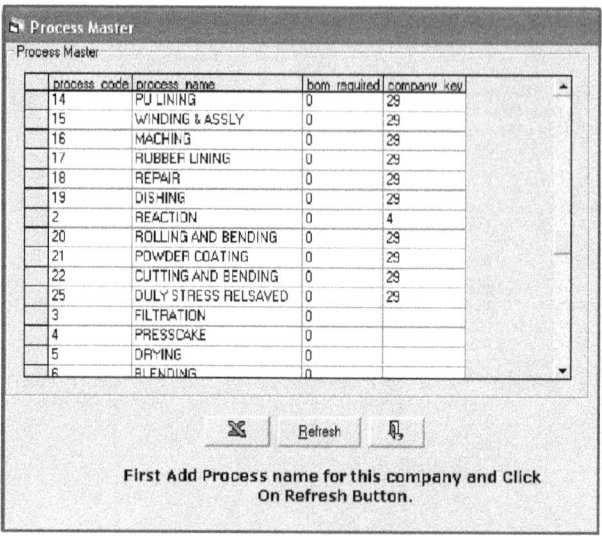

Fig. 3.17: Process Master Menu

The work order (Job Order) is given to production manager by the ERP system, to communicate clearly, what is to be produced, and from which raw material as shown below:

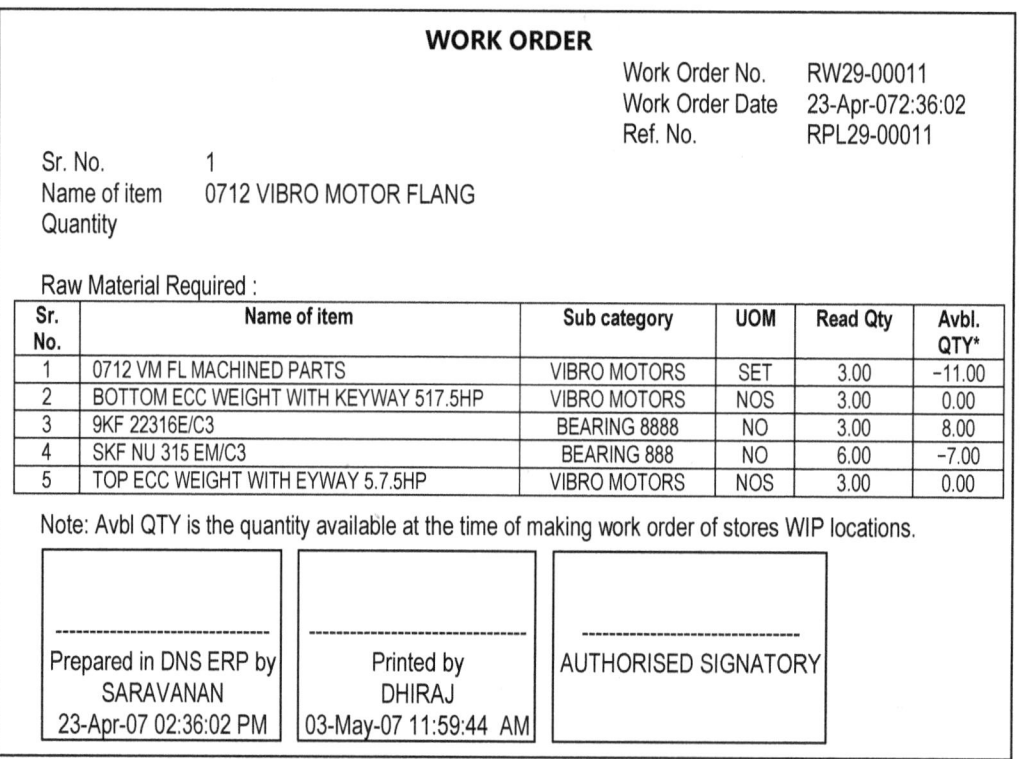

Fig. 3.18: Work Order Transaction Print Out

The sales department is enters all pre-sales transactions in the ERP system. All sales related enquiries received from existing customers, or new prospective customer is entered in ERP system.

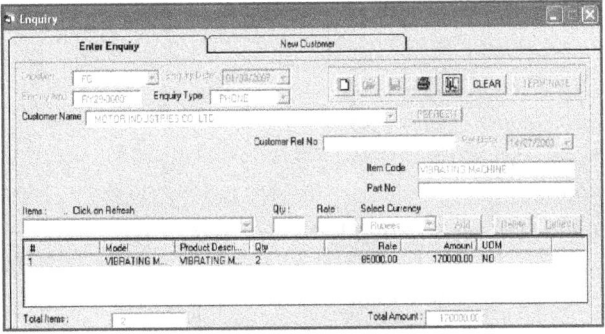

Fig. 3.19: Enquiry Data Entry Screen

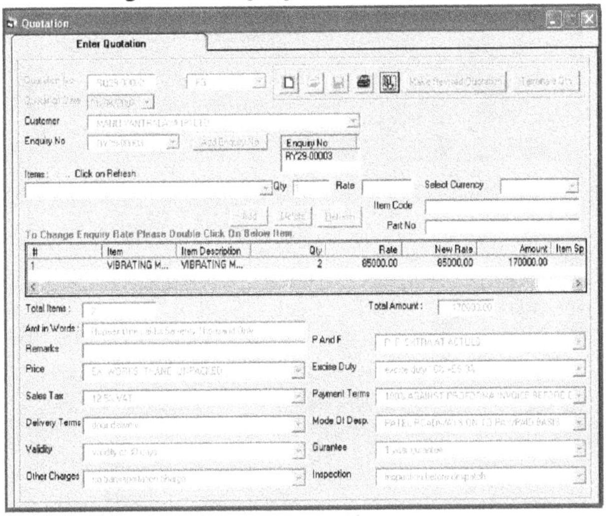

Fig. 3.20: An example of a Quotation Transaction

Quotation is entered by defaulting enquiry that is user cannot enter a quotation without entering enquiry. This will ensure that we get a correct count of number of enquiry and pending enquiry. Next, the sales order is entered, linking the quotation. The SO is also referred to as the OA or the Order Acceptance in some companies. The SO is a parent document, required to prepare the sales invoice. Sales Invoice cannot be prepared without the SO. This will give the count of number of SO and pending SO. Pending SO is order received but invoice not made. In other words the management can get a clear idea about all the important activities, such as enquires, proposals, or orders, and invoice in real-time. The following inputs are required for sales order.

In SO after adding rate, following columns are shown:
(a) Commission paid to agent in ₹
(b) Commission paid to others in ₹

(c) Freight paid by SMS.
(d) Any Other indirect discounts.

In the SO following additional information (fields) are provided:
(a) Sales manager in charge (Drop Down)
(b) Sales Engineer In charge (Drop Down)
(c) Agent In charge (Drop Down)
(d) Customer type (New/ Repeat)
(e) Road permit required (drop down, Y/N)

Cancelling sales order entry: SO can be terminated by clicking on the terminate button. User may enter the reason for terminating the sales order.

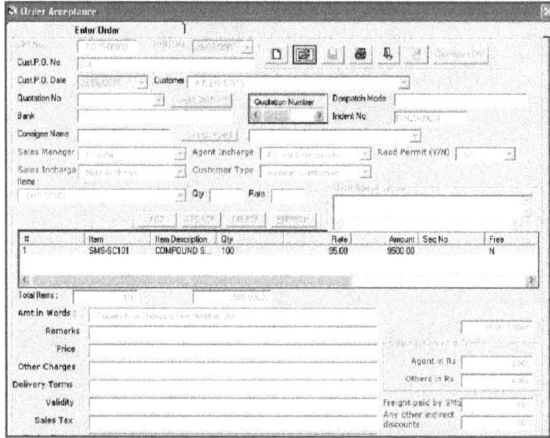

Fig. 3.21: Order Acceptance Data Entry Screen

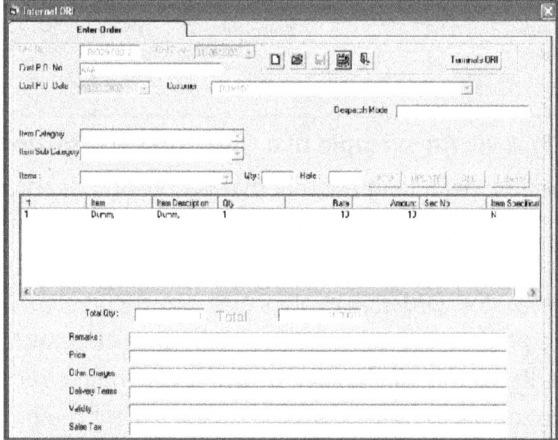

Fig. 3.22: Internal order Receipt Information

This is internal sales order (SO made for stock) for the production, purchase, etc. Here user may not have received a formal purchase order from any customer. The item is produced based on the past trend or projected sales. Scrap Invoice is created to sale the record any scrape material sold.

Proforma Invoice looks similar to the actual sales invoice. However, Proforma invoice is a passive transaction, in the sense that it does not affect accounts or the inventory. Whereas, the sale invoice is an active transaction that affects both accounts as well as inventory.

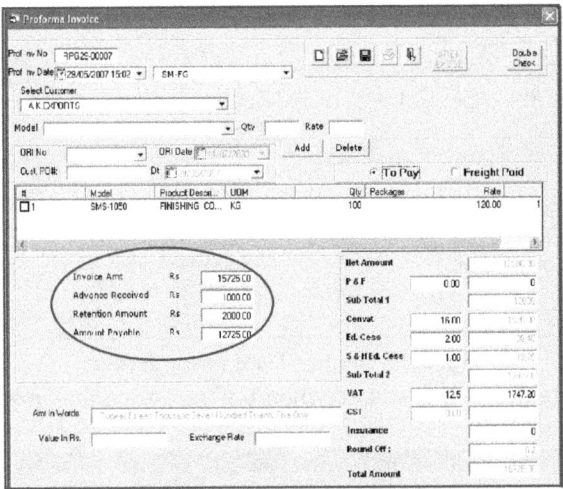

Fig. 3.23: Proforma Invoice Data Entry Screen

If advance is received, retention amount is not null and VAT is applicable then it will display the following business process.

Next the sales invoice is entered in ERP at the time of dispatch of the finished goods (FG). The SO is prerequisite to make sales invoice. User will select the name of the customer from the dropdown. User can print extra copies, usually four copies, of the invoice as required for the excise purpose, transporter copy, etc. Note: Purchase return for excisable goods are sent back to vendor by preparing sales invoice in DNS. For this, user has to select the type of Invoice as Purchase return.

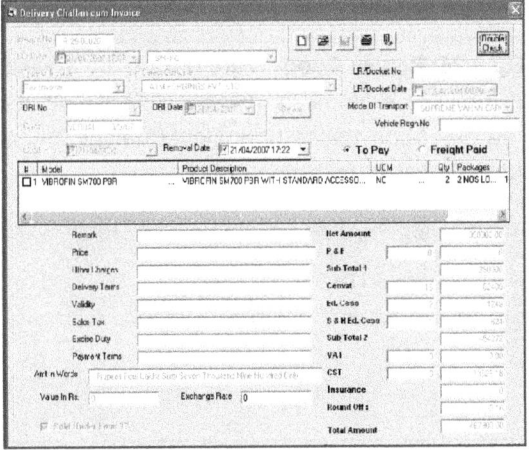

Fig. 3.24: Sales Data Entry Screen

Packing and Forwarding (P & F) amount: User may enter % (percentage) figure OR user may enter lump sum amount (directly).

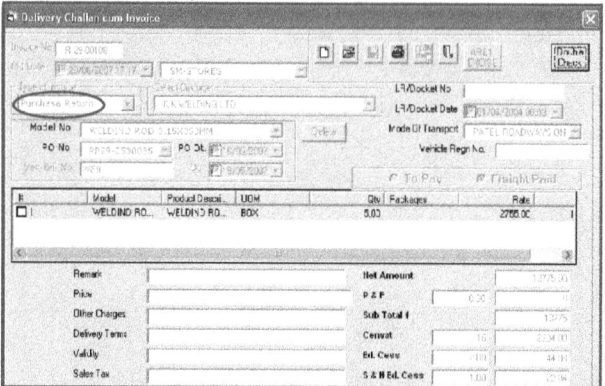

Fig. 3.25: Invoice Data Entry Screen

Return Goods Note (RGN) is prepared when the 'non-excisable' material is received back from customer.

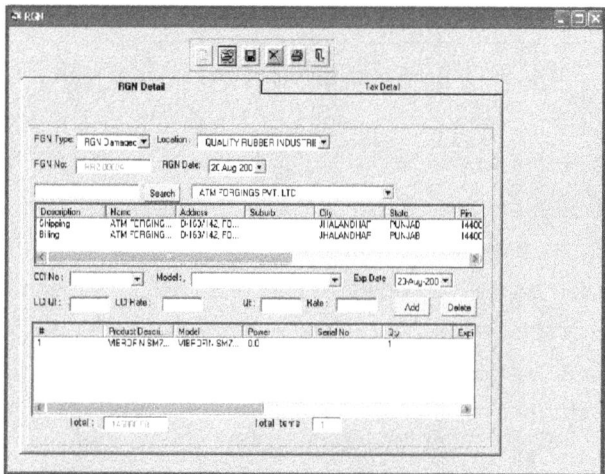

Fig 3.26: Return Goods Note Data Entry Screen

Return Goods Note Register example is given below to list items returned from the customer. This may be an exception transaction. Nevertheless, any exception movement of material, incoming or outgoing has to recorded in ERP.

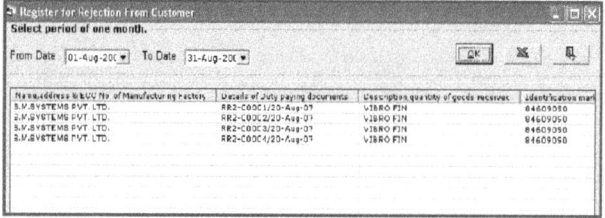

Fig. 3.27: Sales Rejection Register

3.4 Human Resource Management

To compete effectively, an organisation needs to align all corporate resources, including employees with business objectives. All companies must efficiently manage the staff, operators, officers, etc., now referred as the human capital. The personnel department, which is now called the HR or the Human Resource department must keep them happy. The most extreme view is that the employees must be treated as first internal *customer*. For this the HR module in the ERP gives real-time reports to the HR managers to manage the man-power of the enterprise.

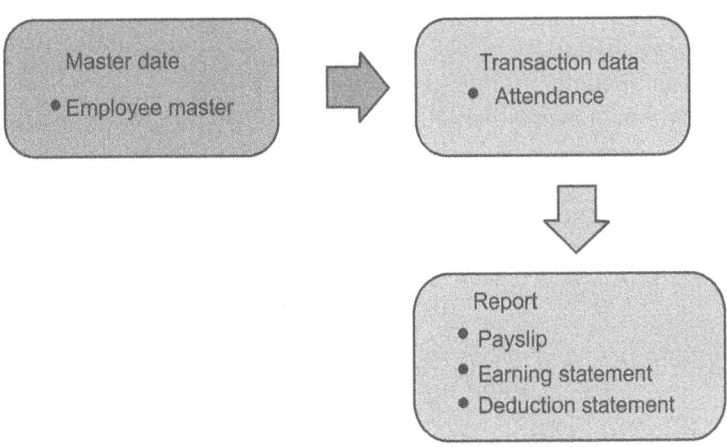

Fig. 3.28: HR Module Concept Diagram

Human Resource Management ERP Module scope is as follows:
1. **Master**
    (a) Employee Master
    (b) Earning heads Master
    (c) Deduction heads Master
    (d) Department master
    (e) Designation master
    (f) State Master
    (g) City master
    (h) Accounts from General Ledger Master
2. **Transactions**
    (a) Employee Attendance Transaction
    (b) Monthly Earning
    (c) Monthly Deductions
    (d) Income Tax Monthly Entry
3. **Reports**
    (a) Salary Slip
    (b) Employee list

(c) Payroll Register
(d) Earning head wise register
(e) Deduction head wise register
(f) Attendance Register
(g) ESI Report
(h) Provident Fund Report
(i) Leave Encashment report
(j) Professional Tax Statement
(k) Form 16 for each employee for returns filing
(l) Bank Statement
(m) Employee Joining Report
(n) Employee Left Report

While calculating the pay it is necessary to identify daily wages and monthly wages type of employee. In the attendance master various kinds of leave is stored, e.g. paid leave, sick leave, unpaid leave, etc. Some employees may have taken advance or loan from the company, which also is recorded in the employee master and monthly instalment can be deducted from the pay.

ABC COMPANY

EL 31/1, Electronic Zone, U' Block, M.I.D.C., Bhosari, Pune - 411026. Phone 27125198

PAY SLIP FOR THE MONTH OF DECEMBER 2008							
Emp Id S17-0002				**Pf No.** 159734		**Esic No.** 121	
Employee Name ABHIMANYU SURYAVANSHI							
Department ACCOUNTS							
Designation ACCOUNTS MANAGER				**ICICI BANK No.** PP4273918			
Present Days	21.0	**PL**	0.0	**CL** 0.0	**SL** 0.0	**Paid Holiday**	1.0
W.Off	0.0	**Absent**	0.0	**LWP** 2.0	**COFF** 2.0	**Paid Days**	24.0
Earnings ₹					**Deductions ₹**		
Basic		9,000	8308	ESC			0
House Rent Allowance		3,000	2769	Provident Fund			997
Education Allowance		300	277	Professional Tax			200
Medical Allowance		500	452	Advance / Loan			0
Transport Allowance		700	646	Labour Welfare Fund			12
LTA		300	277	Income Tax			146
				Bond			1000
				L.I.C.			200
Gross Earnings		16,100	14,862	**Total Deductions**			2,855
Net Salary Payable		12,010					

Balance Loan / Advance : 500

Balance PL : 20

Balance CL : 20

Fig. 3.29: A sample Pay Slip showing Net Pay = Earning – Deductions

Let us have a look at the information stored in one record of the employee master that is called 'fields'.

Employee name is the first field that will come in our mind. However, name is not just one field. It is necessary to store the name in four fields. It is a common mistake to store name as Prof. Jyotindra J. Zaveri in one field. The title such as Mr., Mrs, Dr., Prof, needs to be separated. Otherwise, it will be difficult for the payroll module to arrange the employees list in the alphabetical order. If all entries start with Mr. or Mrs., all name will be sorted under M. To avoid such problems the title field is kept separate.

Fig. 3.30: Salary Calculation in ERP

Another common mistake is about the age. In ERP, the age is not stored but the date of birth is stored. Remember age is output, which is calculated instantly based on the date on which the report is required and it changes every day. Once the server computer knows today's date and the date of birth it will compute exact age and display. Similarly, date of joining, or date of retirement or leaving the organisation is stored. The date is stored in three-separated field as, dd, mm, yyyy. If you check the history, IBM mainframe computers started giving wrong results because the year was stored in a two-character field as yy and the 19yy was not stored. In the turn of the century, the year became 20yy and the payroll program was confused. This was the biggest jolt software industry got and was referred to as Y2K problem.

One more common mistake is while storing the address. Remember the address is not one or two fields only. First, there are two addresses, permanent address, and current address.

Here is a sample/generic list of employee master database record:
1. Employee code
2. Title
3. Family name or surname
4. Father or middle name
5. Name
6. Basic pay
7. Earning code 1 e.g. Travel Allowance

8. Earning code 2 e.g. Dearness Allowance
9. Deduction code 1 e.g. TDS (Tax Deducted at Source)
10. Deduction code 2 e.g. Profession Tax
11. Address field 1
12. Address field 2
13. Address field 3
14. State
15. City
16. Country
17. Date of birth dd mm yyyy
18. Date of joining dd mm yyyy
19. Male / Female
20. Married / Unmarried
21. If married – Name of spouse
22. If married – Date of marriage
23. Blood Group
24. In case of emergency – Contact number
25. In case of emergency – Name of person to be contacted
26. Bank branch
27. Bank account number
28. Provident Fund number
29. ESI number (Employee Scheme Insurance)
30. PAN number
31. Number of dependent children
32. Paid Leave
33. Unpaid Leave
34. Previous employment history
35. Designation
36. Department
37. Leave encashment details
38. LIC Premium Details (Life Insurance Corporation)

Performance review is done by a senior manager every year. For advanced employee appraisal requirements, HR Module also offers web-based performance appraisal and 360-degree review options that make it easier than ever to conduct employee appraisals and implement formal 360-degree feedback procedures. This captures colleague's feedback. For instance whether a person is a good team player or not, his leadership qualities, etc. can be assessed through such feedback.

Finally, we can say that ERP is used to manage four M's - Money, Material, Machine and the Manpower. ERP system ensures that all HR policies are streamlined with the mission statement of the enterprise. MIS is for aligning employees, processes, and strategies for business success. At the end of the day, money matters most. If a question is asked to define the HR management goal in one line, I would say *'HR is to manage people from Hire to Retire'.*

3.5 Inventory Control System

ERP software is used to manage online inventory. The inventory is divided into three major categories:

3.5.1 Raw Material Stock

Items that are purchased from suppliers (also called vendors), bought out items, or consumables fall under this category. For example, steel is raw material for an automobile manufacturing company. Fruit and vegetables are raw materials for a company, which is engaged, is manufacturing pickles. Alternatively, for that matter, a company that is manufacturing computers will purchase monitor, hard drive or keyboard, etc., as the bought-out items. Usually, these raw materials are stored in the location labelled 'raw material stores' after checking for quality.

3.5.2 WIP Stock

Work-in-Process inventory or the semi-finished goods fall under this category. For example, sub-assembly such as the Gear Box or the Brake assembly is the WIP inventory for the car.

3.5.3 Finished Goods (FG) Stock

The final product is the FG item. The item that is made and sold falls under the FG category. FG items usually appear in the Sales invoice. The Finished Goods is housed in the FG store or warehouse after the quality check.

3.5.4 The most important master is the Item Master in an Inventory System. Item master shows details of the item such as item code, item name, item description, item specification, Unit of Measurement, various rates, etc. It also includes the picture of the item.

The first step in the inventory system is to prepare Item Category and Item sub-category master. This is classification done based on the type of item. The most important report of the inventory system is the Stock Ledger. Managers can locate any item instantly using the ledger and find the stock status.

Usually, the R and D (Research and Development) department is authorised (password is given) to create a new Item / Finished Product in the item master. Item master is the prerequisite for preparing the Bill of Materials (BOM) master.

For efficient inventory management, all items in the stock are classified into Category → Sub-category → Sub-group.

The inventory module master database consists of the following information:
1. Item details master.
2. Item classification master – item group, category, subcategory.
3. Bought out item master such as Raw Material, packing material Items.
4. Sub-assembly master or Work-in-Process items information.
5. Product Master also referred as FG (Finished Goods) item.
6. Stores location Master.
7. Accounting unit or UOM (Unit-of-Measurement) Master.

3.5.5 The inventory system captures all material movement using the following main transaction data

1. Item Issue Note for material issue from the stores location.
2. Goods Receipt Note for material received in the stores.
3. Purchase vouchers that for crediting the purchase bill in the creditor accounts ledger.
4. Stock transfer transaction for transferring material to a given location.
5. Stock Adjustment transaction to match the book stock and the physical stock.

At end of the day, the inventory system should be able to provide reports to the materials manager or anyone who has the password to access the output. Some of the major online and real-time reports generated are as follows:
1. Stock Statement for a given month or week or even for a day.
2. Goods Receipt Register.
3. Stock Transfer Register.
4. Material issue Register for every store location.
5. Stock adjustment transaction register for every store location.
6. Item Ledger that gives quantity for any location that shows opening balance, receipt, issue and closing balance.
7. Item Ledger that gives both quantity and value, for any location that shows opening balance, receipt, issue and closing balance.
8. Inventory variance report.
9. Item list with last purchase rate and the standard rate for valuation.

The inventory system provides various cost rates stored on Item master if required, such as Weighted Average Rate, last pure purchase rate, etc. In some cases, the item is purchased in Kg., but issued in numbers. To get the correct inventory the system stores the conversion factor. For example, Steel plate is purchased in Kilograms from the steel supplier company but while issuing to the shop floor the same is issued in 'Numbers'. The system stores the conversion factor, that is, half a kilogram is equal to one number.

It is possible to attach a graphic file (picture) to every item in the item master file. This helps in identifying the item to the user. It is also possible to prepare the product catalogue *automatically* using this feature of attaching the photograph to every product. In case of an engineering company, machine drawing is prepared for the finished goods using SolidWorks or AutoCAD or similar software package. Such a drawing file is stored on the server computer and can be linked with the item master in the ERP system. This helps the operator in locating the correct drawing file on the shop floor.

3.5.6 ISO 9000

When the item is received from the supplier, the same needs to be checked before storing in the stores location. There is a possibility that the stores clerk may not be qualified to inspect the technical specification of the raw material being received. The 'Quality inspector' who is trained to check will perform the 'Quality Check', and mark the item as accepted or rejected after checking. The ERP system then captures the name of the person, date and time of inspection and stores for future audit. Some organisations follow certain standard operating procedures. These organisations gets special certificate called ISO 9000 certificate. In simple terms, ISO 9000 says that: "You write whatever you are doing, and then do exactly as you have written." While following the steps, the operator should not miss any of them. Therefore, ISO 9000 procedures once captured in the ERP business logic should be religiously followed without mistakes. This results in high quality of work in the organization, which is why most organisations prefer to deploy ERP software that ensures that they do not lose the ISO 9000 certification. For example, proper documentation which pertains to the quality checks is automatically prepared in the inventory system. While a separate ledger shows items under inspection, items accepted and rejected.

If the item purchased (raw material) is manufactured by another company, then the supplier will have to charge 'Excise duty' over and above the actual rate of the item. As per excise rules in India, if such item is rejected, then it has to be sent back using a sales invoice, thus reversing the excise duty. It may sound amusing, because we are saying 'you have to sell' the item to your own supplier, in case of rejection! Heavy penalty has to be paid if the excise duty is not reversed when the rejected material is sent back to the supplier. ERP helps in streamlining such complicated processes not only from the inventory point of view but also from the accounting and excise regulations point of view.

Typically, in a manufacturing company, it is important to capture and store the 'batch number' of each item produced. This is also called the 'Lot number', especially in the pharmaceutical or the food industry. Similarly, for a discreet product company such as the Television or the laptop, the serial number is important to record in the database. These numbers help in tracking back the production process in case if there is any rejection or issues related with quality of the product. The fast moving consumer goods companies are known as FMCG companies. In an FMCG Company such as soap or toothpaste, items are packed in a small box (inner carton) and in turn again packed in a bigger box (outer carton). The outer box may also be packed in a still bigger box (shipping carton). In short, the inventory system keeps a record of all the items, box, etc. until the same is finally invoiced to the customer.

ERP provides the automatic calculation of 'landed-cost' of item received, and updates the same on the item master for the purpose of inventory valuation. For instance, an item rate may be ₹ 10/- but while receiving, there may be paid, say ₹ 2/-, plus some other components like those that insurance may also be charged, say ₹ 1/- etc. If all these are put together, the actual 'landed cost' of the item may become 10 + 2 + 1 = ₹ 13/-. The landed cost is useful for the inventory valuation as well as for costing purpose. ERP captures and records all this information from the 'purchase voucher' transaction to give accurate cost of the item.

Japanese automobile companies were the first to start practicing the JIT or Just-in-Time inventory management. The idea is to keep optimum inventory. Neither more nor less. Overstocking is not good because it blocks working capital. This results in more borrowing from the bank and the company has to pay more interest on the loan to the bank. To reduce interest (expenses), it is important for the company to practice JIT. At the same time, if less stock is maintained, the company may lose the order from the customer. ERP software system helps company in maintaining the JIT inventory. This is achieved by using the MRP module or the Material Requirement Planning Module.

ERP gives item wise consumption report based on the Bill of Materials of the products made. ERP gives Branch wise, Location wise, or Plant wise Stock status of each item at any given time, without asking another human being. Thus, ERP is managing business without depending on people. ERP logic depends on the business process and not humans. The trick is in defining the business rules properly during the ERP implementation stage.

Some items are perishable, especially in case of Pharmaceutical or Food items. The ERP software captures the date of manufacturing. ERP server knows 'today's' date, and based on it, gives a quick report of the item which are likely to expire next month. This report is important for the materials manager to push such items that are likely to expire in the near future. Thus saving lakhs of rupees for the company, because once an item, say medicine, has expired, it has to be discarded or scraped, which is a straight loss.

Alias: ERP helps in standardising the name of an item. Let us say a company is manufacturing 'ball pens'. The item name in the item master is 'ball pen'. However, customer calls it 'pen'. The system helps in storing the sales order and informs the department concerned that the order for 'pen' is actually an order for 'ball pen'. This is also called 'alias'. Some other company may call 'ball pen' as 'writing instrument'. But the alias name is also stored in the item master to avoid any confusion.

In ERP, material is received in the stores as per the purchased order (PO). The PO quantity and the GRN quantity (Goods Receipt Note) should be same. For example, if the purchase officer has ordered ten numbers of chairs, the store cannot and should not receive more than ten numbers of chairs. The PO transaction *defaults* (is shown) on the computer screen of the stores officer, while making the GRN entry. In other words, PO is the parent document, and the GRN is the child document.

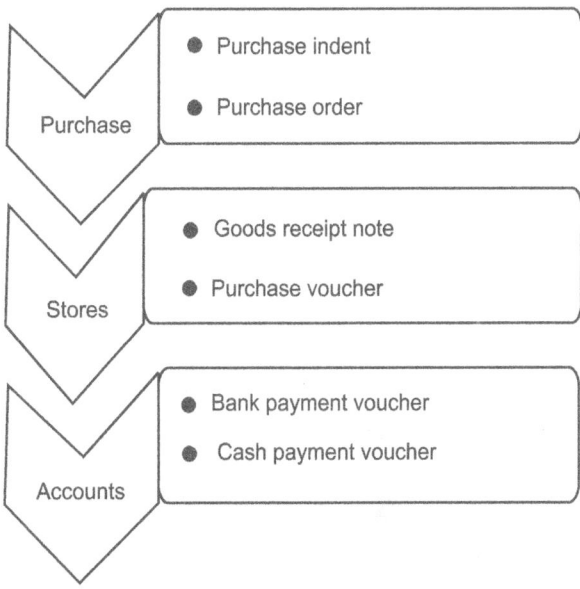

Fig. 3.31: Purchase, Stores and Accounts are linked

The diagram shows that in ERP, business processes are linked automatically. Usually, there is always a parent document linked with the child document. This reduces human error and gives reports that are more accurate to the decision makers.

As explained earlier, the GRN quantity should be less or equal to the PO quantity. However, there could also be an exception to this rule. In actual practice, it is not possible to supply some item as per exact PO quantity. Consider that the purchase officer wants hundred tons of steel bars. The PO quantity is 100 and accounting unit (unit of measurement) is ton. Now, the vendor (the steel mill) cannot supply exact hundred tons, may be vary it slightly more or little less. Therefore, it is necessary to add one more field called 'tolerance' in the item master for such item. Let us say tolerance for the steel bars is plus or minus ±10%, meaning the stores officer is allowed to receive 90 ton or 110 ton.

3.6 Quality Management

The quality control is one of the most important functions in the company. Some companies take the rejection very seriously. To ensure this all relevant details in ERP, the quality assurance or the QA module is integrated with the material movement.

The QC or the Quality Check is done in the following three major areas:

(i) QC at the time of receiving material from the vendor.
(ii) QC at the time of producing the goods on the shop floor.
(iii) QC at the time of final dispatch of the FG to the customer.

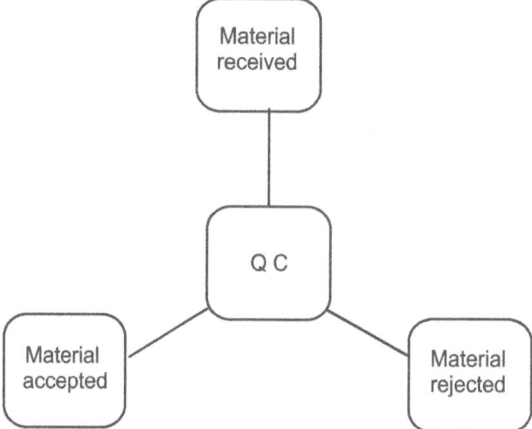

Fig. 3.32: Quality Check Concept Diagram

Fig. 3.33: Dabbawala in Mumbai

3.6.1 Six Sigma

Six Sigma is a very popular quality management concept. For quality management, it is necessary to count defects every time a rejection occurs. Six Sigma is a methodology to manage process variations that cause defects and to systematically work toward managing variations to eliminate defects. The objective of Six Sigma is to deliver high performance, reliability, and value to the end customer. It was originally defined as a metric for measuring defects and improving quality, and a methodology to reduce defect levels below 3.4 defects per million opportunities (DPMO). That is 3.4 rejections in ten lakhs products. Six Sigma works to minimise the difference between what your customers need, and the product or service you deliver.

Six Sigma's goal is the near elimination of defects from any process, product, or service. The numerical goal is 3.467 defects per million opportunities. To achieve this kind of very high quality standard 'attitude' is more important as compared to the technology. You may be surprised to note that the Mumbai Dabbawala are awarded the Six Sigma status, the highest standard of quality, that is service of delivery of the lunch box practically without any error.

> I would like student to recall the example of the stamping manufacturing company. On the shop floor, the quality inspector will check the production. Punched coils will by default get in Production QC for accept / reject purpose. In Production QC first punched coil will get selected as 'Location before QC' and then other location could be 'Location after QC'. Production QC will be done for that particular date. Once the date is selected then machine wise and shift wise or all Production QC can be done. Accepted quantity will be put in accepted quantity column and accordingly rejected quantity will be computed by ERP system.

Six Sigma : Practical Meaning

99% Good (3.8 Sigma)		99.99966% Good (6 Sigma)
• 20,000 lost articles of mail per hour.	⟶	• Seven articles lost per hour.
• Unsafe drinking water for almost 15 minutes each day.	⟶	• One unsafe minute every seven months.
• 5,000 incorrect surgical operations per week.	⟶	• 1.7 incorrect operations per week.
• Two short or long landings at most major airports each day.	⟶	• One short or long landing every five years.
• 20,000 wrong drug prescriptions each year.	⟶	• 68 wrong prescriptions per year.
• No electricity for almost seven hours each month.	⟶	• One hour without electricity every 34 hours.

Seven essential steps to implementing **high quality management** under Six Sigma are:

1. Understanding and commitment to 'Quality' by the top management.
2. Access to current information on customer needs using the ERP software.
3. A process-management system to measure current performance and identify where you need to make improvements.
4. Resources: Black Belts and Green Belts trained to design and improve processes and to assist process owners.
5. Ongoing management involvement and review to reinforce process management, improvement, and design.
6. Communication to ensure that customer focus and Six Sigma methods is embraced throughout the enterprise.
7. Assigned responsibilities for Six Sigma within the organisation.

3.7 ERP market, Comparison of Current ERP Packages and Vendors, like SAP, Oracle, PeopleSoft, BAAN etc.

Fig. 3.34: ERP Vendors

ERP Vendors

Broadly speaking, Software companies may be of two kinds:

(a) Companies that develop Software package.

For example, a Company called SAP that develops ERP software package.

(b) Companies that implement Software packages.

For example, Wipro that implements the SAP ERP software package.

Let us first discuss ERP software companies:

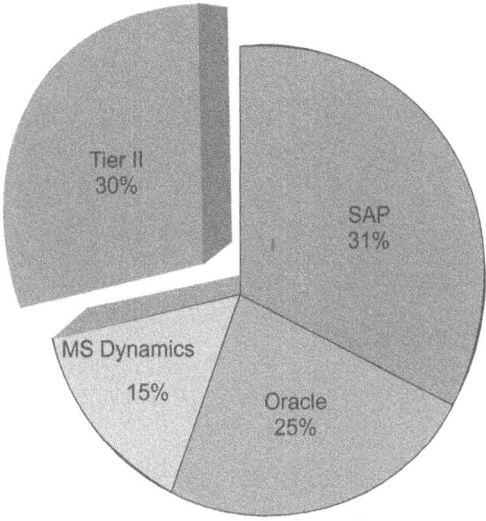

Fig. 3.35: SAP has major market share

There are hundreds of software companies that has developed ERP software package. Here is a list of few large companies that are operating worldwide. I have grouped them in three Groups based on their size as follows:

Group I
   Oracle
   Oracle eBusiness Suite
   Oracle JD Edwards
   Oracle Peoplesoft
   Microsoft Dynamics
   SAP

Group II
   Epicor
   Sage
   Infor
   IFS
   QAD
   Lawson
   CDC Software

Group 3
- ABAS
- Activant Solutions
- Bowen and Groves
- Compiere
- Exact
- NetSuite
- Visibility
- CGS
- Hansa World
- Consona
- SysPro

Let us consider three of the most successful and top ERP companies in the world.

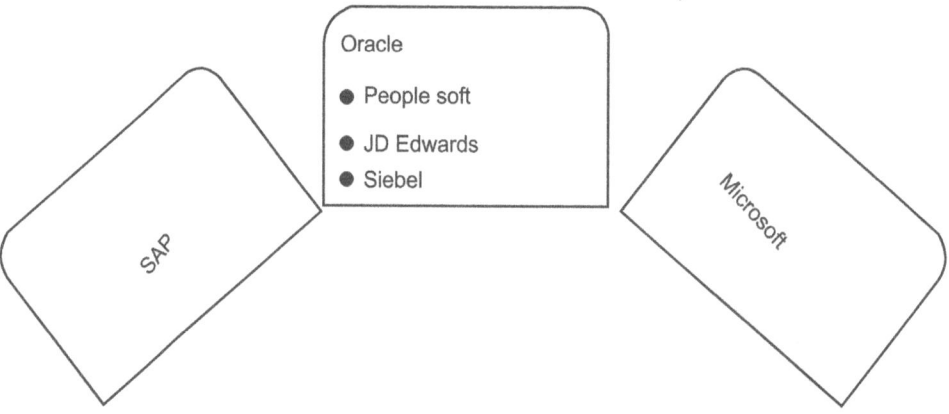

Fig. 3.36: Three Giant ERP Vendors

1. **SAP AG**

SAP is a multinational software corporation which has designed and developed ERP software, called SAP. Note that the name of the company is SAP and the name of the software is also SAP. The head office is in Walldorf, Baden-Württemberg, Germany. SAP has offices in 130 countries, around the world. SAP is the market leader in enterprise application software. SAP also has enterprise data warehouse solution, known as SAP Business

Warehouse (SAP BW). SAP Business Objects software is now very popular amongst large MNC. Sybase mobile products and in-memory computing appliance SAP HANA are recent developments. SAP is one of the largest software companies in the world. About SAP North America has more than 14,500 employees.

The number one package is SAP R/3. This is an acronym for Systems Applications and Products in data processing. The "R" is for "Real-time data processing" and 3 is for 3-tier.

From back office to boardroom, warehouse to storefront, and desktop to mobile device, SAP empowers people and organisations to work together more efficiently – and use business insight more effectively. SAP does this by extending the availability of software across on-premise installations, cloud and on-demand deployments, and mobile devices.

SAP plus points are as follows:
- World class fully integrated ERP software
- Global leader
- Faster Speed

SAP was founded by five former IBM employees in 1972. Number one vendor of standard business application software, with a worldwide market share of 31%. The world's leading provider of business software offering applications and services to more than 100,000 customers located in over 120 countries. SAP is one of the largest independent software suppliers in the world. SAP ERP is available in more than 14 languages, e.g. English, German, Japanese, etc. SAP Business Objects.

SAP Business Objects is a French enterprise software company, specialising in business intelligence (BI), now merged with SAP. Since 2007, it has been a part of SAP AG.

SAP offers more than 25 industry solution portfolios for large enterprises and more than 550 micro-vertical solutions for mid-size companies and small businesses.

SAP focuses on six industry sectors as follows:
1. Process manufacturing industries.
2. Discrete product manufacturing industries.
3. Consumer industries (FMCG).
4. Service industries.
5. Financial services.
6. Public services.

Examples of above vertical industries that use SAP ERP system are given below:
1. Aerospace
2. Automotive
3. Banking
4. Chemicals
5. Consumer Products
6. Construction
7. Defence and Security
8. Healthcare
9. Engineering

10. High Tech
11. Insurance
12. Life Sciences
13. Logistics Service Providers
14. Media
15. Mill Products
16. Mining
17. Oil and Gas
18. Pharmaceuticals
19. Postal Services
20. Professional Services
21. Public Sector
22. Retail
23. Railways
24. Telecommunications
25. Utilities
26. Wholesale Distribution

SAP ERP Functional Modules that are most popular are as follows
1. SAP FI - Finance
2. SAP CO - Controlling
3. SAP SD - Sales and Distribution
4. SAP HR - Human Resource
5. SAP MM - Material Management
6. SAP PP - Production Planning
7. SAP PS - Project Management
8. SAP QM - Quality Management
9. SAP PM - Plant Maintenance

ABAP

ABAP is short form of Advanced Business Application Programming. Originally Allgemeine Berichts-Aufbereitungs-Prozessor, German for "general report creation processor". ABAP is a high-level programming language created for customising or tailoring the ERP software. Students with programming background may learn the technical side of the SAP ERP that is the SAP ABAP/4.

Students who aspire to become SAP consultants and for corporate managers should learn more from SAP accredited training courses offered worldwide.

Scope in SAP: You can join a company as a Functional Consultant, during implementation with a software consulting (implementation partner, such as Infosys, Wipro, Siemens, etc.) firm which is implementing SAP in organisations or as a Technical Consultants / developer, if you have mastered the ABAP/4 (Programming language). It is currently positioned, alongside the more recently introduced Java, as the language for programming the SAP Application Server, part of its NetWeaver platform for building business applications. The syntax of ABAP is somewhat similar to the legacy COBOL programming language.

SAP: The Three Tier software architecture is as follows:

Presentation Tier: This is the topmost level of the application. The presentation tier displays information related to such services as browsing merchandise, purchasing, and shopping cart contents. It communicates with other tiers by outputting results to the browser/client tier and all other tiers in the network.

Application Tier (business logic, logic tier, data access tier, or middle tier): The logic tier is pulled out from the presentation tier and, as its own layer; it controls an application's functionality by performing detailed processing.

Data Tier: This tier consists of database servers. Here information is stored and retrieved. This tier keeps data neutral and independent from application servers or business logic. Giving data its own tier also improves scalability and performance.

Top five enterprise applications in SAP's Business Suite are as follows:

1. **ERP:** SAP ERP Software package. This helps managing business seamlessly.
2. **CRM:** Customer Relationship Management. This helps companies acquire and retain customers, gain marketing, and customer insight (sales analysis).
3. **PLM:** Product Lifecycle Management. This helps manufacturers with product-related information.
4. **SCM:** Supply Chain Management. This helps companies with the process of resourcing its manufacturing and service processes.
5. **SRM:** Supplier Relationship Management. This enables companies to procure from suppliers, also called VRM or Vendor Relationship Management.

Competitive scenario

The #1 ERP Company, SAP is facing competition from two other giants: Oracle and Microsoft. We will be discussing about these two top companies in the next section. Meanwhile, it is interesting to note that the Oracle Corporation filed a case against SAP for malpractice and unfair competition in the courts in 2007. In Oracle Corporation vs. SAP AG case, Oracle alleged that SAP provided discount support for legacy Oracle product lines, used the accounts of former Oracle customers to systematically download patches and support documents from Oracle's website and appropriated them for SAP's use. Later SAP admitted wrongdoing on smaller scale than Oracle claimed in the lawsuit. SAP has admitted to inappropriate downloads; however the company denies the theft of any intellectual property!

To fight the competition against SAP, Oracle invested US$ 40 billion, during 2004 to 2010, acquiring many competitors such as JD Edwards ERP, PeopleSoft ERP, Siebel CRM and so on. However, SAP was able to increase its annual profits by 370% since 2002.

A note of caution for students who may get carried away by SAP certification. SAP ERP is business management software, that automates and links business activities automatically, and this implies you should have some business management experience before you learn ERP. It will be a good idea to work in a company for say one or two years and then do a short basic course to learn and get certified. Otherwise it will be difficult to grasp both, first the business management and second the automation of the business management.

SAP ERP users in India:
    ABB Ltd.
    Bangalore International Airport Ltd.
    Bharat Earth Movers Ltd.
    Bharat Electronics Ltd.
    Bharat Heavy Electricals Ltd.
    Bhuruka Gases Ltd.
    Birla Horizons International Ltd.
    Brittania Industries Ltd.
    Cognizant Technology Solutions
    Hewlett-packard India Pvt. Ltd.
    IBM India Ltd.
    Indian Institute of Management
    Intel Technology Private Limited
    Kirloskar Electric Company
    Madura Coats Pvt Ltd.
    MTR Foods Ltd.
    New-Age Business Consultants
    Tata Sky Ltd.
    TCGIVEGA Information Technologies
    Zenith Software Ltd.
    Zuari Cement

2. Oracle ERP

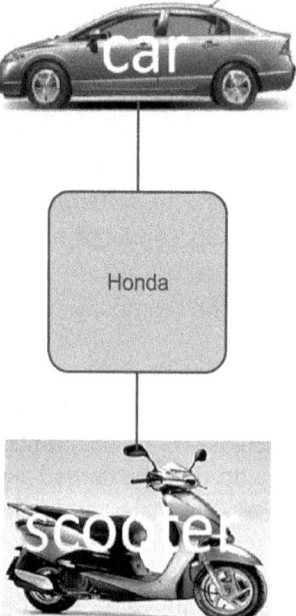

Fig. 3.37: Honda makes car as well as scooter

Let us consider a simple question /answer asked by someone as follows: "Which vehicle are you using"? The answer comes from another person: "I have a Honda". Well, the answer is incomplete. Honda scooter or Honda car? Just by saying Honda does not give complete idea about vehicle.

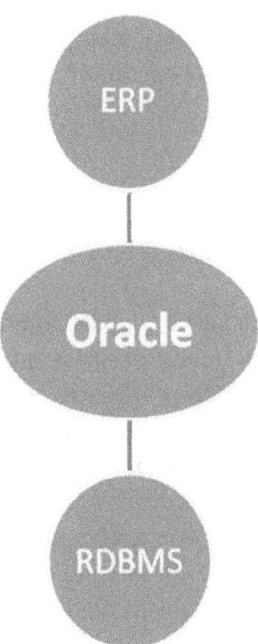

Fig. 3.38: Oracle makes ERP Software as well as RDBMS Software

Similarly, if a question is asked: "Which software do you use?" And the answer is "We use Oracle software". The answer is incomplete. Oracle has two main products category: (1) Oracle Database and (2) Oracle ERP. Oracle Corporation is name of the IT Company.

The Oracle database is very popular as backend of the ERP software. It is a leading RDBMS (Relational Database Management System). To store large chunk of information a stable and efficient database is necessary. The Oracle RDBMS is called 8i or 9i or 10g. These are version numbers. The latest version is called 11g. Oracle Database 11g helps users lower IT costs, and delivers a higher quality of service by enabling consolidation onto database clouds and engineered systems like Oracle Exadata and Oracle Database Appliance. It's proven to be fast, reliable, secure and easy to manage for all types of database workloads including enterprise applications, data warehouses and big data analysis.

Larry Ellison and his friends, former co-workers Bob Miner and Ed Oates, started the consultancy Software Development Laboratories (SDL) in 1977, in USA. SDL developed the original version of the Oracle software.

ORACLE

Oracle ERP

Oracle's Enterprise Resource Planning (ERP) applications commonly referred as Oracle Apps, for mid-size organisations offers enterprise-class technology. With Oracle Apps, user can leverage proven best practices to optimise business processes, reduce costs, and respond more quickly to changing market conditions.

Advantages of Oracle ERP:
- Flexible
- Scalable
- Affordable

Oracle ERP solutions provide a rapid return on investment and a low total cost of ownership.

Users expect the role of modern ERP to handle complex needs, which are broader than the systems they are currently using from a business process perspective. Users expect ERP to truly be a complete, integrated global, enterprise-wide system that manages all of their key business processes across their global enterprise, not just for back office functions like finances, manufacturing, and receiving order. An ERP user extend their current ERP deployment to add new processes as their business changes and grows and as users demand it. Oracle's enterprise-class applications enable this strategy with industry specific functionality within each product suite, with integration with Oracle's other industry leading applications, and with services to integrate with third party solutions.

Oracle ERP Modules

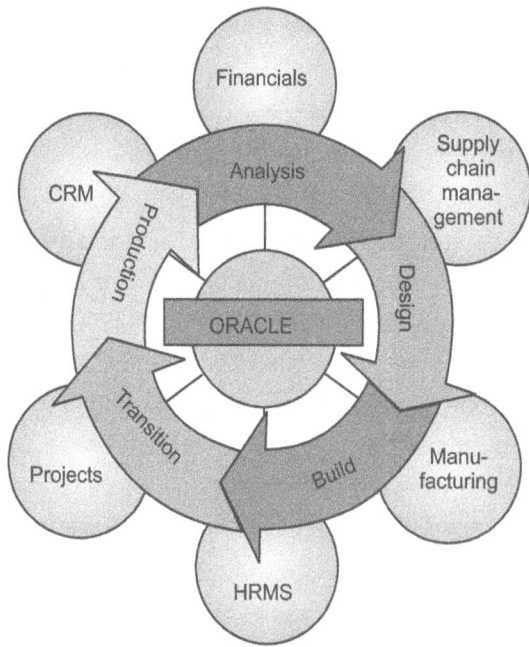

Fig. 3.39: Oracle ERP Modules

Here is list of some of the most popular Oracle ERP modules:
1. Financials
2. Financial Services
3. Projects
4. Public Sector
5. Maintenance Management
6. Manufacturing
7. Order Management
8. Procurement
9. Supply Chain Planning
10. SEM/ABM (Strategic Enterprise Management, Activity Based Management)
11. HRMS/Payroll
12. Global Financials

Oracle is one of the **largest ERP** Company offering ERP solutions refered as Oracle Financials. Oracle is a global software company competing with SAP. In India number of Oracle customers will be over 7,000 using Oracle Database, Oracle Fusion ERP and Oracle applications across financial services, communications, government and public sector, manufacturing and retail segments.

With more than 380,000 customers, including 100 of the Fortune 100, and with deployments across a wide variety of industries in more than 145 countries around the globe, Oracle offers an optimised and fully integrated business solution. Maruti Udyog Ltd with around 800 users is one of the largest customers of Oracle's eBusiness suite in India.

Oracle user – presenting a case study

Fig. 3.40: Tube Investments of India Ltd.

Oracle Customer: Tube Investments of India Ltd., Chennai, India
Industry: Industrial Manufacturing. Employees: 5,000
Annual Revenue: $500 Million to $1 Billion.
What Oracle user says: "Tube Investments of India Cuts Month-End Inventory Closing Time Approximately 67% with ERP System Upgrade that Supports Centralised Core Business Functions".

Tube Investments of India Ltd., is a large engineering company, catering to the automotive, railway, and general engineering sectors. Tube Investments of India Limited is more than ₹ 2400 crores company and the flagship enterprise of Murugappa Group. It manufactures precision steel tubes and strips, car doorframes, automotive and industrial chains and bicycles. The Company has 4 business units i.e. TI Cycles of India, TI Diamond Chain, Tube Products of India and TI Metal Forming.

Although more than one-third of Tube Investments annual turnover is still generated by bicycle manufacturing, the remainder comes from the components it develops and manufactures for the automotive industry, including metal tubes, car door frames, and industrial chains. The company has more than 5,000 employees, 16 manufacturing locations throughout India, and serves almost 15,000 customers.

In 2011, Tube Investments decided to upgrade to Oracle E-Business Suite Release 12.1 and Oracle Database, Enterprise Edition 11g. The company found that Oracle E-Business Suite Release 12.1 was highly suited to the new, centralised accounting processes and improved efficiencies even further. Tube Investments has streamlined its monthly financial reporting processes, cut month-end inventory closing time from six hours to less than two hours, reduced administrative costs, and developed a platform to support further centralisation of functions, such as fixed-assets accounting in the future.

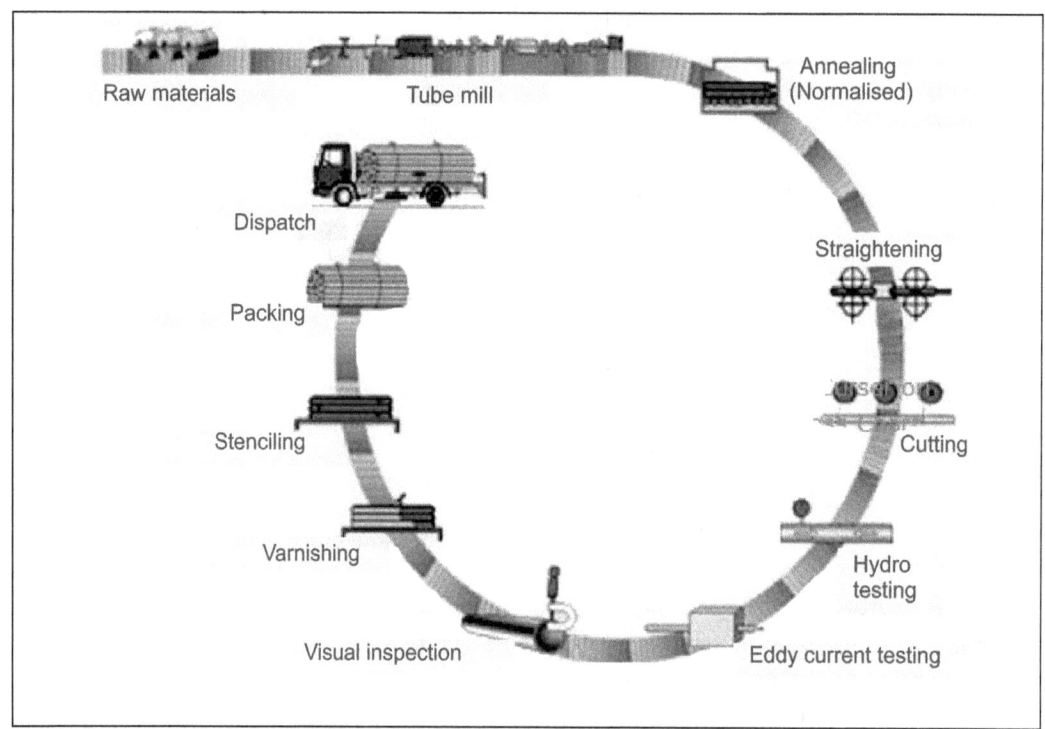

Fig. 3.41: Above figure shows major business process, right from receiving raw material to the final dispatch, that is linked by Oracle ERP

TIIL was facing four major business challenges as follows

1. Support centralised core accounting functions from 16 manufacturing locations to further increase staff efficiency, reduce administrative costs, and improve workflows.
2. Reduce the amount of time taken to close inventory accounting at the end of each month to ensure visibility of stock, such as steel components, at manufacturing locations.
3. Ensure monthly financial reports are made available more quickly to management.
4. Develop the company's existing Oracle enterprise resource planning (ERP) platform to take advantage of advanced features in Oracle E-Business Suite Release 12.1 and support future growth.

Oracle ERP helped TIIL by offering the following solutions:

1. Cut the time taken to complete month-end inventory closing from six hours to less than two hours, by integrating inventory processes across manufacturing locations.
2. Reduced month-end reporting back logs significantly and improved the efficiency of management information systems.
3. Decreased administration costs by reducing the number of hours required to manage month-end inventory and financial accounting processes.
4. Enabled managers to make faster business decisions by providing them with monthly financial reports up to a day faster.
5. Lowered the risk of human error and provided a clearer picture of company finances by better integrating inventory, purchasing, and manufacturing modules with the general ledger.
6. Developed a future-proof ERP platform, by taking advantage of advanced features, such as sub-ledger accounting and a flexible architecture that will support further centralisation of accounting and fixed-asset processes.
7. Provided a fast, stable, and highly accurate database for the new ERP system by upgrading to Oracle Database, Enterprise Edition 11g.

A testimonial from Mr. Kaushik, Senior Vice President of Information Technology, Tube Investments of India Ltd., Chennai, India.

> "We have been using Oracle products for more than 20 years and have great confidence that the upgrade to Oracle E-Business Suite Release 12.1 will assist our future growth. The applications fully support our centralised core business functions, helping us cut month-end inventory closing time by approximately 67%."

The Oracle ERP Implementation Process

Tube Investments upgraded to Oracle Database, Enterprise Edition 11g in September 2011 to provide a stable and highly available platform for its new ERP system. The company then spent five to six months upgrading to Oracle E-Business Suite Release 12.1.

"As we have been working with Oracle software for 20 years, we have developed considerable in-house skills and decided to undertake both upgrades without external support," said Kaushik.

The process was smooth and took place on time and on budget. The new ERP system went live in January 2012.

"Upgrading to Oracle E-Business Suite Release 12.1 and Oracle Database, Enterprise Edition 11g has provided us with the application performance and flexibility that support many of our centralised core business functions," he said.

PeopleSoft ERP

PeopleSoft Company was a leading ERP software Company specialising in the Human Resource Management. Like other industries in IT too, a lot of merger and acquisition have taken place. Oracle was finding it difficult to compete with PeopleSoft and SAP. PeopleSoft ERP Software was taken over by Oracle Corporation in 2005. All PeopleSoft customers are now supported by Oracle.

Infosys is the implementing partner for Oracle / PeopleSoft. Infosys is specialising in deploying, training and customising ERP software. Honda, China is using Oracle PeopleSoft Global Payroll.

For more information about Oracle, students are advised to check their website www.oracle.com

JD Edwards ERP

Even after merger with PeopleSoft, Oracle was finding it difficult to compete with SAP. Eventually, Oracle also took over another leading and successful ERP company called JD Edwards. Students may find the 'All India Oracle Users Group' interesting for further studies. The idea of this group is to share what the Oracle users have learned from using Oracle technology over the years with fellow users who have similar interest. AIOUG is a non-profit organisation, started by likeminded ERP users who think such a community is required in India, where there are a large number of Oracle users.

AIOUG provides Oracle technology and database professionals the opportunity to enhance their productivity and influence the quality, usability, and support of Oracle technology. The AIOUG is composed of Oracle professionals committed to helping fellow IT professionals develop solutions to their business challenges. Browse website http://www.aioug.org.

Siebel CRM

Meanwhile, another large and successful company called Siebel came up and started competing with Oracle, SAP and other ERP companies. Oracle once again, strategically took over the Siebel too. Siebel is strong in the CRM (Customer Relationship Management) module.

Oracle Social CRM Applications harness the latest **Web 2.0 technologies**, empowering sales users to be more effective and productive by leveraging the knowledge and experience of the broader community. These highly intuitive and focused applications work the way sales people do, helping them identify qualified leads, develop sales campaigns, and collaborate with colleagues to close more deals. With Oracle Social CRM Applications, users reap instant benefits to manage customer and prospect. Siebel CRM is one of the most complete customer relationship management (CRM) solution. **Oracle's Siebel CRM** helps organisations differentiate their businesses to achieve maximum top-and bottom-line growth.

3. Microsoft Dynamics ERP
About Microsoft operation India:

Microsoft set up its India operations in 1990, and has since been working closely with the IT industry, the Indian government, academia and the local developer community to partner in India's growth. Microsoft in India is focused on being a key IT partner to the Indian government and the local IT industry; enhancing India's inclusive development; and delighting customers and consumers.

Microsoft runs six business units in India: Microsoft Corporation India (Pvt.) Ltd. (the marketing division), Microsoft India Development Center, Microsoft Global Technical Support Centre, Microsoft IT, Microsoft Services Global Delivery and Microsoft Research India, together representing the complete Microsoft product lifecycle. Microsoft currently has offices in 9 Indian cities: Ahmedabad, Bangalore, Chennai, Hyderabad, Kochi, Kolkata, Mumbai, New Delhi and Pune; and employs about 5,800 people in the country.

The Author has worked closely with Microsoft and was invited to meet Mr. Bill Gates during his first visit to India in 1997.

While the war between two super ERP companies SAP and Oracle was on the peak, third super IT company, Microsoft jumped in the ERP arena. Microsoft, as usual, did not actually developed ERP software from scratch. At that point of time, Navision ERP was one of the most leading ERP companies in the world. As per Microsoft business strategy to compete with existing ERP Companies, Microsoft took over Navision ERP. Later it was renamed as Microsoft Dynamics NAV ERP Software. NAV because it was originally Navision.

Microsoft Dynamics NAV is a cost-effective, customisable business management solution with functionality for financial and supply-chain management, customer relationship management and e-commerce.

Microsoft ERP success story in India

Microsoft ERP steadily created a stronghold in the retail sector, consolidating its customer base to 60+ with majority being in north India including Chandigarh, Jaipur and Ludhiana region.

Some of the significant wins include:
1. Devyani Group (Indian franchisee of global food retail chains Pizza Hut, KFC and Costa Coffee).
2. Ethos (part of the Kamla Dials), a leading brand in luxury watches.
3. Evok (part of Hindware Sanitaryware).
4. Bikanerwala, a prominent food retailing business.
5. Damas, an international chain of Jewellery retailer.
6. Great India Nautanki Company, an entertainment initiative of Wizcraft and IFA.
7. Twenty First Century, a retailer of furniture.

Microsoft Dynamics ERP has helped the Indian Retail industry streamline operations which previously were run as stand-alone systems. With no structured system to manage the POS (point-of-sales), old legacy POS systems were being used for billing sales and product level analysis with zero capabilities to consolidate data and employ it for building efficiency and productivity into internal systems. Microsoft Dynamics ERP has helped many players in this business build an integrated and intuitive system that efficiently manages all POS terminals, captures and consolidates data points for creating an information rich environment, thereby increasing overall productivity and efficiency.

Apart from the three biggest ERP Companies in the world discussed above, there are some other companies that have created a name for themselves. These are discussed below.

Baan ERP

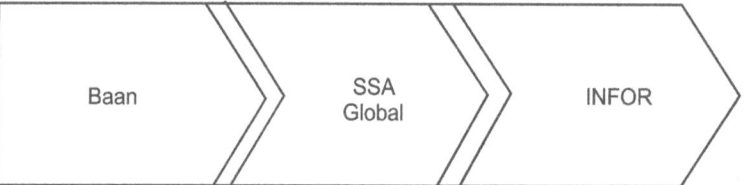

Fig. 3.42: Boan ERP is merged with INFOR ERP

Baan ERP History

Baan was born in 1978 in Holland created by Jan Baan to provide financial and administrative consulting services. Baan has 6,500 customers worldwide and installations at more than 21,000 customer sites.

Baan Customers

In India, Baan ERP users were L & T, Dabur, Godrej & Boyce, Samsonite, Blue Star, Pantaloon, Vulcan, Unichem, Rallis, Goa Shipyard, Bharat Bijlee, Birla Yamaha, Fedders Lloyd, Kirloskar-Copeland etc., and more than 100 companies in India. Overtime Baan Corporation faced financial problems (caused by the owner himself) and was sold to Invensys and now to SSA Global. Baan Company is now merged with the IFOR ERP.

Fig. 3.43: INFOR ERP

Infor ERP

Infor is a leading provider of business software and services, helping 70,000 customers in 194 countries improve operations and drive growth. Their customers include 9 of the top 10 high tech companies.

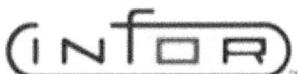

Fig. 3.44: INFOR LOGO

Here is a list of major verticals using Infor ERP software system around the world:
- 19 of the 20 largest aerospace companies.
- 12 of the 13 largest high tech companies.
- 9 of the top 10 pharmaceutical companies.
- 82 of the top 100 automotive suppliers.
- 26 of the 35 largest global retailers.
- 26 of the top 50 industrial distributors.
- 6 of the top 10 brewers.
- *8 of the top 10 U.S. integrated delivery networks.*
- 19 of the top 20 U.S. hospitals.
- Over 1,100 apparel and footwear companies.
- Over 1,200 state and local government agencies.
- Over 3,000 financial services companies.
- Over 4,700 machinery manufacturers.

Fig. 3.45: Logos of some of the companies that uses Infor ERP

It is recommended to study the website **http://www.infor.com/** to know more about the Infor Company.

3.8 Disadvantages of Non-ERP system

Importance of ERP vice versa In-house applications

Let us compare a scooter and a car. Well, you will perhaps think that it is a crazy comparison. Scooter may have certain benefits, but a car is definitely more comfortable and for very long distance one would prefer car. Scooter is affordable, but car is expensive. Scooter is easy to park, whereas car needs more place, so on and so forth.

You must have guessed why I am discussing such a crazy comparison. That's right, it is like comparing a simple account centric software such as Telly and a car. Telly is simple to learn and use, like a scooter. Whereas to learn car one has to have extensive practice, join a driving school perhaps. Telly is fine for small and tiny company but for corporate you need ERP.

A non-ERP software, although easy to use does not give entire business overview. ERP gives bird-eye-view. ERP gives overall status instantly whereas Telly kind of software focuses only on accounts. Non-ERP system does not link all the business processes automatically. ERP ensures that all business processes are linked with the following business process. For example, goods receipt in stores cannot be done unless purchase officer has entered the purchase order. In a small company, there is no such discipline, usually the purchase officer asks vendor on phone to supply the material, without any thing in writing. Such verbal communication is risky, and leads to misunderstanding.

The Focus on using the Information Technology (IT) to 'execute' business processes rather than 'supporting' business processes. Look at how IT can change the 'rules of the game' in the industry, like creating new distribution channels. For long IT has been perceived as a tool for back-office data crunching and account automation rather than a strategic business enabler, which has the potential to transform business models.

Non-ERP system allows editing of transaction. If an entry of a voucher is done on 14th November and saved, later user can change the date to 14th August easily. This kind of practice is not allowed in ERP. Some user who is habitual doing such editing does not like ERP because in ERP user just cannot edit or delete a transaction. If at all an incorrect entry is found, user has to enter a reverse transaction to correct. In the ledger posting there will be two lines. You might have noticed in the ATM statement, when an entry is reversed, there are two entries, debit, and credit. Instead of appreciating such harsh discipline, auditors do not like ERP because it does not allow manipulation of reports. Editing and deleting can confuse Government and management both. Telly kind of package is popular with Chartered

Accountants in India because this 'Scooter' kind of software allows changing of transaction any time. It is difficult to believe that even the document number is not given in Telly and user can enter backdated transactions. In ERP (compare car) every transaction has to be entered sequentially, no backdated entry is possible. This ensures accurate report and dependable output. User cannot take important decisions looking at the computer screen if he or she knows the data is manipulated. So top management uses Telly accounting package just for filing income tax returns and not for finding out correct inventory status.

ERP solves the problem of islands of information. Island is a mass of land surrounded by water and is not connected. An organisation may have hundreds of computers but are used more like a typewriter because it is not saving data in single database on a single computer (Server). It is necessary to deploy ERP software to unleash the real power of computer.

Many companies tried to develop ERP in-house, by employing a few software engineers. Unfortunately this is not a good idea. This may look a cheaper solution, but such in-house ERP software development will not serve the purpose. Managers and users try to automate the business process as they are used to work, and not as they are supposed to work. For example, a senior sales manager will ask in-house programmer to allow to create sale invoice without entering the sales order. In other words, the poor programmer will compromise the logic and will allow, after all he or she is just a junior employee. Who will argue with the boss? ERP system developed without incorporating the best business practices does not give real benefit of ERP. By automating wrong process in computer it can go wrong faster, is that what user wanted? No, I do not think so. ERP offered by a reputed ERP vendor brings in best business practices from companies around the world, which in-house ERP cannot give. ERP vendor such as SAP, or Oracle or Microsoft brings in much more matured business logic that can increase operational efficiency not ten or fifteen per cent but three hundred or four hundred per cent. Unfortunately, even senior executives are not ready to change and adopt proven way of business process. They ask ERP vendor to 'customise' or change the ERP program. This not only increases the cost and time but also dilutes the tight links that is inherent in the ERP system.

3.9 Benefits of Integration

Integration or linking department in ERP helps organisation in many ways. Tight integration of business processes is the real advantage of ERP because without which it is not possible to weed out slow or a weak department.

ERP integrates various business processes automatically. For example, the work order (or Job Order) given to the shop floor is integrated with the sales order on one side and the production entry on the other side. The purpose of the work order is to communicate from marketing department to the production department. For instance, the automobile sales officer says: "I have received order for xyz model of a specific car". In turn, the work order is linked to the Bill of Materials master, and will explode the same to show what and how many child items are required to make the father item (in this case one car).

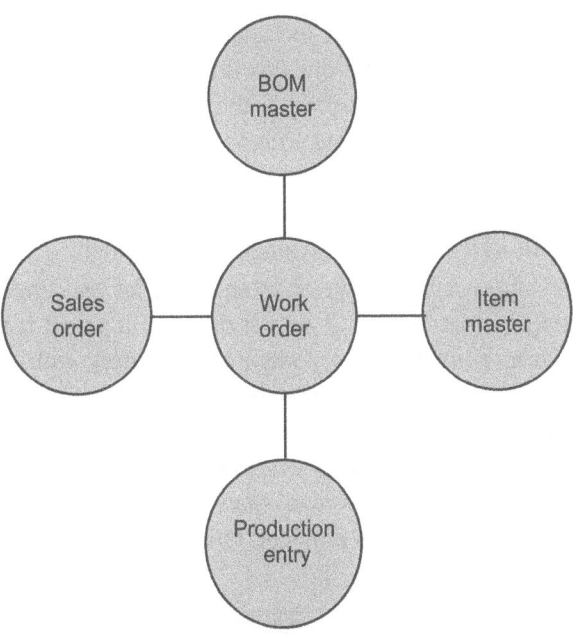

Fig. 3.46: Manufacturing activities are linked

Further, the work order is also linked with the material issue transaction, which is used to issue the child items (raw material) to the production department. Once the product is produced, the production department informs ERP by making production entry. This will close the work order. Work order is the parent document and the Production entry is the child document.

Fig. 3.47: Chain

How strong is a chain? You know that the chain is as strong as the weakest link in the chain. If all links are made of steel and if one link is made of wood, the chain is as strong as the wooden link. In other words, how strong is the organisation? Let us say there are ten departments in one organisation: Accounts, Purchase, Stores, Production, Sales, and so on. The organisation is as strong as the weakest department. Even if all managers of all departments are working efficiently except one inefficient department, the organisation is as strong as that weak (inefficient or careless) manager's department.

To understand and appreciate benefit of integration, let us consider one of the most crucial aspects of managing material. Here we will discuss the latest techniques of inventory control. The CEO can take control of the company's inventory with 'Automated Inventory Management Solutions'. ERP can revolutionise the way the company manages and controls the delivery of consumables, instruments, and tooling to the point of use. Whatever may be the industry, whatever your company, ERP provides substantiated cost savings and increased competitiveness to any business. From two man job-shops to multinational blue-chip conglomerates, ERP software system has provided tangible, proven solutions.

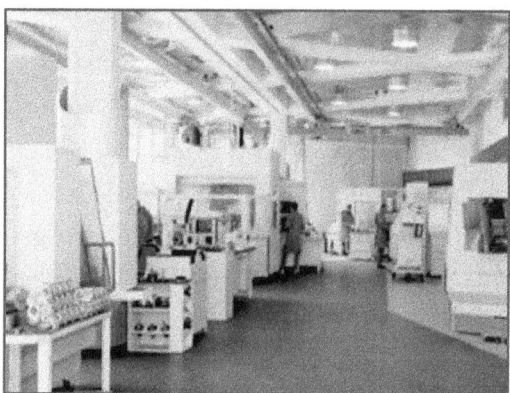

Fig. 3.48: Manufacturing Plant

Case Study of Machine Shops

Let us see how ERP has quickly and consistently delivered quantifiable savings in hundreds of machine shops worldwide. Typically introduced to control carbide inserts, drills, taps and similar high value, consumable, metal cutting supplies, system provides immediate benefits throughout user factory. High product availability combined with point-of-issue supply and user accountability quickly reduces:

1. Theft and stock shrinkage.
2. Wastage through unnecessary replacement of consumables.
3. Hiding of stock in toolboxes and private stores.
4. Wastage due to unidentifiable product or incorrect product identification.

ERP consistently produces savings of 30% to 48% on cutting tool expenditure, whilst simultaneously providing measurable increases in productivity and quality. Processes such as rework and recycling, which can be difficult to implement and manage with traditional manual methods, can be implemented, and maintained easily with automated rationing and restrictions. Report module enables the wealth of automatically recorded information to provide meaningful management information. Once available, such information can be used to implement lean manufacturing, identify poorly trained operators, and detect faulty equipment or incorrect tooling specifications.

In the Engineering Job Shop, prior to the installation of the ERP system, all cutting tool inventory was stored and controlled from the central stores with limited knowledge of the correct use of the tools they dispensed. The focus was on ensuring availability of tooling, through a legacy, and minimum /maximum stocking policy. Cooperation between production and stores to predict demands was limited and cost reduction programs such as optimal tool usage and regrind were limited in scope and success.

In the first four weeks following installation of ERP software, consumption of consumables was reduced by an average of 45% as 'private stores' in cupboards and toolboxes were consumed. Further, the management information recorded allowed the number of different carbide inserts stocked to be reduced from 451 to 306 styles.

Following the success of the initial installation, the system was improved with the introduction of fully automated re-ordering and increased utilisation of rationing and restrictions.

> Stores Manager's feedback: "The way we manage our cutting tool inventory has changed beyond recognition. I can now spend time negotiating with suppliers, streamlining stocks and ensuring quality of supply. None of the improvements could have been achieved without ERP."

Benefit of ERP in hospitals and clinics

> Doctor says "ERP software system has removed many of the problems we had controlling our cupboard based stores. Stock management is now more accurate and less time consuming."

Management of medical consumable is a challenge. With our expanding and aging population in India, medical service providers are facing an ever increasing demand on time and resources. Doctors, nurses, pharmacists and surgeons are now being required to reduce administrative errors, waiting times, and wastage, with simultaneous improvements in primary care quality.

Primarily used for inventory control of consumable medical equipment, ERP Software System is in daily use at a number of leading hospitals across the world. By fully utilising the innovative and adaptable platform, ERP Software System is revolutionising the concept of ward based pharmaceutical inventory management. With its extensive search functionality nurses benefit by faster, more accurate access to life-saving drugs; time-consuming searches for keys or misplaced drugs is eliminated, increasing time available for primary patient care. With expiration date and batch number controls, unnecessary drug wastage can also be reduced. Thanks to accurate, up-to-the-minute inventory records, administration of ward based stores is also improved; by simply producing a stock issue report, pharmacists can restock the ERP software system from the main stores in one operation. Time consuming and error prone manual procedures (stock check - calculate requirements, pick, replenish) are eliminated, whilst simultaneously increasing availability and reducing on-hand stocks.

Case study: Benefits in Office management

Fig. 3.49: Office Automation

Even in the office environment, ERP can control the office stationery cupboard. With recent revolutions, in back office operations, such as email, MRP management systems and improved telecommunications, offices are often regarded as streamlined, efficient environments with little wastage; expenditure on office consumables is often considered minimal or totally overlooked as an unavoidable necessity of operating.

After deploying ERP, usage of 'low value' consumables such as pens and staples has been drastically reduced. "Ownership" of such items is instilled in users, through the knowledge that they are now accountable for the supplies they take; as a result, items such as pens and files are no longer disposed of or misplaced in the knowledge that "There are another ten in my table drawer". Offices are also extensive users of hidden, expensive consumables such as paper, batteries, IT media, files, and printer toners cartridges (costly consumable). A study of print cartridge purchases of a company made during a 12 month period prior to an ERP installation revealed that:

- 20% were for printers the company no longer owned!
- 45% were for printers the company had never owned!

A further detailed study confirmed the latter cartridges were not present anywhere on the company premises! Post installation ERP, automated reordering module was utilised to ensure only legitimate print cartridges was purchased or sent for refilling.

Automated inventory information, coupled with automatic reordering and supply has been used to ensure 100% availability of consumables, reducing expensive disruption through stock-outs and incorrect products.

3.10 Standardisation of Data Code

Standardisation of data code aims for perfect consistency and predictability across the data set; both within and between fields. For example, abbreviation or missing leading zeros can lead to confusion. Program logic is provided for generating standardised product data. The computer system includes a database which maintains data for a plurality of known products, each known product associated with a respective standardised product code. The state of being plural, or consisting of more than one; a number consisting of two or more of the same kind; as a plurality of words; the plurality of a verb. A processing facility, coupled to the database, receives raw data for an unidentified product from a plurality of diverse data sources, each of which has its own separate identifier for the unidentified product. The processing facility compares the raw data for the unidentified product against the data for the plurality of known products. If there is a match between the raw data for the unidentified product and the data for one of the plurality of known products, the processing facility assigns the respective standardised product code of the matching known product to the unidentified product.

ERP Implementation Life Cycle

There are many stages in the implementation of ERP in any organisation. This is called the ERP implementation life cycle. The overall success of ERP would depend on how accurately and seriously, the ERP has been applied at every stage. Therefore, the management of the organisation introducing ERP as well as the Vendor must work as a cohesive team for a fruitful final result. Experience of implementing ERP over a long period of time has indicated that following the steps given below with utmost sincerity would generally yield a good ERP implementation"

A proven path to Enterprise Resource Planning software implementation

1. **First appoint ERP coordinator:** He or she will be exclusively focusing on Enterprise Resource Planning implementation. If possible, identify two persons as backup, the second person will coordinate with users and ERP implementer team. Although it is difficult to spare two senior people exclusively for ERP, it is worth it. By the way, who said ERP implementation is easy? Majority of ERP are under-utilised or have failed to give desired benefits. The ERP coordinator should be sufficiently senior or supported by the CEO / Director.

2. **Appoint 'chief-of-ERP-project':** A senior person with full authority (usually owner) who will not hesitate to throw out a person who is not ready to work in ERP because such a person will always put spanner, and ERP coordinator may not be able to speak up to his or her seniors, whereas the owner can.

3. **Give highest priority to ERP education and training:** Educate all users to understand what can be achieved with the new system. Additional education should include Total Quality Management and Change Management Strategies. Give training to main business process owners (department managers), in how to use the system. Make them train the other users. It is absolutely necessary to take time out from the routine and actually have hands-on training. Don't think ERP software is a magic to produce instant result without necessary ground work.

4. **Conduct Business Analysis to streamline the current processes:** This is done by the implementer team (from ERP vendor side). They will interview main department heads and the CEO to find gaps between what ERP will deliver and what user wants.

5. **Planning, training and education for the IT Support staff:** This will enable them to understand the new hardware, software and network imperatives. For instance, server computer configuration, firewall software, security settings for the user login into the server operating system (e.g. Microsoft Windows Server OS 2008).

6. **BPR or Business Process Reengineering:** (Match business processes with the new software). BPR implies that it is not necessary to do things as you were doing for last several years when ERP is used, rather change. Easy to say, but difficult to change people who are senior, experienced and will not easily change to modern business management logic. Boss is always right will not work, but accepting that the ERP brings best practices will work.

7. **Software modifications:** Carry out software modifications only when business processes exist that do not differentiate you in the market place are not supported by the software. Stick to essential customisation. Do not ask for chopping and changing of the program at every level.

8. **Business Simulation (on a departmental level and at the enterprise level):** Execute Conference Room Pilot or the CRP run. Prepare a 'Proof of Concept' file. Certify the printouts. Yes, each user will have to sign every page and agree that they have understood ERP and are ready to use.

9. **Go Live:** A phased approach may be indicated, based on the amount of change dictated by the new system.

10. **Implementation review meetings:** This is conducted after users have become comfortable with the ERP system. The goal is to ask the software vendor to suggest better ways to use the system.

11. **Have patience:** If you have asked for unlimited customisation then it will take unlimited time! Give sufficient time to ERP vendor to change the programs to do last minute changes. If the changes are coming in bits and pieces then it will take time for ERP to stabilise. Do not get into the vicious circle of change-correct-errors-change.

12. **Increase budget if you have enlarged the scope:** Usually users do not know what ERP is, and therefore they expect moon, well it is necessary to provide enough money for the same. Many times ERP journey halts due to lack of money during ERP implementation.

Whenever there is a requirement to implement ERP rapidly or in a short period of time the following points should be kept in mind.

Rapid Implementation

Whenever there is a requirement to implement ERP rapidly or in a short period of time the following points should be kept in mind:

Get an ERP consultant whose time-tested implementation process, together with **ERP user training**, will help to get your system and employees up-and-running. Many of ERP are implemented in about 180 days. This can be attributed to several factors as follows:

- A good understanding of legacy system and proper gap analysis helps ERP team in implementing.
- High flexibility of the ERP package.
- The ERP consulting services and training provided by experts.
- ERP interface, which makes the product easy for your employees to learn and use.
- Ease of customisation / modification of the ERP system to meet the exact needs of the users.
- Extensive handholding and support in preparing master database.

3.11 Example: ERP modules complete list with details of master, transactions, and Reports

ERP Modules were discussed above in brief. However, there may be numerous ERP Modules that could be required, depending on the nature of the project. Given below is an exhaustive list of ERP modules with details of master, transactions and reports. Students can refer to this while preparing their own list of ERP Modules.

- The following are some key business processes (or procedures) which can be managed using ERP software; in ERP parlance, it is called ERP Module. Some or all of these, modules may be applicable in the user organization, depending on the business requirements. MIS (Management Information System) or the reports are shown for each module in the list given below.
- The reason this is better than in-house of self-made ERP, is due to the fact that the ERP user gets a set of pre-mapped best business practice solutions for their particular industry. These ERP modules represent the best business practices.

3.11.1 Security Module

3.11.1.1 Masters
  (a) User Manager security master.
  (b) User group security master – login ID and Password.

3.11.1.2 ERP features

ERP is a multi user, multi-tasking ERP software. Multi-level security based on User Group and User Level. The following features must be incorporated in this module:
  (a) Create Login id and password for each user
  (b) Assign permissions. Map each user with menu / submenu
  (c) Restricting user access with login and password
  (d) Role based access and password
  (e) Audit trail: ERP ensures accountability of users. Work done by individual users can be easily tracked because all transactions capture the users name automatically.
  (f) Automatic Audit Trail helps top management to know who has updated Masters or transaction and when.
  (g) Each menu and submenu can be locked (allow / deny) including MIS (Management Information System) reports to individual user in a very user friendly screen with tree structure and check box facility.

3.11.2 Accounts Module – General Ledger Accounts

3.11.2.1 Masters
  (a) Account Group Master.
  (b) Subgroup Master.
  (c) General Ledger Account Head Master with Tax, Bank, Cash bifurcation.
  (d) Detail Account Master.
  (e) Narration Master.
  (f) TDS (Tax Deducted at Source) and % fields in the supplier / address (TP) masters. Automatic posting in GL. ERP will create a JV automatically.

3.11.2.2 Transactions
   (a) Cash receipt voucher
   (b) Bank receipt voucher
   (c) Cash payment voucher
   (d) Bank payment voucher
   (e) Service-tax payment (for excise link)
   (f) Journal Voucher
   (g) Contra-entry voucher
   (h) Credit Note
   (i) Debit Note
   (j) Expense PO (for service provider, optional)
   (k) Expense voucher (for service provider bill booking)
   (l) Adjust unlink receipt with open sales invoice
   (m) Adjust unlink payment with open GRN (Purchase bill / expense bill)
   (n) Closing balance for master data (debtor, creditor, and GL accounts)
   (o) Rate of depreciation (as per company act)
   (p) Rate of depreciation (as per I-Tax act)
   (q) Asset installations slip
   (r) Asset sale transaction. (For asset register and deprecation register)

3.11.2.3 Key MIS reports
   (a) Trial Balance. Option of various kinds of formatting, such as - GL wise Tr. Balance. Sub-group wise Tr. Balance. Group and GL wise Tr. Balance. Group and sub-group wise Tr. Balance. (Option of T- format = only closing balance)
   (b) Sub-ledger trial balance. (Supplier / customer)
   (c) Consolidated reports of multiple locations for one company in Accounts Module. E.g. ERP gives factory wise or branch wise plus consolidated for the head office
   (d) Cash Book
   (e) Bank Book (supports multiple banks) with receipts, payments and contra filters.
   (f) Expense voucher register
   (g) Journal Voucher register
   (h) General Ledger. (Account head wise or all accounts with details under General Ledger). Filter available for amounts < than, > than and =
   (i) Credit note register
   (j) Debit note register
   (k) Contra-entry register
   (l) Fixed Asset register

(m) Depreciation schedule (as per company act)
(n) Depreciation schedule (as per Income Tax act)
(o) Profit & Loss account. (GL wise and sub-group wise). For multi-location user can make consolidated P & L report
(p) Balance Sheet. (GL wise and sub-group wise)
(q) Bank reconciliation statement

Exceptional MIS Reports

Dash Board: This will give at a glance the highlights of certain figures to the top management viz. purchase, sales, money receivable, money payable, bank balance, etc.

3.11.2.4 ERP features
(a) Automatic posting in respective G. L., from goods inward and sales invoice, etc.
(b) TDS procedure takes care of automatic TDS posting.
(c) Service tax procedure takes care of automatic posting in related excise ledger.
(d) Help of Standard Narration master saves time to make entries into the voucher.
(e) All reports with drill down facility down to transaction level.

3.11.3 VAT / Sales Tax Module

Key MIS reports

3.11.3.1 ERP takes care of all VAT (Value Added Tax) / CST (Central Sales Tax) related procedures and the same is linked with other relevant modules. The same is customised as per the rules applicable.

Capturing from various transactions taxes details such as Sales Invoice, GRN (Goods Receipt Note), Sales RGN (Sales Return Goods Note, GIN (Goods Inward Note material from subcontractor etc.)

3.11.3.2 Capturing VAT / CST / Service tax components in PO, GRN, JO, GIN, Exp, PO, Exp. Voucher, etc. Can default from item master.

3.11.3.3 Sales Tax – VAT & CST statements.

3.11.3.4 Link to the GL (General Ledger Accounts).

3.11.3.5 Store CST number / TIN number etc. on the masters. In Invoice, ask for TIN number of consignee and display on invoice.

3.11.3.6 C Form tracking – Sales.

3.11.3.7 C Form tracking – Purchase.

3.11.4 Excise Module

3.11.4.1 Masters
- (a) Opening Balance Entry (For PLA, CENVAT – 'Input' & Capital and Service Tax)
- (b) Excise Tariff Heading Master

3.11.4.2 Transactions
- (a) Excise Debit Entry with GL postings
- (b) GAR 7 for CenVAT (Excise)
- (c) GAR 7 for Service Tax
- (d) Form ARE 1 for Export items

3.11.4.3 Key MIS reports
- (a) ER 1 register
- (b) DSA Register
- (c) CenVAT Credit Register (INPUT)
- (d) CenVAT Credit Register (CAPITAL Goods)
- (e) Service Tax Credit Register
- (f) PLA Register

Personal Ledger Account (PLA) is an account current through which the Assessee pays Duty to the Government of India. The PLA register is credited when the duty is liable to pay and when the Duty is discharged (by CENVAT Credit /Payment) the PLA register will be debited. The Duty Payable if any will be displayed as Balance. PLA and CENVAT Credit should be used only for payment of excise duty and not for any other payments like rent, fines, penalties etc.

- (g) Excise Tariff wise sales report
- (h) Rule 4 (5) (A) CenVAT credit. (57 F 4 Register)
- (i) Sales rejections register
- (j) Purchase rejection register

3.11.4.4 ERP Features
- (a) Company Excise details – Excise registration code number, range, division.
- (b) Account master integration – under duties and taxes in GL account.
- (c) Capture excise duty, Education Cess, SH Cess (Secondary Higher Education Cess) in excise related purchase and sales transactions
- (d) Debit entry from PLA & Input, 'Capital & Service Tax (single entry)

(e) Form ARE 1 for (Export) items
(f) ERP features Excise module is tightly integrated with other modules such as purchase, sales, accounts, etc. The service tax is availed at the time of payment automatically. All relevant details captured at the time of creating the sales invoice automatically such as Excise duty, Cess, Excise Tariff heading. Prepare Annexure VI – subsidiary Challan (for sending goods) is automated if applicable. Automated means, this statutory document will be generated automatically by ERP. In case materials on which excise duty is applicable, and if it is sent to sub-contractor ERP prepares the required 57 F4 challan automatically.
(g) Capturing Service Tax at the time of bank / cash payment of advance and after the bill is received.

Material Management (MM) Module

This includes the following business processes:
- Inventory Management Business process.
- Purchase Business process (Local procurement within India).
- MRP (Material Requirement Planning) with drill down to last child level.
- Import Purchase Business process.

3.11.5 Inventory Management Business Process Module

3.11.5.1 Masters
   (a) Unit-of-Measurement (UOM) Master
   (b) Category Master / Subcategory Master / Sub-group master
   (c) Item Master
      (i) Raw Material (Bought out) Item Master and list
      (ii) Packing Material Item Master and list
      (iii) Factory Made (SFG or Semi-Finished) Material Item Master and list for WIP inventory
      (iv) Finished Goods Item Master and list
5.1.4 Main Location Master – (sub-contractor location)
      (vi) Sub-location master (stores, shop floor) and subcontractor location.

3.11.5.2 Transactions

(a) GRN or Goods Receipt Note. Linked to Stores as well as creditor accounts.
(b) Stock transfer challan. For transferring material from one location to another location
(c) Stock Transfer Challan. material issued to shop floor link to the Work Order as per BOM. (Optional)

(d) Material Issue Note (MIN) to consume / material from a 'given' location.
(e) Stock Adjustment (SAN) to increase or reduce stock from a given location. This transaction is useful to match physical inventory with stock reports.
(f) Physical stock slip to enter actual stock in a given location.
(g) Closing balance master entry (as of cut-off date, one time entry).
(h) Conversion process Purchase return for *non-excisable goods or Return to Supplier*. RTV. This is linked with the material received and accounts entries are automatically generated by ERP. This will debit the supplier in supplier ledger or the user may create Tax Invoice (sales -for excisable goods).

3.11.5.3 Key MIS reports
(a) List of category, sub-category, and sub-group
(b) GRN register (list) of items under "inward inspection"
(c) Stock Transfer Challan register (STC) - Filter provided for 'normal' STC and STC with Work Order
(d) MIN (Material issue note) register. (Location wise)
(e) SAN (Stock adjustment note) register. (Location wise)
(f) Stock Statement for all types of material as well as WIP, a given period
   (i) With quantity (location wise and category wise filters)
   (ii) With quantity and Rate (location wise and category wise filters)
(g) Item Ledger (location wise)
   (i) With quantity (location wise and category wise filters)
   (ii) With quantity and Rate (location wise and category wise filters)
   (iii) Item ledger summary gives the stock of material at all locations – Drill down to ledger for any given location
(h) Physical stock and system stock (book stock) variance report
(i) Stock Valuation report. (With option to generate WAR – weighted average rate)
(j) RTV Register (Return to supplier – non-excisable items)
(k) Item List. (With option to select any or all fields from item master)

3.11.5.4 ERP Features
(a) Various cost rate stored on Item master if required, such as Weighted Average Rate, last pure purchase rate, etc.
(b) Conversion Factor (relation between Purchase UOM and Issue UOM). Payment UOM and Payment conversion factor
(c) Optional Online link with picture of an item (.JPEG file)
(d) Optional hyperlink with an AutoCAD drawing

(e) ISO 9000 Facility to keep material in HOLD location – i.e. item under inspection, QC person can login and enter Accepted / Rejected Quantity to transfer material to Stores. Separate ledger shows item in Hold, Stores and Rejection location
(f) Lot number / Batch number / Serial number / heat number tracking of inventory (Optional)
(g) For FMCG products user can store Inner Box / Outer Box data for shipping, or volume / weight of the box on item master (Optional)
(h) Automatic calculation of landed-cost of item received and updating the same on master for valuation purpose
(i) Just-in-time (JIT) inventory management by linking the MRP (material requirement planning) module and inventory module
(j) Pending list of returnable items - RTV (return to Supplier with auto debit feature).
(k) Item wise consumption
(l) Branch wise / Location wise / Plant wise / wise Stock status
(m) Expiry / Near Expiry inventory for perishable goods (Optional)
(n) Calling a given item by a different name (alias) because different customers call different items with different names (Optional)
(o) Excess material received can be accepted (Percentage tolerance given in sub-category master)
(p) Serial No. applicable flag in Item Master
(q) PFD (Process Flow Diagram) selection in Item Master

3.11.6 Purchase and Pre-purchase Module

3.11.6.1 Masters
(a) Supplier Master (Supplier List)
(b) Supplier Type Master

3.11.6.2 Transactions
(a) Purchase Requisition (Linked further to Purchase enquiry)
(b) Purchase enquiry
(c) Purchase quotation
(d) Preparing Purchase Order. This can be saved as .PDF file and email to Supplier

3.11.6.3 Key MIS Reports
(a) Purchase requisition Register
(b) Purchase Order Register
(c) Purchase Order status Register with optional alert flag – when delivery period elapsed, P.O. being highlighted

(d) Creditor Ledger
(e) Supplier master list
(f) Supplier Performance Rating / Supplier Rating based on quality, delivery
(g) Warning letter generation based on poor performance/service

3.11.6.4 ERP Features
(a) Auto transfer of Rejected Quantities to rejection stores location
(b) Link to payment voucher with required validation to the GRN (Goods Receipt Note)
(c) Item specification document as per ISO 9000 requirements can be linked to PO (.pdf) file; Drawing number, etc. can be shown automatically
(d) Capturing of Excise, Cess and S & H Secondary and Higher Education Cess information
(e) Item 'accept / reject' quantity to be put by a separate password - by QC person
(f) Purchase officer can make PO based on Material Requirement Planning report, or based on ROL based report
(g) Purchase Indent 'Automatic' alert to Purchase Department
(h) Purchase Order 'short-closed' facility
(i) Purchase Order Revision Provision (Amendment)
(j) Purchase Order Expiry Provision (Option)
(k) Make Similar Purchase Order
(l) One Purchase Order – Multiple GRNs

3.11.7 MRP - Material Requirement Planning Module / Supply Chain Management (SCM)

This module is applicable for the Finished Goods (products), where the first level child item is shown. For example, if a Ball pen is finished goods, it is called the Father item. Whereas, the refill, body and cap are the child items.

3.11.7.1 Transactions
(a) Sales Order (Export or Domestic) or Projection based input
(b) Sales Schedule – from date and to date and quantity given by the customer

3.11.7.2 Key MIS reports
(a) Material Requirement Plan - MRP based on production indent and link to BOM to get raw material required (bought out items) based on stock in hand and buffer stock.
(b) ROL based Material Requirement report (items below Re-Order Level).

3.11.7.3 ERP Features
(a) Pre-requisite: Customer Master. Item Master. Customer Master. BOM Master.
(b) Purchase Requisition (purchase indent) can be prepared based on the MRP report – shortage quantity MIS.

(c) MRP based on the Re-Order Level (ROL).
(d) MRP considering stock in hand.
(e) Automatic calculation of ROL depending upon consumption.

3.11.8 Import Purchase Module

3.11.8.1 Masters
(a) Foreign supplier Master (Supplier List)
(b) Foreign supplier type Master

3.11.8.2 Transaction
(a) Import purchase Order for foreign supplier (in foreign currency).
(b) Import GRN (Goods Receipt Note) when material is received from foreign supplier (in foreign currency).

3.11.8.3 Key MIS reports
(a) Import Purchase order register
(b) Import GRN register – supplier wise information
(c) Import GRN register – item wise information

3.11.8.4 ERP Features
(a) Capturing custom duty, CVD, Education Cess, etc., and other relevant information in ERP
(b) Indian Rupees and Foreign currency exchange rate stored at the time of importing.

3.11.9 Job working IN module – Customer's material received for processing

Subcontractor IN or job-working for customer. Customer gives material.
After processing (say, machining) the same is returned back to the customer.

For example, in Thane there are many factories manufacturers for some big OEM customers such as Eicher Motors. The raw material is not purchased but is supplied by the customer (Eicher Motors). After processing (turning, milling) the material is returned back to the customer with a Labour charges only bill.

3.11.9.1 Masters
(a) Sub-location master for customer's material location (separate stores)
(b) Customer master

3.11.9.2 Transaction
(a) Material Inward Challan. To capture information about when and what quantity material was received
(b) Annexure VI Challan (subsidiary Challan)
(c) Labour charges only sales invoice (cum Challan)

3.11.9.3 Features
(a) Linking customer's material (inward Challan quantity) with sales invoice quantity.
(b) Zero value invoice (Customer's defective material returned as it is).
(c) Capturing heat code / lot number / serial number etc.

3.11.10 ISO 9000 – Quality check
(a) Quality check for inbound material. The Goods received with respect to purchase order are kept in a 'HOLD' location or location for material under inspection. The stores will enter challan quantity and received quantity. The QC inspector will reopen the GRN with his / her password and enter the accepted quantity.
(b) Quality check for outbound material / Finished Products. At the time of shipping, QC check and relevant certificate can be fetched as standard word document file.
(c) Throughout the process production manufacturing process, the output (production) of each stage is captured and can be issued to next stage after the QC pass procedure. The quality supervisor has to verify the produced quantity at each stage until the packing stage, and record the entries in ERP. Rejected material can be monitored location wise.

3.11.11 BOM – Bill of Materials Module
Prerequisite: Item master. (Inventory module).

3.11.11.1 Masters
(a) Bill of Materials Master - using user friendly GUI interface (drag-and-drop)

3.11.11.2 Key MIS Reports
(a) BOM Master Printout category wise / subcategory wise
(b) List of Finished Goods items for selected F.G. item

3.11.11.3 ERP Features
(a) Save the BOM instantly in MS Excel format showing Father / child relation up to N level
(b) BOM Master is used for Production Module Work order is linked to BOM master. Material consumption in own shop floor and Sub-contractor - during production is linked to BOM

(i) Costing / Estimation - Product cost estimation is linked to BOM master.
(ii) Material Requirement Planning to compute the shortage quantity the BOM is exploded automatically.
(c) Automatic tracking of changes in BOM (engineering changes) with auto Revision Number and revision date.
(d) Adding similar BOM features allows creating a BOM from existing BOM of a similar product and then saving after minor changes as new BOM – tremendous time saving features for large BOM.

3.11.12 Cost Sheet Module – preparing estimate
3.11.12.1 Masters
(a) Overhead Master
(b) Export / Domestic Expense Master
(c) County / currency master

3.11.12.2 Transactions
(a) Enquiry (optional link)
(b) Cost sheet for the product. Raw Material / Packing Material costing / Labour Material
(c) Quotation (optional link).

3.11.12.3 Key MIS Reports
(a) Cost sheet Register

3.11.12.4 ERP Features
(a) Costing to arrive at the ex-factory price (can be based on BOM)
(b) Preparing estimate in multiple currency (US $, Euro, etc.)
(c) Option of saving of costing / quotation suggested price with mark-up instantly in MS Excel Sheets

3.11.13 PPC – Production Planning & Control Module
For process production. Not applicable for assembly kind of production.
3.11.13.1 Masters
(a) Process Flow Diagram (PFD) master
(b) Production planning as per PFD selected in item master
(c) Stage-wise inspection.
(d) Serial number generation in last (Production) entry [For tracking each product manufactured]

3.11.13.1 Key MIS Reports
   (a) Make work order - link with BOM and sales order (ORI)

3.11.13.2 ERP Features
   (a) BOM Master - One father item and *one* child item are considered in process production. However, the raw material undergoes many processes, such as cutting, bending, etc. [unlike assembly BOM, where there are many child items and one father item]
   (b) First a work order is prepared. This work order is is linked to the sales order (or sales schedules). User can plan the production that is linked to the work order (job card). Work order is a pre-requisite to PPC, for process-production.
      (i) PPC links the production plan for machines (from machine master).
      (ii) PPC links the production plan for process (from process master, such as drilling, plating, cutting, etc.).

3.11.13.3 Production plan further links (next procedure) with the actual production entry.

3.11.14 Production Module
ERP captures both kinds of manufacturing – 'Process production' as well as 'Assembly production' whether some of the following may be applicable or not will depend on the kind of manufacturing process.

3.11.14.1 Masters
   (a) Shift Master
   (b) Machine Master
   (c) Operator Master
   (d) Process Master

3.11.14.2 Transactions
   (a) Production Slip. (Production without link to BOM)
   (b) Work Order
   (c) Production Entry

3.11.14.3 Key MIS reports
   (a) Production issue and production slip register
   (b) Work Order Register
      (i) Work Order status – open, close and terminated or all with ORI / User filter. Users filter to capture Work Order prepared by each User

(ii) Work Order type – In-house or sub-contractor or all

(iii) Work Order Register with ORI Filter. To select sales order for a given work order

(c) Production Register with shift-wise, machine-wise/ operator-wise filter

3.11.14.4 ERP Features

(a) Pre-requisite: Item Master, Customer Master

(b) Captures scrap generated during production – end piece, etc.

(c) Production Indent integrated with inventory and Finished Goods produced

(d) Production QC

Order Fulfilment Module: This would normally have two parts:-
1. CRM – Customer Relationship Management
2. Sales Module.

3.11.15 CRM Module (Customer Relationship Management) and pre-sales module

3.11.15.1 Masters

(a) Marketing Master – Commercial terms

3.11.15.2 Transactions

(a) Sales Enquiry

(b) Sales Quotation (as per ISO format)

(c) Internal Order Acceptance (Internal ORI).

(d) Order Acceptance or OA or Sales Order, (Customer Purchase Order link). Order Receipt Information (ORI). [With Sales Schedule - Optional]

(e) Proforma invoice (optional).

(f) ORI status entry by Marketing/Production/Dispatch Department

(g) Quotation

3.11.15.3 Key MIS reports

(a) Enquiry Register. Automatic report of enquiries for which quotation not given

(b) Quotation Register. Automatic report of quotation for which order not received

   (i) Automatic Pending Quotations Report (Quotation given but order not received)

(c) Order Acceptance (Sales Order) Register. ORI register – (i) All; (ii) Open; (iii) Used; (iv) Amended; (v) Booked; and (vi) Terminated

   (i) Automatic Pending Orders Report (order received but not dispatched)

(d) Proforma invoice register

(e) Customer rating based on share of business, payment promptness

3.11.15.4 ERP features

(a) State wise 'Road permit' information. (Master)

(b) Sales Officer wise Order booking

(c) Multiple contact names for one customer can be stored with their individual email id and cell number. This helps in follow-up with the right person

(d) Sales schedule linking (optional)

3.11.16. Sales Module (Shipping)

F. G. inventory (dispatch) and sales accounting.

3.11.16.1 Masters

(a) Customer Type Master.

(b) Customer Master.

(c) Enquiry type master.

(d) Delivery mode master.

(e) Sales coordinator master.

(f) Officer Master (engineer or staff name can be attached to customer.

3.11.16.2 Transactions

(a) Commercial Invoice

(b) Sales Invoice. Preparing Challan cum Sales Invoice (CCI)

   (i) Tax Invoice (Domestic). Link to Order Receipt Information (ORI)/Internal ORI (Projection ORI for stocking)

   (ii) Scrape sales Invoice.

   (iii) Trading Invoice. (Optional)

   (iv) Invoice with zero sales value (free samples). Complementary.

   (v) Purchase return invoice. (For excisable material returned to supplier).

(c) Sales Return transaction. Goods returned from Customer.

(d) Automatic Inspection Report (QC) for finished goods along with sales invoices (ISO 9000).

(e) Replacement Challan non-excisable (linked to sales and RGN).

(f) Stock Transfer Invoice. (To transfer material to own stock locations, such as branch, franchises, etc.).

(g) 'Repairing Invoice' (Sales bill towards repair service charges).

(h) Packing Slip

3.11.16.3 Key MIS reports
- (a) Invoice register – Customer details.
    - (i) Invoice register – Product (item) details.
- (b) RGN (Return Goods Note) register.
- (c) Transfer Invoice register (optional).
- (d) Trading Invoice register (optional).
- (e) Ledger. (Debtor Ledger).
    - (i) Customer ledger.
    - (ii) Age-wise outstanding report
    - (iii) Age-wise overdue report
- (f) Product-wise invoice list.
- (g) Customer Master List. User can select fields to prepare excel file, e.g. to prepare phone book, select customer name, phone number, email id.
- (h) 'Repairing Invoice' Register.
- (i) Price List – with filter to select a given category or subcategory.

3.11.16.4 ERP features

- (a) Multiple Delivery Sales Schedule (Sales Order) Report.
    - (i) Sales invoice link to sales schedule (for OEM).
- (b) Replacement management – linked with inventory and sales accounting.
- (c) Sales Returned Goods Note (RGN) for item received back, link to sales account and excise.
- (d) Sales Invoice Link with sales order (ORI) to ensure accurate and fast billing preparation.
- (e) Automatic posting to Customer Account, Excise Books, VAT / Sales Tax, and Inventory.
- (f) Information about the Contact details such as multiple contact person names, telephone numbers, email id, etc., for each Customer.
- (g) Classification of customer Geographically (Region, state, city, Country), Segment wise.
- (h) Credit control. Credit Limits for the customer. Automatic pop-up based on link with credit limit of Customers and outstanding amount, while preparing sales invoice.
- (i) Capturing CT 3 information (optional).
- (j) Customer Grading, for preferential treatment as part of CRM

3.11.17. Sample Management Module
3.11.17.1 Master

(a) Customer master
(b) Item master

3.11.17.2 Transactions
(a) Sample received
(b) Sample sent

3.11.17.3 Key MIS reports
(a) Sample received register
(b) Sample sent register

3.11.18 Sub-contractor OUT Module

Complete Inventory tracking of sub-contractor inventory fully integrated with creditor accounting. Outsourcing. (Also referred as off-loading).

3.11.18.1 Master
(a) Sub-contractor or Address Master (for account with inventory location)
(b) Address Type Master

3.11.18.2 Transactions
(a) Job Order (Labour Purchase Order)
(b) Goods Delivery Note (GDN) – integrated with excise – 57 F4 Challan
(c) Goods Inward Note (GIN) – Material received back after processing with creditor accounting integration. QC – accept / reject.
(d) Special P. O. where the unloading location is direct at the sub-contractor (in ERP the subcontractor factory is also an inventory location). Automatically ERP will do the GDN along with the GRN entry. (optional).

3.11.18.3 Key MIS reports
(a) Job order register
(b) Job order status wise – Open JO, close JO, terminated JO
(c) GDN register
(d) GIN register
(e) GDN / GIN register. (Item sent to subcontractor and related material received duly after processing)
(f) Sub-contractor master list (sub-contractor list).

3.11.18.4 ERP features
(a) Pre-requisite: Location Master, BOM Master.
(b) Fully integrated with BOM master to ensure material given to the sub-contractor is the correct child items.

(c) Auto-production to consume material from sub-contractor
(d) Auto GDN. Purchase Order is placed on a supplier with 'unloading location' as sub-contractor. Material is directly sent to sub-contractor's factory by supplier. ERP can automatically capture the twin-transactions – material received from supplier and immediately transferred to sub-contractor
(e) Stock ledger for sub-contractor location gives information about stock lying with the TP
(f) Creditor accounts ledger for the accounts payable
(g) Money payment to sub-contractor after deducting TDS
(h) Scrap accounting

3.11.19 Export Sales Module

3.11.19.1 Master
  (a) Country – currency master
  (b) Customer Master (with country information)

3.11.19.2 Transactions
  (a) Export Order – captures foreign customer's sales order information and is linked to the Export invoice
  (b) Foreign Currency export invoice
  (c) Form ARE 1 is prepared automatically with the export sales invoice. (ARE = Allowed to Remove without paying Excise duty).
  (d) Packing List (automatically prepared with export invoice).
  (e) Commercial Invoice
  (f) Export Proforma Invoice

3.11.19.3 ERP features
  (a) Facility to enter current Exchange rate
  (b) Foreign Currency Order Receipt Information (export ORI)

3.11.20 Distribution Module for standard products sold through channel partners / distributors / stockists / agents / franchises

Sales through franchises / channel partners / distributors / dealers / agents / stockists / CFA. (optional).

3.11.20.1 Dispatch Order created by Head Office to factory for dispatch of material to channel location.

3.11.20.2 Transfer Invoice. Preparing online Stock Transfer Invoice (to Depot / franchises / Branch transfer). From factory to own inventory location linked to Dispatch Order.•

3.11.21 Project Tracking Module

Every order can be considered as a 'project' in ERP.

3.11.21.1 Masters
   (a) Project name Master
   (b) Drawing Maser

3.11.21.2 Transactions
   (a) Key transactions are captured and stored with the sales order number (Order Receipt Information – ORI)
   (b) Work order and production entry link to the project

3.11.21.3 Key MIS reports
   (a) Project Work Bench – This, at a glance will give activity status of a particular project (Sales order or ORI). Discipline needs to be maintained to enter the ORI in all the respective fields to capture data.

3.11.22 Warranty / After Sales Service Module

AMC /spares management / Customer Engineer (C.E.)

3.11.22.1 Masters
   (a) Customer Master
   (b) Item Master
   (c) Types of service call Master
   (d) Fault Master
   (e) Commercial Terms
   (f) Type of Contract
   (g) Key components master (Main spares)
   (h) Engineers Master (Customer Engineer)

3.11.22.2 Transactions
   (a) Call Sheet for the products. To register complain
   (b) Annual Maintenance Contract [AMC after warranty period]
   (c) Old History Card Entry (Legacy)
   (d) History Card
   (e) AMC Bill
       (i) VAT Bill (Include only VAT)
       (ii) Service Bill (Include only Service Tax)

- (f) Contract proposal
- (g) Agreement Generation
- (h) FOC (Free of Cost) Bill
- (i) VAT Bill
- (j) Expense Voucher to for Service
- (k) VAT Bill without link to Service Report.

3.11.22.3 Key MIS reports
- (a) Call Sheet Register
- (b) Service Report Register. [2nd, 3rd and 4th Quarterly Service Provided]
- (c) Annual Maintenance Contract Report [Engineer Wise, City Wise, Customer Wise]. AMC Register
- (d) Call Analysis Report
- (e) Daily Service Report
- (f) Annual Maintenance Report
- (g) Engineers Wise Revenue
- (h) Components Replacement Details
- (i) History card register. Filters - Category, Sub-category, Item, Service Engineer
- (j) VAT Bill Register. Filters - Category, Sub-category, Sub-Group, Item, Customer Type, Customer
- (k) Service Bill Register. Filters - Customer Type, Customer
- (l) Contract Proposal / Agreement Register. Filters - Customer, Status
- (m) Preventive Maintenance Report. Filters Under Warranty / AMC, Category, Sub-category, Sub-Group, Item
- (n) Expense Voucher Register for Service. Filters –Service Engineer
- (o) Service Expense voucher register.
- (p) FOC (Free of Cost) Bill Register. Filters - Category, Sub-category, Sub-Group, Item, Customer Type, Customer

3.11.22.4 ERP features
- (a) Call Sheet to arrive at the number of complaints or faults registered.
- (b) Services provided to the complaints or faults.
- (c) Machine Level Components used.
- (d) Report on Fault Analysis
- (e) Reports on Components Replacement Details

3.11.23 Helpdesk Module

Tracking customers calls / Without spares management

3.11.23.1 Masters
- (a) Customer Master

3.11.23.2 Transactions
- (a) Point data entry

3.11.23.3 Key MIS reports
- (a) Point Register
- (b) Point (call) status

3.11.23.4 ERP features
- (a) Email alerts for points pending for more > nn days. Here nn may be for example 15, means ERP will send automatic email if points are pending for over 15 days.

3.11.24 Automatic Email Alerts Module

3.11.24.1 Email id Master for sending auto emails

3.11.24.2 Alerts user for items falling below ReOrder Level (ROL)

3.11.24.3 ORI pending since defined days. Order received but dispatch pending alert

3.11.24.4 Pending Purchase Order since defined days

3.11.24.5 Pending customer Bills since defined days/Months

3.11.24.6 Bank balance going below defined amount

3.11.24.7 Non-Moving Items

3.11.24.8 Daily Sales to TOP Management

3.11.25 Plant Maintenance Module

3.11.25.1 Master
- (a) Machine Master
- (b) Machine and its spares Master with Activities Integrated
- (c) Activity Master (Includes cost)
- (d) In-charge Master (Includes cost)

3.11.25.2 Transactions
- (a) Work Order for Machine Maintenance
    - (i) Corrective Maintenance

(ii) Preventive Maintenance
(b) Production Entry for Machine Maintenance

3.11.25.3 Key MIS reports
(a) Machine Master Report (With Spares)
(b) Works Order Register with filters as
    (i) Maintenance Type (Corrective/Preventive)
    (ii) Work Order Status (Open, Closed, Terminated, All)
    (iii) Machine Wise
    (iv) In-charge Wise
(c) Production Entry Register (Cost is calculated) with filters as follows:
    (i) Maintenance Type (Corrective/Preventive)
    (ii) Machine Wise
    (iii) In-charge Wise
(d) Spares List

3.11.25.4 Features
(a) Automatic popup for maintenance to be done in next 2 days is shown when you login in into the system
(b) Automatic Email Alert for maintenance to be done, in next 2 days is prepared and send by ERP

3.11.26 Multi-location

This module is applicable for multi-location organization. For instance, Head office and Factory are situated in different geographical locations. Static IP address server and broadband internet connection allows user to access ERP database from anywhere / anytime. Pre-requisite Server with fixed IP address from your ISP (Internet Service Provider) and firewall software is required. You can also opt for 'thin-client' technology.

3.11.26.1 Remote Connection from another computer using Internet.
3.11.26.2 ERP also supports Remote Login where user can access ERP Server using Internet.

3.11.27 Payroll and HR

3.11.27.1 Master
(a) Bank master
(b) Bank-Branch master

- (c) Attendance Bonus setting
- (d) Bank master
- (e) Bank-Branch master
- (f) City master
- (g) Department master (Cost Center)
- (h) Designation master
- (i) Employee master
- (j) GL account Master
- (k) Grade master
- (l) Income Tax – Bank master
- (m) Income Tax – Earning and deductions (Section 80C, 80D, 80 U, 17(2) (V) etc.)
- (n) Income Tax – Form 16 - Signing authority master
- (o) Labour Welfare Fund master (LWF)
- (p) Salary Heading - Earning heads and deduction heads Master
- (q) State Master

3.11.27.2 Transactions
- (a) Attendance – The number of days that an employee was present will have to be punched in the system by the concerned official of the HR Department.
- (b) Income Tax Monthly Challan Entry
- (c) Income TAX Quarterly Acknowledgement Entry
- (d) Monthly Deductions.
- (e) Pay slip

3.11.27.3 Reports
- (a) Attendance Register
- (b) Attrition Report
- (c) Bank Statement
- (d) Deduction head wise register
- (e) Earning head wise register
- (f) Employee Joining Report
- (g) Employee list
- (h) Employee resignation
- (i) ESI Report
- (j) Form 16
- (k) Gratuity register
- (l) Income Tax Yearly Report per Employee wise (Automated)

(m) Leave Encashment Statement
(n) Loan register
(o) Pay Slip
(p) Payroll Register
(q) PF statement
(r) Professional Tax [Professional Tax] Statement

3.11.27.4 ERP features
(a) Daily wages, monthly wages – salary calculations.
(b) Attendance types – absence, paid leave, unpaid leave, etc.
(c) Loans and advances to employees
(d) Employee type – manager, operator, etc.
(e) Automatic calculation of income tax in pay-slip every month based on Earning and Deduction fed into the system.
(f) Modify all the transaction as many times as needed.
(g) Salary lock. (After this no Modification is allowed, once an Account have audited.
(h) User Matrix – By which each user is given/denied access to particular Report/ Transaction resulting is high Security and blocking un-authorised access.
(i) Every Report can be easily transferred to Excel.
(j) Very User Friendly GUI and Easy to understand procedures which require minimum Training.
(k) Leave allotment master

3.11.28 Resource Matrix Module

3.11.28.1 Master
(a) Activity Master
(b) User Master
(c) Customer Master

3.11.28.2 Transaction
(a) Daily Time Card entry

3.11.28.3 Key MIS reports
(a) Resource wise (User wise) time spent report for a given period
(b) Activity wise time spent for a given sales order (ORI)

3.11.28.4 ERP features
(a) Activity or Task Tracking of individual in the organization – for example draftsman hours, salesman hours
(b) Can also be linked to enquiry or quotation (pre-sales) time spent by staff
(c) Department wise, controlling and monitoring indirect time (hours) spent by staff

3.11.29 e-Business

This module depends on the website based interface for receiving orders. Necessary secure payment gateway is integrated with the bank to process money transactions.

The internet security is provided by encryption which is done based on the Secured Socket Layer (SSL) technology.

3.11.29.1 ERP Database contains various information such as 'Product List' or 'Price List'. This can be now uploaded to a **website**.

3.11.29.2 User can restrict some web pages for internal use (Extranet / Intranet). Show stock position online, etc.

3.11.29.3 E-Catalogue. The rapid development of B2B and B2C e-Business shows that the internet is not just a new place to do business but constitutes a completely new method for commerce. E-Business is the most significant area of the new 'Digital Economy'. Once you have ERP database in place, the same can then be published to the World Wide Web. For instance, we can prepare an active website.

3.11.29.4 For example, channel partners (dealer) Finished Goods (FG) item master can be synchronized with the FG being shown on the e-commerce website for the shopping cart, or while booking sales order (with option of showing stock).

3.11.30 Automatic SMS / Text to mobile phones (cell phones)

3.11.30.1 Reports or transactions such as Order Acceptance can be send as SMS (short message system) to mobile phones directly.
3.11.30.2 B2B or B2C communication anywhere anytime from ERP.
3.11.30.3 SMS Gateway is designed to integrate seamlessly with ERP. Third party integration with a telecom company to provide text gateway.

3.11.31 Plant Connect - Web-based solution for Support, Maintenance and Monitoring of machines.

Monitor equipment: Located anywhere, anytime (24x7), continuous monitoring, or need based monitoring. Any equipment fitted with a Controller / PLC / HMI and which can communicate using a published protocol. E.g. CNC machines, Boilers, Pumps, Chillers, Generator, Engines sets, etc. Usually this is a third party solution integrated with ERP software.

Practice Questions

1. List Masters and Transactions of the Finance Module.
2. What is JIT?
3. Which departments are linked automatically in the inventory system?
4. Describe disadvantages of non-ERP system.

Activity

1. Visit any service business organization, for example a Bank, Travel agent, Hotel or similar.
   (a) Find out if Server is installed or not, find out what kind of business management software they are using and a make a note and share with the class.
2. Additional online study material:
   (a) Register with professional networking site LinkedIn.com
   (b) Join ERP LinkedIn Group 'ERP, E-business Forum' to get automatic updates about ERP. Tip: Use LinkedIn search engine to locate this group, select Group and search. Click on 'Join Group' button.

***

Chapter 4...

ERP IMPLEMENTATION LIFE CYCLE

4.1 Evaluation and Selection of ERP Package
4.2 Project Planning and Implementation
4.3 Team Training and Testing
4.4 End User Training and Going Live
4.5 Post Evaluation and Maintenance
4.6 Role of Organisation Management and ERP Vendor
- Practice Questions
- Activity

Learning Objectives

After going through this unit, you will be able to:
- Evaluate and select ERP packages
- Discuss planning and implementation of projects
- Examine the importance of team training, testing and end user training
- Assess the role of organisation management and vendor

Introduction

ERP software is a complex software that changes the 'brain' of the organisation, like a brain transplant. ERP implementation implies the deployment (installation) of ERP in the organisation. This is not like an accounting package, say Tally. You acquire the CD, do the setup and begin using it in a couple of days. However, ERP takes a much longer time than other software and can even take three to twelve months to commence. This is because it not only automates the manual methods but also forces to amend the manual method if found wrong.

In this chapter we will examine the ERP implementation life cycle. There are many stages in the implementation of ERP in any organisation. This is called the ERP implementation life cycle. The overall success of ERP would depend on how accurately and seriously, the ERP has been applied at every stage. Therefore, the management of the organisation introducing ERP as well as the vendor must work as a cohesive team for a fruitful final result. Experience of implementing ERP over a long period of time has indicated that following the steps given below with utmost sincerity would generally yield good "ERP implementation".

A proven path to Enterprise Resource Planning Software Implementation:

1. **First appoint a ERP coordinator:** He or she will exclusively focus on Enterprise Resource Planning implementation. If possible, the organisation must identify two persons, as a backup, the second person will coordinate with the users and the ERP implementer team. I know it is difficult to spare two senior people exclusively for ERP, but trust me it is worth it. Majority of ERPs are under-utilised or fail to give the desired benefits because of improper implementation. The ERP coordinator should be sufficiently senior and/or supported by the CEO / Director.

2. **Appoint 'chief-of-ERP-project':** A senior person with full authority (usually owner) who will not hesitate to remove a person out of the project because he is not ready to work in ERP (because such a person will always put a *spanner*), and the ERP coordinator may not be able to speak up to his or her seniors, whereas the owner can.

3. **Give highest priority to ERP education and training:** Educate all users to understand what is going to be achieved with the new system. Additional education should include Total Quality Management, Change Management Strategies and so on. Give training to main business process owners (department managers), in how to use the system. Have them train the other users. It is necessary to take time out from the routine and actually do hands-on training. Don't think ERP software is like magic which can produce instant results without necessary ground work.

4. **Conduct business analysis to streamline the current processes:** This is done by the implementer team (from ERP vendor side). They will interview the main department heads and the CEO to find gaps between what ERP will deliver and what the user wants.

5. **Planning, training and education for the IT support staff:** This will enable them to understand the new hardware, software and network imperatives. For instance, server computer configuration, firewall software, security settings for the user login into the server operating system (e.g. Microsoft Windows Server OS 2008).

6. **BPR or Business Process Reengineering:** (Match business processes with the new software). BPR implies that it is not compulsory to do things as were being done for the last several years. Once ERP is implemented, change has to be accepted. Though it is easy to say, it is tough for people who are senior and experienced to modify their working styles and adapt to modern business management logic. "Boss is always right" may not work every time, but accepting that "ERP brings best practices" will always work.

7. Software Modifications: Carry out software modifications only when Business Processes exist that do not differentiate you in the marketplace are not supported by the software. Stick to essential customisation. Do not ask for *chopping and changing* of the programme at every level.

8. Business Simulation (on a department level and at the enterprise level): Execute Conference Room Pilot or the CRP run. Prepare a 'Proof of Concept' file. Certify the printouts. Yes, each user will have to sign every page and agree that they have understood ERP and are ready to use it.

9. Go Live: A phased approach may be indicated, based on the amount of change dictated by the new system.

10. Implementation Review Meetings: This is conducted after users have become comfortable with the ERP system. The goal is to ask the software vendor to suggest better ways to use the system.

11. Have patience: If you have asked for unlimited customisation then it will take unlimited time! Give sufficient time to the ERP vendor to change the programmes to carry out last minute changes. If the changes are happening in bits and pieces then it will take time for ERP to stabilise. Do not get into the vicious circle of change-correct-errors-change.

12. Increase budget if you have enlarged the scope: Usually users do not know what ERP is, and they have very unrealistic expectations. If you want the moon then it will be now necessary to provide enough money for the same. Many a times the ERP journey halts due to lack of money *during* ERP implementation.

Rapid Implementation

Whenever there is a requirement to implement ERP in haste or in a short period of time, the following points should be kept in mind:

- Get an ERP Consultant whose time-tested implementation process, together with **ERP user training**, help to get your system and employees up-and-running. Many ER Plans are implemented in about 180 days. I attribute this to several factors:
    - (i) Understanding of Legacy system and proper gap analysis helps the ERP team in implementing the ER plan.
    - (ii) The flexibility of the ERP package.
    - (iii) The ERP consulting services and training provided by experts.
    - (iv) ERP interface, which makes the product easy for your employees to learn and use.
    - (v) Ease of customisation / modification of the ERP system to meet the exact needs of the users.
    - (vi) Extensive handholding and support in preparing the master database.

4.1 Evaluation and Selection of ERP Package

Introduction: ERP software is a sophisticated business management software that has evolved over a period to a million line codes. One has to be very careful while selecting an ERP software package because once the organisation selects and starts implementing the ER Plan there is no going back. It is a one way street. Wrong selection of ERP may cause loss of money and time that no organisation can afford.

In the next few sections in this chapter we will learn more about evaluation and selection of the ERP software package.

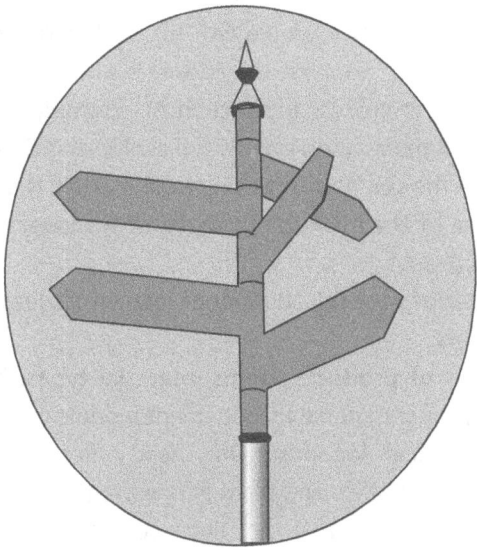

Fig. 4.2

A farmer who had seen a Mercedes car in his village came to the city and began asking about buying a Mercedes. Obviously, friends explained to him that Mercedes is not the only car available and is an expensive car. There are many other makes and models in the market. Depending on the budget, and his needs the farmer should buy a car more suitable to him and his lifestyle, may be a TATA Nano or Maruti Alto would be better suited to him. However he was keen on a car which would seat at least ten people in the car. He was then advised to think of a mini bus or a similar vehicle.

Similarly, an executive may have heard of SAP and would ask for SAP for his small company. ERP is a generic name and SAP is a specific make and model of ERP. The user company must dwell on selecting the right ERP and ERP modules.

The first step is to jot down what do you expect from ERP. Define goals clearly, write down what return on investment you expect. It should not be the other way round; people commonly ask what ROI is expected, but when asked what returns they would be expecting, they are very vague in their answer.

For instance, a CEO can say, our rejections should be reduced and customer complaints must be taken care of, can ERP solve these specific objectives? This is a good way to select the ERP, because the user already has the end objective in mind and knows what to expect. Yet, another Director says, 'Can ERP reduce my inventory by 10%"? One can now select an ERP and implement this main objective in mind.

ERP is a business management software system. However, there are many flavours of ERP and many kinds of ERP Companies, small and big. Well sometimes, the board of Directors may get carried away with impressive PowerPoint presentations without asking details of each module. One should follow the points given below to select an ERP:

1. First question to ask is are you a Service company or manufacturing company. For example, a service sector ERP will be further different for each kind of business. For example ERP for Bank is different as compared to the ERP for an Airline. Suppose the answer is a manufacturing company, then the next question is process production or assembly production, OEM (Original Equipment Manufacturer) or FMCG (Fast Moving Consumer Goods) product?
2. Next define the size of business operation: Here is a checklist:
   (a) **Volume of the business in terms of turnover:** Annual sales in India and Export (if any).
   (b) **Number of people:** Number of total employees, and number of possible ERP users.
   (c) **Number of products, items, material types:** This will be important to select proper material management module and its flavours.
   (d) **Geographical location:** One head-office and two factories, or one location with office and plant in one premises.
   (e) Sales is performed to the direct customer or channel partners, agents, stockist.

Documenting the above details will help in selecting the ERP vendor and specific flavour of ERP. That's why I took the example of buying a vehicle, car or bus?

3. The best way to evaluate is to simulate the ERP requirements by way of preparing a file of current reports. A list of expected reports will help in evaluating ERP. However do not expect all reports to be available in ERP. This is a common mistake. A user becomes greedy, and asks for everything, without realizing that inputs will be given to ERP or not. Most ERPs will meet eight out of ten requirements, which is acceptable. If the ERP vendor says yes to all ten reports (100%) there may be a catch.

4. It is important to start with preparing an SOP manual - Standard Operating Procedures. How you want to do your business is known best by you. However that is all in your head and needs to be written down. Unfortunately, the top management is reluctant to write. In fact, they will even argue and say "What is there to write, it is understood, it is common sense". Nevertheless, you see, common sense is not so common! SOPs are mandatory, to start evaluating ERP, because users are then clear about what they want, and how the operations details are well defined.

Consider the example of a process called 'Receiving order from customer'. This has to be written in detail. What if the order is cancelled? How will the system handle change in the quantity? Is the term of payment to be linked with the order. This means, 100% advance must be received with the sales order before dispatch (invoice), and so on. If these details are not defined in a systematic manner, ERP will be unable to automate the process of 'receiving order'. Many companies such as Amazon.com conduct sales through a e-commerce website. It is one of the most successful e-commerce companies with Lakhs of customers buying and giving advance money. This is possible because they have well-defined and tightly-integrated business processes, right from receiving orders, money and shipping. Without ERP, it would not have been possible to do such a large business.

Companies that wish to buy ERP software must do lots of homework before installing ERP. This implies that lots of time needs to be invested in the evaluation and selection of an ERP system. Any shortcuts taken will prove to be costlier in the long run. It may therefore be wise to take help of experienced ERP consultants in the selection process. Many companies take emotional decisions without putting much thought and try to save time and money in the selection process. Eventually they land up buying a truck in place of a TATA Nano! In other words, they buy a large and complicated (sophisticated) ERP software and find it difficult to implement.

4.1.1 ERP System Requirements Specification – Joke

Official New Year invitation e-mail from the Director was sent by e-mail to all staff:

"All members of staff - please note that due to recession, there will only be one drink per person at the new year's Annual Party. And please bring your own cup!

And what happened at the annual party?
The specifications were missing in the e-mail-memo - size of cup.
Everyone brought very large glasses!

Fig. 4.1: High expectations!

Moral of the story

Be very specific in your daily life, including ERP project work. Give precise specifications, during the SRS meetings (system requirement specification). User will often prepare a "wish list" with unrealistic expectations. On the other hand top management will have to learn to draw a line and put stop to customization. Similarly, knowing exact requirements and laying down proper system specifications is very important from ERP perspective also.

Before proceeding further it would be worthwhile to familiarise with certain commonly used phrases. Otherwise, these have a good potential to be misunderstood.

4.1.2 Paperless Office

Paperless office is next step or shall we say 'Less-paper-office'? Now that you have understood that entire office work, documents, etc., are on Server Computer, in other words electronic format. This not only reduces cost by saving paper but is also good for the environment. Usually ERP transactions are printed and if they are pertaining to customer or vendor the same is sent out. Traditionally this is sent by post, by courier or by fax. In addition to printing on paper one can also make a .PDF file and send the same as an email attachment.

- **For example:** Purchase Order, Sales Order, Dispatch Order, Sales Invoice, Transfer Invoice, Proforma Invoice, Dispatch note, Account statement, etc. can be printed as .PDF file and send by email.

- **Document-based communications is made more efficient:** ERP enables businesses to automate and streamline paper-less communications. ERP replaces islands of information with a unified program that delivers a single real-time vision of the enterprise. By printing Portable Document Format (PDF) from ERP, users are enabled to create easy-to-use, paperless documents that extend ERP to colleagues, partners, vendors, and customers. Using this solution, one can - Improve productivity, streamline communication, sharpen one's competitive edge and improve CRM.

4.1.3 CxO

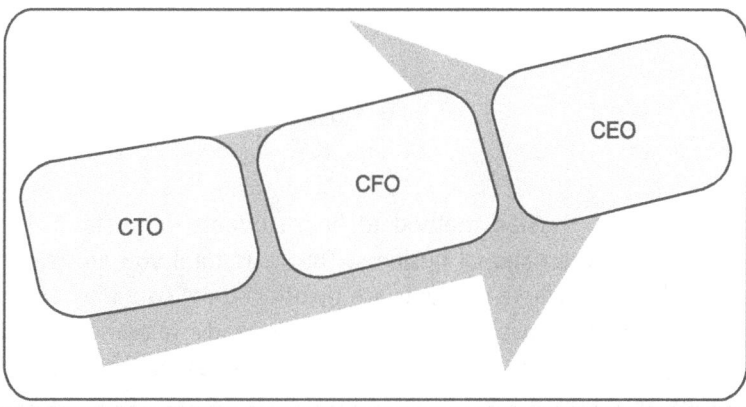

Chief x Officer: For ERP project you need to involve all C x Os. That is chief of all functions.

CIO is Chief Information Officer: The chief information officer is called the CIO, this is a job title for the head of the information technology group within an organisation. The CIO is important person for the ERP project. The CIO typically reports to the CEO (Chief executive officer). The prominence of this position has risen greatly as IT has become a more important part of business. No specific qualification is typical of CIOs in general. Many had degrees in computer science, software engineering, or Certified ERP Professional, but this is by no means universal. Many were technical staff. More recently CIOs' leadership capabilities, business acumen and strategic perspectives have taken precedence over technical skills. It is now quite common for CIOs to be appointed from the business side of the organisation. Typically CIO is responsible for ERP implementation.

CTO is Chief Technical Officer: A chief technical officer or chief technology officer (abbreviated as CTO) is an executive position whose holder is focused on scientific and technical issues within a company. The BOM Module in ERP is controlled by the CTO and his / her technical team. They know the design, Bill of Materials or the Recipe. Often, the CTO will oversee technical staff at a company, particularly those building products or creating services that embody industry-specific technologies. In some cases, the CTO will also oversee the work of the research and development organisations.

4.1.4 Lakhs and Crore to Millions and Billions

- For a company outside India targeting customers in **India** for marketing their product or service, it may be a good idea to learn the system of putting *comma* in large figures as per Indian style. The meaning of *Lacs* or *Lakh* or *Crore with respect to Million or Billion should also be understood*. Or the other way round, Indian organisations possessing a web site for export, should maintain comma style used in other countries and mention million or billion instead of Lacs and Crores. It should be noted here that the new symbol for Indian currency is changed from Rs. to ₹.

- Here is a quick conversion method to help students understand the importance, especially for the international business. This is useful if you are reading articles or financial statements, where amounts are mentioned as "so-many" Millions / billions. This conversion table has been provided for ready reference. Please note that the **placement of comma** in India, is after two zeroes, and in international is after three zeroes, as shown below:

Indian term	International term	Indian coma position	International coma position
1 Lakh	100 Thousands	1,00,000	100,000
10 Lakhs	1 Million	10,00,000	1,000,000
1 Crore (100 Lakhs)	10 Million	1,00,00,000	10,000,000
10 Crore	100 Million	10,00,00,000	100,000,000
100 Crore	1 Billion	1,00,00,00,000	1,000,000,000

Note: 'Digit grouping' settings in control panel of the Microsoft Windows allows user to place comma in the desired position. This is useful if you are showing figures in Lacs or Crore in MS Excel spread sheet in India.

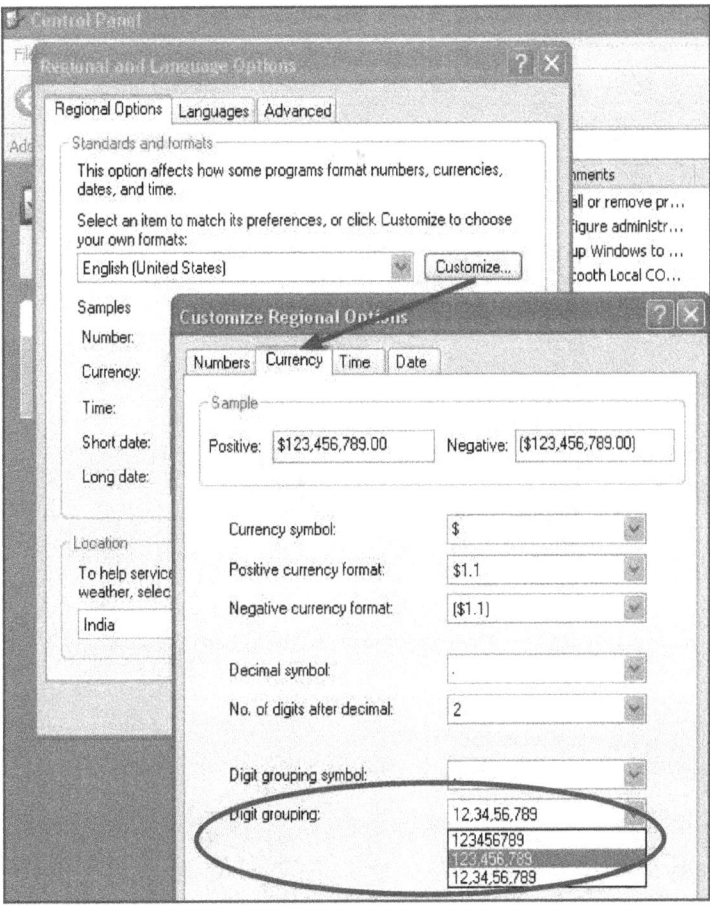

Fig. 4.2: MS Windows Control Panel Settings

Due care should be taken in the *ERP software* to indicate the figures properly. Since Tally kind of software package is very popular in India it gives an option to set the comma in the desired position.

- In some countries such as Bahrain, a three decimal currency is used in the accounting system. E.g. BHD or Bahraini Dinar BD 345.678/-.
    - Minor Unit is 1/1000 = Fils.

Indian terms for Very Very large numbers are given below:

Indian term	1 and number of zeroes	International term
Arab	One with nine zeroes	One billion
Kharab	One with eleven zeroes	One hundred billion
Neel	One with thirteen zeroes	Ten trillion
Padma	One with fifteen zeroes	One quadrillion
Shankh	One with seventeen zeroes	One hundred quadrillion

On the lighter side do you know what the meaning of name Google is?

10^{googol} ($10^{10^{100}}$) is called a googolplex.

- In 1997 Larry and Sergey gave the name of their search engine 'Google', from the word "googol," a mathematical term for the number represented by the numeral 1 followed by 100 zeroes. The "Googleplex" is the Google company headquarters, located in California, near San Jose, USA.

4.1.5 List of IT infrastructure, Computer Hardware, and Software Recommended for ERP Software

Given below is a schematic layout of a typical ERP framework. The various IT, Computer and Hardware requirements for ERP software are listed below.

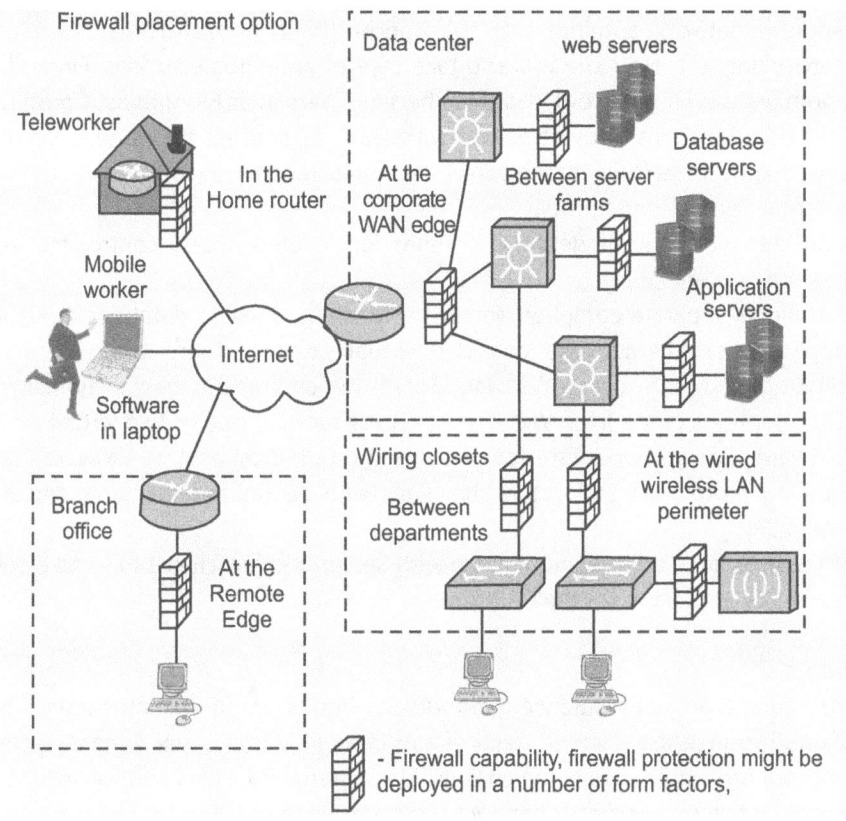

Fig. 4.3: Firewall

1. One High performance (Xeon) **Server computer** with Minimum 16 / 32 GB RAM 1 TB Hard disk drive (HDD). With DVD writer for taking periodical backup. With at least ONE node (8 GB RAM) with the latest Operating system.
2. Other client sides **PC** (user's nodes) with MS Windows 8 and at least 4 GB RAM. Thin client terminal may also be considered.
3. System software: MS Windows 2012 *Sever* Operating System and MS SQL 2008 Server RDBMS software. MS Excel.
4. **UPS** for the Server and switch (hub) is required for at least two / three hours battery backup.
5. You may add as many PCs as many users are planning to use ERP. The PC (nodes) may be networked using wired LAN or wireless LAN (Wi Fi) technology.
6. LaserJet printer is recommended for hard copy printouts.
7. You will appoint ERP Coordinator who is available during the ERP testing, implementation and deployment activity.
8. There will be a 'Chief-of-Project' to monitor and review the progress during the ERP software implementation. (Usually a very senior person with necessary authority to take crucial decisions).

9. Appoint network administrator to support the IT infrastructure, such as Server, networking, etc. He / she will also take care of anti-virus solutions, Firewall settings, Login and secret password, etc. (May be same person as ERP project Coordinator).
10. For multi locations: Provide Server with static IP address for remote login. A good broadband connectivity at the server location is recommended.
11. Internet / Email connectivity.
12. Consider biometric (fingerprint) scanner for secured access control for server and user computers.
13. Additional separate computer server for Machine drawing database or similar other applications. Alternatively, consider virtual servers. There are several VMware offerings that can replace VMware Server depending on the functionality needed. These options range from VMware Player for running one or two virtual machines to VMware vSphere Hypervisor for virtualizing on physical host, to VMware vSphere for running more than 100 virtual machines with centralized management and cloud scalability.
14. If possible, provide a separate room with Server and few clients PC, and a conference table, LCD Projector, for the CRP run.

Conclusion

Incorporating a project assurance methodology into your ERP implementation helps you to identify and resolve the strategic, tactical and intangible issues - and manage the human factors - before project gaps become chasms. The incremental costs you will incur by having an additional resource periodically conduct project assessments will be far less than the cost of project delays caused by unrealized project gaps and will provide the peace of mind that the project is on the right track.

4.1.6 A Step-by-Step Approach to Business Automation

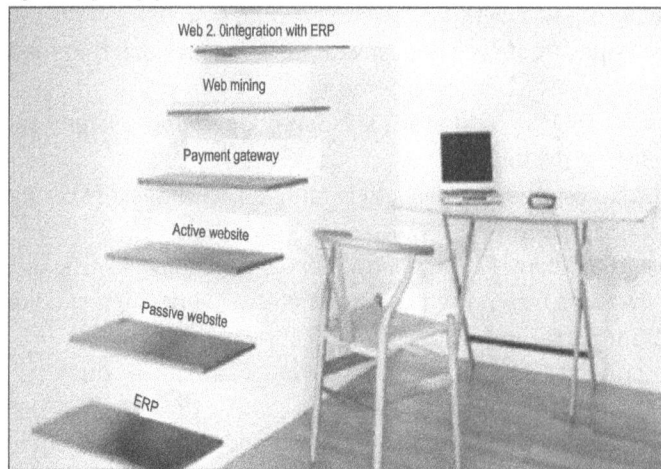

Fig. 4.4: First step is ERP

Many companies have made a mistake of first publishing a website, and then deploying ERP. However, it is only later that they realize that the website is bringing much more business than they are able to manage with the legacy systems. So, they try to hurriedly implement ERP, as second step. It is recommended that you streamline your business processes first, by deploying ERP, and then tap the power of the internet to expand the business.

The figure above shows the schematic of an automation process. *The first step is ERP.* That lays the foundation to manage growth. How can you do web mining without ERP or a website? Without using the internet, business will be limited to geographical location.

Progressive organisations use the internet to connect to the office using remote access. Depending on the business model, some organisations opt for payment gateway i.e. an interface with the bank server computer. Business Intelligence (BI) software solution depends on the 'On-Line Transaction Processing' (OLTP). The ERP software meticulously captures the transaction and stores it in a database.

Most multinational companies, as well as many public sector organisations, have adopted ERP and increasingly small and medium sized enterprises have been following suit. Indeed, by 2003 ER Planning formed the backbone of many application architectures and was being extended into developments such as e-business and e-Governance. After ERP, the next step is, to publish a simple website (passive), followed by a more interactive site, and later a payment gateway for transacting money (Digital money). All this leads to next step of data mining and web mining. The next plan is to integrate ERP with web 2.0.

Robust ERP is the foundation of the successful E-commerce website such as Amazon.com. Amazon is one of the largest stores in the world, without any physical store. Without ERP, it is not possible to manage such a large business.

4.2 Project Planning and Implementation

At this point, the reader must have understood that ERP project planning and ERP Implementation is a big challenge. As mentioned earlier, it is not like a Tally accounting software, that you get a CD of and in a couple of days begin using it. In fact sometimes it takes three to six months to implement ERP, and sometimes even up to one year.

The first step is to plan the ERP Project. Below is the step-by-step procedure:

Step 1: Give the name of the project: ERP Implementation.

Step 2: Decide ERP Project Start Date and Target Completion Date.

Step 3: Do homework to estimate TCO – Total Cost of Ownership.

Step 4: Fix total Budget based on TCO exercise: Maximum ₹ NN Lakhs.

Step 5: Define Objectives: Implement ERP in Head office and Plant 1, then in plant 2.

Step 6: **ERP Project Calendar:** 6 Days a Week, Thursday weekly holiday (due to power staggering).

Step 7: Identify **Project Holidays:** Sept. 6, Oct. 2, Oct. 21-24, Dec. 25, Dec. 31

Step 8: Define **Phases:**
- (i) Initiation and Planning
- (ii) Implementation and training – Pilot Run
- (iii) Acceptance test
- (iv) Go Live

Step 9: Identify and appoint the 'ERP Task Force'

Step 10: Write Milestones

Step 11: Write Task for each milestone with resources

4.2.1 ERP Implementation Process

A detailed approach to the ERP implementation process is described below. The duties, responsibilities and progress monitoring can be carried out as described below. Once it has been decided to implement a particular ERP package, one should commence with naming the ERP Task force Team.

ERP Task Force Team

Sr. No.	Name	Initials	Department	Role
1	Jyotindra Zaveri	JJZ	CEO	Leader
2	Sachin Joshi	Sachin	Marketing	Member
3	Amrapali	ACG	Accounts	Member
4	Kedar Joshi	Kedar	Production	Member
5	TS Nair	TS	Purchase	Member

Project Management tool for monitoring and control: Microsoft Project Management Software.

Resource Calendars:
- Marketing - 5 D/Week, Sat-Sun Off
- Others - 6 D/Week, Thursday Off

Leaves: Nair Oct 3-7, Sachin Oct 16-20.

It is interesting to note that majority of ERP projects are delayed due to lack of planning, lack of teamwork, or lack of leadership. Most ERP project implementation is started without a roadmap (plan) and fails miserably.

> **"If you fail to plan**
>
> **you plan to fail**

Remember:

Progress Report example:

ERP Project	As of	30/09/2006
Task Name	Actual Start	Actual Finish
Project Announcement	2-Sep-06	2-Sep-06
Kick Off Meeting	12-Sep-06	12-Sep-06
Project Planning	14-Sep-06	23-Sep-06
Collecting Legacy data	18-Sep-06	28-Sep-06
Master data entry	26-Sep-06	27-Sep-06
Transaction data entry	28-Sep-06	28-Sep-06
Customization	30-Sep-06	30-Oct-06
Review Meeting 1	21-Sep-06	21-Sep-06
Review Meeting 2	27-Sep-06	27-Sep-06

Summary of the MS Project software procedure:

1. Define the project.
2. Define general working times.
3. List the tasks in the project.
4. Organize tasks into phases.
5. Schedule tasks.
6. Link to or attach more task information.
7. Add columns of custom information.

8. Set deadlines and constrain tasks.
9. Identify risks to the project.
10. Add documents to the project.
11. Publish project information to the Web.

It may be appropriate to assign responsibilities for this project (most of that should be Vendor's responsibility but with the help of the ERP customer). There are many softwares for managing project. Let us take the example of one made by Microsoft.

About Microsoft Project (MSP) Software

MSP is a project management software program, developed and sold by Microsoft, which is designed to assist a project manager in the following steps:
1. Developing a plan.
2. Assigning resources to tasks.
3. Tracking progress.
4. Managing the budget.
5. Analysing workloads.

See examples of an ERP Project Plan given below:

ZAVERI ERP PROJECT ROADMAP	133 days	16/08/2007 08:00	21/01/2008 17:00		Resource (Person)
ERP Initiation & Planning	26 days	16/08/2007 08:00	14/09/2007 17:00		Puneet
Scope list printout and softcopy	5 days	16/08/2007 08:00	21/08/2007 17:00		Dhiraj
SRS	5 days	22/08/2007 08:00	27/08/2007 17:00	2	Dhiraj
ERP Preparation	15 days	28/08/2007 08:00	13/09/2007 17:00	3	Amol, Dhiraj, Kalindi, Mani, Puneet, Sachin
Kick-off meeting	1 day	14/09/2007 08:00	14/09/2007 17:00	4	Amol, Dhiraj, Kalindi, Mani, Puneet, Sachin
Begin Implementation	91 days	15/09/2007 08:00	02/01/2008 17:00	5	
Collect Legacy	2 days	15/09/2007 08:00	17/09/2007 17:00	4	Kalindi
First cut by ERP	21 days	18/09/2007 08:00	11/10/2007 17:00	7	Dhiraj, Mani
Business Blueprint - first draft	7 days	12/10/2007 08:00	19/10/2007 17:00	8	Dhiraj, Mani
POC spiral based on first cut	7 days	12/10/2007 08:00	19/10/2007 17:00	8	Dhiraj, Mani
Documents given - two spirals	5 days	20/10/2007 08:00	25/10/2007 17:00	9,10	Dhiraj, Mani
Training	5 days	20/10/2007 08:00	25/10/2007 17:00	10	Dhiraj, Kalindi, Mani, Puneet, Sachin, Amol

ZAVERI ERP PROJECT ROADMAP	133 days	16/08/2007 08:00	21/01/2008 17:00		Resource (Person)
Training Completed	25 days	26/10/2007 08:00	23/11/2007 17:00	12	
Internal CRP - S1	5 days	26/10/2007 08:00	31/10/2007 17:00	8	Mani
Internal CRP - S2	10 days	01/11/2007 08:00	12/11/2007 17:00	14	Dhiraj Purusha
POC file S3	10 days	13/11/2007 08:00	23/11/2007 17:00	15	Mani
ERP EXE Ready for first cut	30 days	24/11/2007 08:00	29/12/2007 17:00	16	
First cut by Task force / users	10 days	24/11/2007 08:00	05/12/2007 17:00	16	Amol, Kalindi, Mani, Puneet, Sachin
Essential customization	5 days	24/11/2007 08:00	29/11/2007 17:00	13	Mani
CRP by Task force / users	15 days	06/12/2007 08:00	22/12/2007 17:00	18	Amol, Kalindi, Puneet, Sachin
Customization	5 days	24/12/2007 08:00	29/12/2007 17:00	20	Mani
ERP EXE freeze	1 day	02/01/2008 08:00	02/01/2008 17:00	21	
User Acceptance ceremony	1 day	02/01/2008 08:00	02/01/2008 17:00		Puneet, Dhiraj Purusha
Go Live	15 days	03/01/2008 08:00	19/01/2008 17:00	23	
Post Go Live support	15 days	03/01/2008 08:00	19/01/2008 17:00		
Closure	1 day	21/01/2008 08:00	21/01/2008 17:00	25	

Note that certain tasks are dependent on previous tasks. If the previous task is delayed, the next dependant task will also get delayed. This will affect the project completion date. The Project Leader must take care of the bottlenecks and expedite the task to keep the project timeline as per the plan. For example, master data entry is a bottleneck. No further transaction data can be entered unless the masters are ready.

Sometimes people (resource) are constraints. Unexpectedly, someone maybe absent or busy with other work, or his or her computer maybe down; this can hamper the project deadline. A very systematic and professional approach will not only save time but also money.

The critical path is the series of tasks that dictates the project finish date. Tasks on the critical path are called critical tasks, and they cannot be delayed without affecting the project finish date.

MS Project (for that matter any good similar software) will give the Gantt chart automatically as shown as follows.

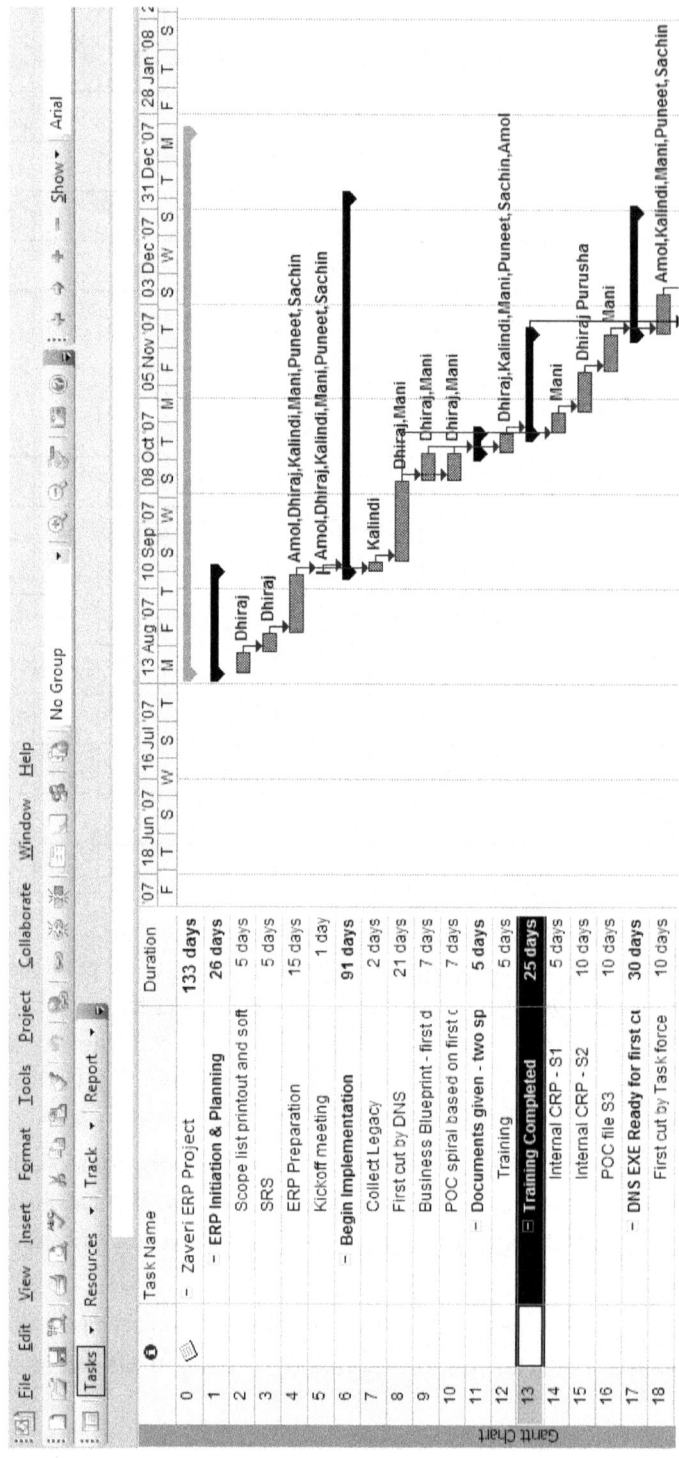

Fig. 4.5: ERP Gantt Chart

The previous figure shows an example of an ERP Project Gantt Chart.

Here is a review-meeting format

Purpose: Review ERP software implementation based on the following format. It can be used for internal review meetings.

Project goal of team: To implement ERP.

The team comprises of all stakeholders of the ERP project such as, the chief of ERP project or owner (project sponsor), ERP coordinator, users, ERP implementer team.

1. Name of the enterprise:			Xyz Manufacturing Ltd.	
2. Name of ERP sponsor (Owner)			Mr. ____	
3. Name of ERP coordinator:			Mr. ____	
4. Name of ERP implementer:			Mr. ____	
Date ERP project start:	DD MM YYYY		Planned Date ERP project 'go-live':	DD MM YYYY
5. Daily Back up on CD / DVD available: Yes / No taken by (name). Backup taken to different premises and kept in secured drawer.				
6. Letters to creditors (vendors) sent informing about ERP **(Y/N). Date?**			Y	
7. Letters to debtors (customers) sent informing about ERP **(Y/N). Date?**			Y	
8. Inventory Closing balance updated Y / N. As on date? Locations:				
9. Debtor (customer) Closing balance updated. Y / N. As on date?				
10. Creditor (Supplier) balance updated. Y / N. As on date?				
11. Invoice sent out to customer? Y / N. Dates?				
12. Purchase Order sent out to vendor? Y / N. Dates?				

13. Job Order sent out to Third Party? Y / N. Dates?	
14. Is Sales Order prepared when customer's purchase order is received? Is SO printed and signed by the marketing executive. Printout attached with the customer's PO copy. Y / N. Show the updated physical box file.	
15. Is GRN prepared when vendor's material is received? Is GRN printed and signed by the stores-in-charge? GRN printout attached with the vendor's bill copy. Y / N. Show the updated physical box file.	
16. Expense Voucher is prepared when service provider's bill is received. Is EV printed and signed by the accounts executive. EV printout attached with the bill? Y / N. Show the updated physical box file.	
17. Is GIN prepared when Third Party material is received? Is GIN printed and signed by the stores-in-charge? GIN printout attached with the TP bill copy. Y / N. Show the updated physical box file.	
18. Task Force members and module matrix as follows:	

It is necessary to review who (authorised user) is using ERP and whether sample printouts of the current 'avatar' of ERP is put in the POC (Proof of Concept) box file for review. The Proof of Concept file implies all users have received ERP training and understand how business processes are linked, how reports will look like after printing, and so on, because they have taken the hardcopy and put in the POC file. In other words, the POC file proves that users are now ready to go live. Even if the format needs change, it should be printed and kept in the POC file for review, duly endorsed. *Write NA if the module is not applicable or not part of the current scope.*

#	Module or Business Process	User 1	User 2	Training given (Y/N)	CRP checklist updated (Y/N)	POC file updated (Y/N)
1.	Accounts Module –					
2.	BOM – Bill of Materials Module					
3.	Costing Module					
4.	CRM Module / pre-sales module.					
5.	Excise Module					
6.	Export Sales					
7.	Import Purchase					
8.	Material Management (MM) Module					
9.	MRP - Material Requirement Planning Module for FG					
10.	Multi-location					
11.	Order Fulfilment – Sales					
12.	Payroll and HR					
13.	Production (Assembly / Process)					
14.	Purchase					
15.	Security Module					
16.	Sub-contractor OUT Module					
17.	VAT / Sales Tax Module					

Change Management or BPR

While implementing ERP it is necessary to change to adopt the best business practice. Please state what changes you have made (Business Process Reengineering or BPR) in the way you have been doing business management: You may use separate sheets to document the changes in legacy business processes. E.g. before ERP, material was received only on challan, now purchase bill is given by vendor with the material, and so on.

It is recommended to conduct the review meeting at least once in a month, or more frequently, documenting proceedings in the above format.

4.2.2 ERP Project Assurance Methodologies are based on the following best practices

1. At the leadership level, objective project assessments establish an executive dialog that allows business and organisational issues to be identified and analysed with clarity and without emotion. By continuing this dialog throughout the ERP system implementation process, the CEO will eventually remove organisational barriers both within the organisation and with the ERP software supplier, and align all the stakeholders with the common goal of ERP project success. This process will also help set realistic expectations upfront and keep expectations current in the mind of project team members.

2. Proactive monitoring of work-streams interdependencies.

Many organisations will set overly optimistic go-live dates in spite of the realities and limitations of the actual project. For example, the design phase extends ... but the time line does not. By monitoring project progress throughout the implementation, you can start discussions regarding key project dates early in the project's lifecycle to avoid downstream impacts.

This can be achieved by identifying, aligning and continuously monitoring work streams to ensure smooth progress throughout the organisation. Understanding the dependencies between work streams during project plan development can help ensure proper resource allocations and project time frames.

3. Looking beyond the project dashboard

Realistic monitoring and analysis of progress of the implementation can show that even though all project management indicators are green, warning signs indicate endangered components. If indicators are only addressing past phases, but not addressing readiness for upcoming project tasks and activities, they are definitely trailing indicators and not trustworthy predictions of the future.

To assist in the process, seek objective project assessments from someone outside the project team. This person can be either internal to the organisation or an independent expert. In either case, the assessments should be conducted by an executive project manager who has managed enough projects successfully to know how to recognize subtle indicators, intervene to accommodate the situation, and adjust expectations accordingly. These assessments will add value to the project implementation and protect against project failure by delivering the know-how and objective oversight through a different point of view.

4.2.3 Golden Guidelines for Good ERP Implementation

Majority of ERP implementations have not gone live, because of lack of budget planning, or proper estimate not done before starting the project.

Let us examine some root because that is usually overlooked by the industry, i.e. Inaccurate ERP implementation estimations. Some important guidelines follow for a successful ERP implementation.

Guideline # 1

Do the homework first to get the right type of information to compute the TCO (Total cost of ownership). Preparing an accurate estimate for a major customization or an ERP implementation can be a challenge for both an ERP Consultant and a new ERP Organisation. An ERP implementation budget is based upon your current understanding of the following areas:

1. **Scope**
   (a) ERP Project Goal should be discussed and written down, with a roadmap, what you expect from ERP and what is timeframe, how many people (man-hours) you can spare for ERP project.
   (b) Project Scope – Identify ERP Modules and Master, Transactions, and Reports for each module. ERP Vendor offering the ERP Module and – its Master, Transactions, and Reports for each module. Match both list and find gaps. If too many gaps then that ERP is not what you want.

2. **Assumptions**
   (a) IT Infrastructure.
   (b) Licensed Software such as Microsoft Operating System or the RDBMS.
   (c) Modification expected in the ERP software – Customization. Caution: This is a bottomless pit.
   (d) Existing data accuracy and completeness and its migration.

(e) Make a phase wise plan and time schedule.

(f) Change management training and its impact – BPR Exercise should be done seriously with help of a BPR Consultant (Business Process Reengineering).

3. **Identify Constraints**

   (a) **Government compliance**, Excise rules, Sales Tax and other Income tax rules must be understood and incorporated in the ERP business logic.

   (b) **Technical constraints** must be identified and resolved to the extent possible. For instance, Server computer or the Internet speed requirements.

   (c) **People Constraints:** The number of senior persons has to be identified and given in writing to confer high priority to the ERP project. Data entry operators must be identified, however if they are not available they may be hired temporarily.

   (d) **Time Constraints:** Time plan is important, when is the year-ending, when will you get year-end physical stock balance, closing balance as on the go live date is important. Debtor and Creditor closing balance, with bill wise outstanding bills information is required to go live. Depending upon how long the project will take and when the audited balance sheet will be available one can plan the cut-off date, which is time to *rollout* the ERP.

   (e) **Implementing Partner Company:** Usually SAP ERP Company gives the SAP software licences but implementation is carried out by its partner company, such as Infosys or Wipro, or Siemens. Identify a proper partner and budget. ERP user organisation has to pay the ERP vendor (e.g. SAP) and separately to the implementer partner company (e.g. Infosys). Estimate for this is necessary before embarking onto the ERP Journey. Remember, the ERP Journey is a one way street, once started you cannot go back or stop.

   (f) **Identify Risk:** Risk of losing on-going business for a few months because people are busy with the CRP run, risk of extra hours working and over-time money to be given during the parallel (CRP) run. ERP enforces harsh discipline, which senior managers may not appreciate and may leave, or may oppose because they are afraid of computers.

Let us focus on some specific areas that are generally ignored:

Region	Explanation
Senior managers Participation	Implementation partners are generally good about estimating their level of effort to support ERP implementations but would not estimate the effort for the customer. In ERP implementations, the customer must make available their best and senior managers for the implementation. The ERP estimate should include any need to temporarily substitute existing business managers.

Region	Explanation
ERP Project implementing activities	The implementation activities that need to be performed and who is responsible for performing the tasks. ERP user should not see this as an area to reduce implementation costs by taking on activities that they do not have the skills / resource availability to complete. Remember 'People make ERP successful and not Information Technology'. All ERP works fine on a demo machine.
Product Scope	Too often business processes and product scope is defined only at the product level. E.g., "we are implementing the ERP's Purchasing module. How can I tell what business activities and features are out of scope"? Developing focus is much harder to develop and maintain.
Implementation Partner Constraints	Every implementation partner has constraints! It is a just a reality that should be factored into any ERP estimate. For example, how much lead time should be given for an Implementation partner to replace their implementer?

Guideline #2

Understand the type of ERP Estimate you are calculating, there are three types of estimates for a project. These estimates are based upon your level of understanding for project scope, constraints, and assumptions.

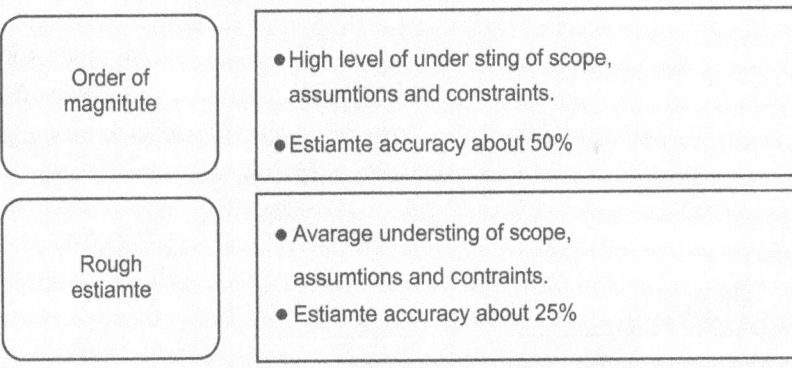

Fig. 4.6: ERP Budgeting

Guideline #3

Drive to validate and refine your ERP estimate. Estimates can and should change as you learn more about the ERP project. However, there is an expectation that these estimates should be defined once and they should be completely accurate. Once an ERP Implementation partner communicates an estimate too often the ERP user company will latch on to it and consider it as a *promise*. The key reason for this phenomenon has more to do with the Implementation partner setting the wrong expectation when an estimate is communicated.

Best Practices for obtaining ERP Estimates from your Implementation partner.

- **Fixed Price versus Time:** Have the Implementation partner provide a Time and Materials estimate for project planning, requirements gathering, and fit/gap. Once the Fit/Gap is performed, you should know exactly what you are up against and then ask for a competitive bid/fixed price estimate to complete the remaining work.
- **Complete Information:** Always as the Implementation partner to provide an estimate with the following information
- Product Scope
- Project Scope
- Assumptions
- Constraints
- Estimate accuracy – let ERP user company know up-front that the estimate will change

Finally, the CFO or the CEO (top management) from the ERP user organisation must also be realistic and understand that estimates created in the early stages of an ERP implementation may change and focus on making the right decisions for mutual success.

Level of effort estimations for ERP implementations are based upon the current understanding of the ERP implementation. Some ERP estimates are easier to calculate given a predefined implementation scope, however, there will always factors unique to a customer that must be explored, defined, and refined during key milestone implementation activities.

4.3 Team Training and Testing

It is of utmost importance to identify the team and provide them with proper training. About one hundred hours of class room training is recommended for each member of the task force. Some of the important points during the team training and testing phase of the ERP implementation to be considered and discussed are given below.

The pilot run or the test run is also called the parallel run because users are using both software parallel, (1) The legacy (Telly) software and (2) New ERP software. The pilot run (CRP run) is carried out in a special exclusive room called the CRP Room.

POC or Proof of Concept

POC is like a 'Delivery Challan' (delivery note) in ERP. ERP implementation tips during the CRP run.

- In small and medium size organisations, implementing ERP is very challenging for both implementers and the ERP coordinator.
- When a supplier delivers goods (say, a computer) the receiver will first check, and test this item. The receiver will check, e.g. if the item received is as per the specification (given in Purchase Order), and is working fine, etc. The supplier will then request the customer to sign a Delivery Challan. In the challan it is written that **"Received in good and working condition".** The supplier will now be in a position to raise the final bill since he has received the challan duly signed.
- How can one sign a Delivery Challan in ERP - **"Received in good and working condition"?** How does one certify that you have received the goods, in ERP?
- In ERP, we have a 'proof of concept' file or **POC**. The POC contains printouts of all the inputs and outputs of each module / procedure covered in the scope of ERP. Each page needs to be signed and certified by (i) an ERP coordinator and (ii) by the concerned user. The POC file is the delivery challan of ERP software.
- The ERP team will keep one such file with the ERP coordinator. Once the page is certified and signed, that means that procedure is now **"Received in good and working condition".**
- Now, suppose a customer changes his mind and asks for a different item (in the earlier example of PC, say he wants a different kind of monitor or simply wants to change the colour of the cabinet, etc.), the supplier may carry out the changes (replacement) to please the customer.
- However, in ERP such changes means additional customization, this will not only lead to additional time, but money as well in the ERP project. The user cannot simply change his mind after the **POC** is signed off.
- In the first place the user is not in a position to spell out clearly (in writing) what he wants, then once the POC is made, he is simply afraid of signing the POC because if he does so, it means he is now bound, which if a choice is given, he would not like to do so. Therefore, in other words the so called 'challan' remains unsigned. In fact, even after the user has received the required module he **will use it merrily** but will hesitate to sign the POC. That means the software company is left to his mercy for receipt of money.
- One cannot simply ignore the **POC** file. Some customers are mature enough to understand this and are ready to sign the POC (i.e. delivery challan), and pay the money to the software company, whereas others will simply *play ignorant* about the

importance of POC. Some ERP software companies are *charging 'per day'* basis towards the ERP resources that are being used at the ERP implementation site. This will automatically put brakes on the job and ensure that the ERP is taken up seriously. Otherwise, ERP implementers and developers are taken for granted.

- Some of the problems that the ERP implementation team faces are:

    (a) No clear logic sheet is given by the user in writing. Because the user himself doesn't know what he wants, how one can supply and satisfy him?

    (b) After carrying out the customization the user hesitates to test and sign. He would nicely say 'he is too busy'! Unless a person at the higher management (Director) level intervenes, this will go on. TATA Motors is a leading company manufacturing trucks and cars. They decided to implement ERP for efficient business management. During the ERP Project implementation Mr. Ratan Tata, the Chairman, himself was sparing his time to review the ERP project. His presence ensured presence of other senior managers during the reviews meetings

    (c) After the POC is signed off, new changes will have to make on a continuous basis in bits and pieces. The software engineer will now chop-and-change the program and the system thus will not stabilize.

- The purchase bill given by supplier and such documents need to be entered in the ERP Software. After the same is entered in the computer a rubber stamp is used and is signed by the user. The rubber stamp carries is a simple mark of 'DATA ENTERED'. Otherwise, it is difficult to find which document was entered, and which was not. Not even one document should remain without data entry. When the ERP implementer asks user to sign, they are unnecessarily reluctant, so he or she is asked to just write their name in uppercase, instead of signing. This is because, it is difficult to identify the name of the user from the graphic signature, or just initials.

Frequently Asked Questions – (FAQ)

1. Q. What if I have signed the **POC** hardcopy, of say PO, and later after two months I realise that some change is necessary?

    A. Please write down the change and email or write on the printout and put your name and date, give to our DNS team. Rest-assured, we will do any essential customization.

2. Q. I cannot give any specification in writing because there is no such procedure in legacy (business process is new). We will verbally explain.

    A. You will have to take time out and prepare an example (may be in Excel) and explain in writing, based on which we will to changes in DNS Exe. Verbal communication should be avoided.

3. Q. Are POC and CRP related?
   A. Yes. CRP is Conference Room Pilot. **CRP run** is simulation of all kinds of scenarios. Before going live, it is necessary to enter at least one-month data including all kinds of transactions and take printouts. Signing of this printout will ensure that there are no surprises when the system goes live. Therefore, it is necessary to make POC file during the CRP run. See separate not on CRP run given in the DNS Reference Manual.
4. Q. What if the ERP coordinator does not find time to carry out CRP run (e.g. he is busy with ISO project also) and users are not cooperating? What if, users are already overloaded and do not wish to enter data twice.
   A. ERP project will not be a smooth experience. The owner (Director level person) will have to intervene and direct all concerned to find time (give highest priority). Otherwise, the ERP project is likely to be delayed and that means cost of implementation also will be high.

4.4 End User Training and Going Live

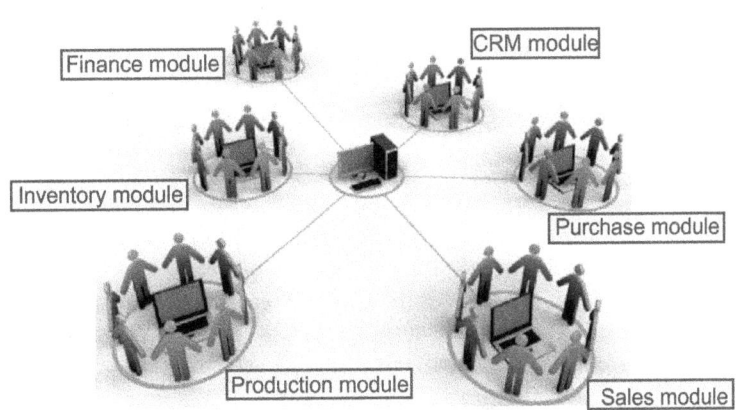

Fig. 4.7: ERP Modules

ERP end user is the one who is actually going to create the master data, enter transaction data, access reports for making decisions. These users must know how ERP will work and benefit the organisation. They have to be given sufficient training to get required confidence in the ERP Software System.

The training to the end user will also eliminate the fear of losing his job. This is very important because when any automation is carried out the first doubt that comes in the mind of the user is related with the security of his or her job. Top management must ensure all end users are trained in their respective module for about 100 Hours.

Successful implementation of any ERP requires change in attitudes and old habits of end users. As it builds a good foundation for information flow in the ERP user organisation, the importance of linking all the business processes has to be understood at all levels. Conference Room Pilot run is the key to success. At end of the CRP run a POC file is prepared. Proper CRP will also ensure that the cost and time will be minimal for all concerned. The ERP coordinator's role is crucial in organising and imparting training to the end user. He is also responsible for keeping a log to record the training imparted, for how many hours and so on.

The ERP vendor will impart the necessary training to the 'coordinator' on the various aspects of ERP, especially on the MIS and data structures. This is to reduce dependability on the vendor and gain confidence in the ERP system even after implementation is over. In turn the coordinator will train other end users. This will ensure a smooth handover of programs from the vendor team to the user organisation.

4.4.1 During ERP Implementation the End User should follow this Important Checklist

1. Increase budget if you have enlarged the scope. Usually ERP users do not know what the new system is, therefore during implementation new requirements surface, which had not been spelled out earlier.
2. The ERP vendor team must explain various modules so that users will understand the new way of working. It is necessary to attend these training sessions without exception.

(i) Security Module

Next the login Id and secret passwords are given. Importance of a unique password must be explained to the end user so that each user will keep it secret and not share it with anyone. User access rights are decided. Who is authorised to create the Master database, who will access what all reports and so on is discussed and decided by the chief of the ERP project. Master data deleting or modifying rights are given to a couple of senior responsible users only. Security levels are explained so that end users will understand their role and responsibility.

Here is a checklist that is based on years of experience for the Enterprise Resource Planning software implementation:

(ii) Education and Training

1. Educate all users to understand what is going to be achieved with the new system. Additional education should include:
   - Total Quality Management
   - Change Management Strategies.
   - Government compliance, such as Excise, Sales Tax, etc.

2. Train process owners (department managers) in how to use the system, in turn have them train respective users from his or her department. It is necessary that end users take time out from the routine and actually do hands-on training.
3. Perform Business Analysis to streamline the current processes. For instance, in an organisation a user was maintaining a register without really knowing the purpose. It is not necessary to incorporate obsolete procedures in the new system.
4. Planning, training and education for the IT Support staff to understand the new hardware, software, and network imperatives.
5. BPR or Business Process Reengineering. (Match business processes with the new software). Once the ERP is in place, it is not necessary to do things as you were doing them for the last several years.
6. Software modifications are done only when Business Processes that do not differentiate you in the marketplace are not supported by the software. Do only *essential* customization. Do not ask for changes or modifications in the program at every level. Change and adapt new procedures.
7. Business Simulation, on a department level and at the enterprise level is done to learn the new system. Prepare a 'Proof of Concept' file. Certify the printouts, during the CRP run. A phased approach may be indicated based on the quantum of change dictated by the new system.
8. Implementation Review meeting is recommended to fine-tune the CRP run. Ask the software vendor to suggest better ways to use the system. Have patience. If you have asked for unlimited customization then it will take unlimited time. Give sufficient time to the ERP vendor to change the programs to make last minute changes.

4.5 Post Evaluation and Maintenance

'Go Live'

Go Live or Rollout means are used when the entire organisation starts using the new ERP system. This means, users stop using the legacy system and all start using the new software. Care should be taken that once the ERP goes live, no one should fall back and use the old software.

After ERP is implemented successfully, it is necessary to carry out an evaluation of the new system. A meeting of all the task-force members meeting is called and everyone notes and evaluates what was expected and what is achieved. They must jot down the benefits of the new system. During the meeting, some gaps also may be observed. After due diligence, the maintenance phase of the system begins.

There are two areas of the maintenance phase of ERP system, (1) Master data maintenance and (2) Software settings. After going live, the user may realise that the master data was incomplete or inaccurate. However, this point should not arise if proper checking is done during the implementing phase. Some new ideas or reports may also crop up.

4.6 Role of Organisation Management and ERP Vendor

The top management and the ERP vendor play a very central role before, during, and even after the ERP is implemented. It is rightly said that prevention is better than cure.

Evidence suggests that majority of ERP software projects are delayed or doomed by cost overturns. Even when ERP projects are completed on time and within budget, users often complain that the software they have paid for does not meet their expectations in terms of quality, or features or both. In other words, a great deal of software that is developed never gains user acceptance. No respectable field of engineering has comparable failure. That would be a catastrophe, and construction and automobile engineers would not make a living!

- **Wish list is a big problem:** Why does the distinguished software industry have such an awful track record? A big part of the answer is 'scope definition', a phenomenon that causes users to be highly inconsistent and unpredictable, about what they wish their software to do. Experienced software engineers often say that users are notorious for their inability to articulate their expectations from the software. As a result, it is alarmingly common for the development (construction) of software applications to begin with insufficient requirements and ambiguous specifications. Most top management believes that they can ask for everything especially because they are paying so much money. There is thus a big wish list. Unfortunately, the vendor (salesperson) also commonly agrees to provide everything, to obtain the order and the advance money.

- Organisation management take up the ERP project as a 'by-the-way' project, whereas in the true sense it should be the only priority during the implementation phase. In one company, the ERP coordinator was asked (by the Executive Director himself), to go to another city, to get the some odd job done, leaving ERP implementation half way. In other words, top management must give the highest priority to ERP and not ask users to be involved in other tasks while ERP is being implemented. It can wait; because once the momentum is lost, the ERP project is delayed.

> Because software is intangible (impossible to see and touch) while it is under development (unlike other forms of construction such as bridges and cars), it is normal for needs to keep evolving as the software gets built. With every round of change and clarification, the scope of the project changes (as earlier assumptions are negated and new ones introduced). In addition, timelines are pushed out to accommodate new expectations. This is analogous to building a house for which the architectural design keeps shifting with the changing priorities of the owners. Human experience suggests that moving-targets do not lend themselves to happy outcomes. In addition, it is true with the timelines and budgets of numerous ERP projects.

- **What top management and ERP vendor should do:** Untreatable as it may seem on the surface, *scope changes* is an eminently treatable problem. For example, world-class ERP organisations now employ the *use case* (case study) method to manage user requirements. Instead of asking users what features they want in their software, the user case method guides them to describe their current and future processes and behaviours in terms of *stories* and scripts (much like playwrights write plays) that are stuffed with actors, actions, and entity. It turns out that humans are fundamentally better at narration than specification, and the requirements that originate from this method are decidedly more robust.
- Further, the software implementation and development process has itself become less linear and more cyclical. Recently, it has been observed that the large ERP projects are broken down into a series of short projects that last for 30-60 days each. Sometimes, module wise implementation helps building up confidence.
- Only a small set of requirements are addressed in each sub-project, and no changes in scope are permitted while the same is in progress. Finally, users themselves play an active role in software evolution. As each iterative cycle draws to a close, representative users (or focus groups) interact with the 'live' (albeit partially complete) system, and provide critical feedback. The feedback is analyzed, course corrections are done, and any major scope changes can now be managed in a controlled fashion.
- Even with advanced techniques and best practices at our disposal, scope changes can at best be contained, not eliminated. In fact, scope changes also called *scope creep* is as natural to software engineering as bad weather is to sailors. It is a professional hazard that professionals in the field must learn how to manage. There are professional 'case tools' available such as IBM Rational Rose to simulate systems and prepare documentation, which is used by ERP vendors. Software engineers can develop early warning systems that will allow them to predict well in advance how serious the downstream effects of unmanaged scope creep can be. An innovative measure that is gaining popularity is the requirements clarity indicator, a metric that allows a panel of ERP software experts to review a set of project requirements early in the lifecycle and determine how well the stakeholders even understand what they want from their stability indicator. Low scores on requirements clarity or requirement stability ought to be sufficient to assume that a project is headed for serious trouble.
- **ERP Demo CD is not a good idea:** Many ERP vendors give a demo program to sell their ERP. Therefore, the customers may play with it at their leisure. An ERP package is an advanced and complicated system; it is not like Microsoft Office, or an iPhone. You cannot simply turn it on and expect it to run without training. The deployment of an ERP

software system can involve considerable business process analysis, employee training, and new work procedures. Just looking at the PowerPoint presentation or a glossy looking demo management cannot help apprehend the depth of ERP.

Here are some points organisations ought to note to prevent ERP delays or ERP failure.

1. **Lack of top management commitment:** Director or CEO says: "I am busy with export orders, let ERP be handled by some junior manager".
2. **Unrealistic expectations:** "Give me this, give me that, and if possible give me the moon also"!
3. **Poor requirements definition:** Managers do not know what they want or rather what ERP can give them. Mr. Ford had once said "if I ask users what they want, they will say we want a better horse". So Henry Ford did not ask them at all, and went ahead to make his car, which eventually replaced horse driven carriages.
4. **Improper package selection** is a big issue because the owner usually asks for a discount and although the vendor will oblige he will cut corners. Since it is an intangible product, it is difficult to identify if everything is not as it should be. To avoid such a situation it is better to pay an experienced ERP consultant for the selection of the ERP software package.
5. **Gaps between software and business requirements** are another reason for ERP failures or ERP underutilization.
6. **Inadequate resources** are provided, for example, proper IT infrastructure is not installed. Senior people are not part of the ERP task force. Remember it is compulsory to provide the best people, sufficient time and money for the success of any ERP project.
7. **Underestimating time and cost** is very common. Users commonly are under the misapprehension that ERP can be installed overnight like other software packages.
8. **Poor project management and lack of professional planning** causes ERP failures.
9. **Underestimating impact of change by top management** is a problem that has nothing to do with Information Technology per se. Impact of change is related to human behaviour. It is matter of cultural change rather than technological change.
10. **Lack of training and education** is the most common dilemma since these are not given enough importance. Most people think training is just a waste of time and there are better things to do than sit in the classroom.
11. **Poor communication or incomplete communication** is the biggest problem, again related to human nature, which causes delays and ERP failures.

In conclusion, scope change and not knowing ERP, remains a major threat to the success of every ERP software project. However, its impact can be minimised by leveraging best practices, and avoid the pitfalls cited above. Good software engineering is all about understanding what users need, and *not getting distracted by what they demand*. It is also about managing scope creep intelligently. Using cases, iterative brainstorming meetings, task group feedback, as well as indicators that measure requirements clarity and stability are some points that will ensure success of an ERP project before, during and after implementation.

Practice Questions

1. Give steps for project planning and implementation.
2. What is the importance of training ERP users?
3. What is 'Going Live'?
4. What is the role of top management while implementing ERP Software?

Activity

1. Interview two Chief Information Officers (CIO) or similar persons who is heading the IT department of a large corporate and find out how details of their ERP software, how many users, what all ERP Modules they are using, and so on.
2. Additional online study material:
    (a) Study Video Lectures http://www.youtube.com/dnserp
    (b) Subscribe to get automatic updates about ERP.

***

Chapter 5...

ERP CASE STUDIES

5.1 Post Implementation Review of ERP Packages
5.2 Case Studies in Manufacturing, Services and Other Organisations
5.3 Customisation of ERP for Different Types of Industries
• Practice Questions
• Activity

Learning Objectives
After going through this unit, you will be able to:
• Discuss how ERP can be used to integrated various functions of an organisation.
• Discuss post implementation review of ERP system of well established companies.
• Discuss different issues addressed by the ERP system.
• Explain customisation of ERP for industries.

Introduction: To understand ERP better, in this chapter, we will take a closer look at some of the real companies that have deployed ERP Software system. First we will take a look at post implementation review of ERP packages of some well established companies. Thereafter, some case studies of Manufacturing, Services and Other organisations will be discussed. In the end the need to customise ERP for different types of Industries will be brought out.

5.1 Post Implementation Review of ERP Packages

Here you will find large as well as small and medium size enterprises facing issues and challenges before ERP is used and how the same is resolved by using ERP. Let us now take a look at the status of some ERP packages post their implementation. These would be seen as case studies.

5.1.1 SAP ERP in Coca Cola

(i) Introduction

With such a large scale of operations, it is evident that Coca-Cola has the need for Information Technology enabled business management solutions that go far beyond individual finance processes. It requires an integrated business management system to handle the different aspects of their worldwide corporation. Coca-Cola started off using the legacy system like many other old companies. Soon, they realised that to sustain their ever growing business, they would have to find a more integrated system to manage their global processes.

Coca Cola falls under consumer products – beverages industry. Their main products and services are non-alcoholic beverage production, sales, and distribution. Coca Cola here being considered as a case study has a revenue of € 6.8 billion and has 42,505 Employees. The reader will find additional information on their Web site: www.coca-colahellenic.com

Today, Coca-Cola is the most recognised brand in the world. Three things helped bring Coca-Cola to world-wide popularity:
1. Unique taste.
2. Uniform quality.
3. Universal accessibility.

(ii) About the Company
- With operations in 28 countries, Coca-Cola Hellenic of Maroussi, Greece, serves a population of approximately 560 million people. Its product portfolio consists of 613 different beverages, of which 485 are noncarbonated drinks.
- In 2010 the company employed 42,505 people and sold over 2 billion unit cases, generating net sales revenue of nearly €6.8 billion.

Let us have a closer look at Coca-Cola Hellenic Bottling, Maroussi, Greece.

To facilitate global expansion of the company, Coca-Cola decided to incorporate SAP ERP Strategic Enterprise Management (SEM ERP) and implemented mySAP financials into their business in order to handle the financial processes of the corporation.

SEM ERP created a single environment to make financial data accessible to management across the globe. MySAP financials are tightly integrated with other SAP systems. SEM provides Business Planning Simulation for finances, Data Warehousing for information collection and data analysis, and can also generate financial reports and monthly sales forecasts. MySAP financials has allowed Coca-Cola to consolidate business and planning, and the data warehousing insures that all financial records can be kept without taking up valuable space on company hard drives.

This project is fully implemented in the company's headquarters, and every field location is equipped with intranet capabilities so that information can be given to and looked up from the centralised website. Data is organised so that intercompany transactions are eliminated and other adjustments can be made so that the information can then be consolidated to draft financial reports.

This system is especially helpful at the end of the month when Coca-Cola is able to consolidate information needed for monthly reports promptly. All of this data provides baseline information so that Coke can track the financial health and growth of the company. In addition to mySAP financials, Coca-Cola uses mySAP BI as a common repository for every location worldwide.

(iii) Challenges and Opportunities

The major challenges and consequently opportunities that were faced by Coca Cola in its global expansion endeavour are listed below. Successfully addressing these would result in better integration of all its business processes which would result in effective centralised control over such a vast corporation.

1. Develop end-to-end process support.
2. Expand capabilities to cover new business requirements.
3. Provide a single solution for all countries and markets.

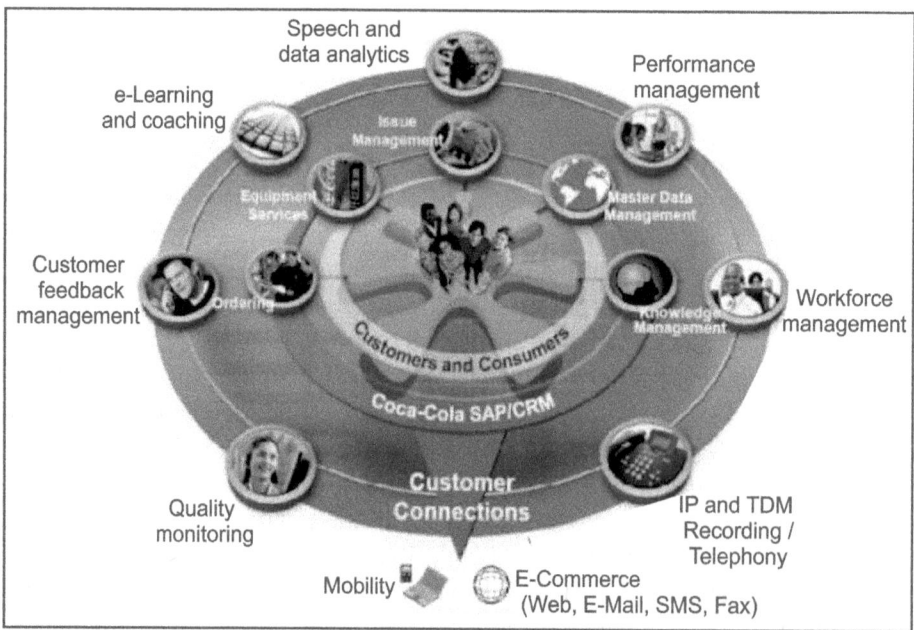

Fig. 5.1: A part of the SAP CRM System that Handles the Contact Centres Around the World

The Customer Relationship Management (CRM) system also handles and integrates customer service. This includes reaching out to representatives in the company for any issues relating to the products. The diagram above shows part of the SAP CRM system that handles the contact centres around the world. Here, not only is service provided to the customers through feedback, email, and telephone services but also through quality monitoring and different types of analyses to ensure the best service practices. Therefore, the CRM system ensures efficiency in all aspects of customer service.

(iv) ERP System Objectives

The ERP system objectives that were laid out were as follows:
1. Build an end-to-end solution.
2. Deliver, to the extent possible, a single solution.
3. Define and formalise best practices in a template and then roll it out in a pilot implementation (CRP Run).
4. Build new capabilities to support retail customers.
5. SAP Solutions and Services.
6. SAP NetWeaver technology platform.
7. SAP NetWeaver Mobile component.
8. SAP Customer Relationship Management application.
9. SAP ERP application - SAP Mobile Direct Store Delivery application.
10. SAP Mobile Asset Management application.
11. SAP Safeguarding services, delivered by the SAP Active Global Support organisation.

(v) Implementation Highlights

1. Business-driven project, starting with an end-to-end process approach to the technical details.
2. SAP consulting services for business process design and solution implementation.
3. Benefits:
   (i) Efficiency improvements in several business processes.
   (ii) Implementation of the latest SAP technology.
   (iii) Support for organisational and process change.

Through the implementation of a technology initiative called "Wave 1," Coca-Cola Hellenic moved from a decentralised IT system to a centralised system. It introduced the SAP Advanced Planning and Optimisation module to assist management with all aspects of business planning. The SAP NetWeaver Business Warehouse module was also added at that time.

Coca-Cola Hellenic is first and foremost a sales company. The company needed to address issues involving promotional activities. There were also business-strategic direction in customer services and growth in the complexity of the product portfolio – in fact, there was a whole range of strategic imperatives that touched the commercial processes, and most of these could benefit from software integration across the group.

The sum of those considerations led to **a complete transformation of the information systems**, processes, and people at Coca-Cola Hellenic.

If you want end-to-end processes, you need integration rather than individual best-of-breed applications. Integration also has implications for flexibility – that is, your ability to change your process and to add new capabilities.

> Kiril Topalov, SAP programme director at Coca-Cola Hellenic says: "In the end, Coca-Cola Hellenic reviewed and revised some 341 processes, 151 of them commercial. We're really talking about massive organisational and process change here. Accordingly, we are paying special attention to change management. If somebody places an order, immediately there's an availability-to-promise check using the whole warehouse management functionality."

(vi) ERP benefits as seen by Coca Cola

Many benefits are already beginning to appear. Coca-Cola Hellenic expects to achieve improvements in the following areas:

1. Advance account management.
2. Customer asset management.
3. Trade promotion management.
4. Distribution and order management.
5. Overall field sales management.

Coca-Cola Hellenic estimates that the second phase called 'Wave 2' implementation will roll out to the last of the 28 countries it serves in 2013. "At the moment, we are running deployments in four countries, two of them the biggest in our group," says Topalov. "Wave 2 represents a major transformation in the Coke environment.

This is the first end-to-end SAP software implementation in the Coca-Cola bottling system. As such, it provides a sustainable platform for future growth and enhancements. SAP technology is moving us into a totally new, integrated environment. From there, from a pure IT perspective, we expect significant efficiency improvements. And on the business side, it provides a foundation for future enhancements and future expansion.

(vii) Business Management Solution

The Coca Cola team decided it was time to derive more performance from the business-critical SAP applications, while driving down hardware and software costs. Instead of upgrading Oracle, the team decided to introduce IBM DB2. As part of the SAP upgrade project, Coca Cola SAP R/3 system would require a conversion to Unicode.

SAP R/3 denotes a version of SAP ERP software. The SAP R/3 System has three-tier client/server architecture. All data is stored in a database, and the data is processed in the application layer on the application servers. The SAP GUI (Graphics user interface) frontend, presentation layer, is the interface to the user. All three layers are connected to each other with networks.

Combining the database migration with the SAP Unicode conversion saved time and money. Initial results show that DB2 delivers a reduction in storage needs of approximately 40 per cent. The duration of manufacturing runs was reduced by more than 65 per cent. The migration was completed under budget and ahead of schedule. The company has reduced licensing and maintenance costs by avoiding the purchase of additional Oracle licenses, and predicts savings in the next five years of about US$750,000.

(viii) Architectural Overview – Migration Project at COCA COLA

For the migration, COCA COLA used four logical partitions (LPARs) on an IBM Power Systems server (model p5-560). Three LPARs were used to handle database export processes from the source system, and one LPAR was running the target system for the import processes.

The export partitions consisted of a Central Instance / Database partition, which had 16 CPUs of 1.5GHz and 64GB of memory, and two other partitions that had four CPUs of 1.5GHz and 12GB of memory each.

The import partition had 16 CPUs of 1.5GHz and 64GB of memory.

(ix) Direct Store Delivery, Full-Service Vending and Equipment Service

Coca-Cola's needs continue to change with their growing demands. And with every change, Coca-Cola has the customer at the core of the decision. They will focus on how to best satisfy the needs of their customers in all available markets. New technology for their SCM, ERP, and CRM systems will be vital to maintain their position at the top of the beverage market. So, the company decided to install DSD or the direct store delivery system.

Direct Store Delivery (DSD), full-service vending and equipment services are key components of bottlers' business operations and profit centres. With tight integration between bottlers' back-end IT systems and mobile devices, field sales representatives, delivery drivers and equipment service staff can quickly and more effectively respond to a comprehensive range of customer requests. Specifically, DSD from SAP helps companies improve logistical performance and efficiency and better monitor, analyse and integrate data in near real-time from sales to settlement. By eliminating unnecessary paperwork, ensuring proper cash settlement and minimising wasted cargo space, DSD improves delivery productivity and reduces costs.

With DSD, companies also can identify and profitably acquire and manage new customers and market opportunities. The initiative with Coca-Cola Enterprises will result in enhanced capabilities to manage price lists and promotions in a mass customer environment. Further, merchandising and customer prospecting capabilities will be addressed with new, improved handheld application support.

Coca-Cola is sure to run into new problems as they fight to maintain their position at the top, but as former CEO E. Neville Isdell said in 2005, "As we have always done in the past, I know that this industry will rise to the occasion."

Fig. 5.2: Coca Cola Plant

5.1.2 Bajaj Electricals, India

Fig. 5.3: Bajaj Electricals Lamps

Bajaj Electricals, a known name in consumer electronics for almost 65 years in India, was confined to legacy systems for most of their business processes. This was causing hindrance to core business operations, as growth was fast but the legacy systems weren't able to support it. At places, these systems were more than 12 years old and it was becoming costly and difficult to maintain them. Even the supporting technology platforms had become outdated. Hence it was decided by the management to initiate a project that will focus towards improving business processes with IT systems. They decided to implement ERP, SCM, CRM & BI applications together with complete integration taking a big-bang approach.

The Oracle Business suite of applications was selected for implementation, and the project was named 'Project SMILE.' This is an acronym for the objectives to be achieved:

- S – Simplify the business processes
- M – Migration to newer technologies
- I – Innovative and Integrated Business applications
- L – Create learning orientation across the organisation
- E – To make entire organisation Effective and Efficient

Before implementation of this project, inefficient processes resulted in revenue loss as there were no forecasting or planning tools available. In addition, legacy systems were not built to support current business processes. These challenges were overcome by implementation of the following products: Oracle E-business Applications (ERP), Oracle

Siebel CRM Applications, Oracle Demantra Demand Management Tool for demand forecasting, and on top of these applications, business intelligence solutions like Oracle Daily Business Intelligence and Oracle Business Intelligence Enterprise Edition for Sales Analytics, Dashboards & Reporting (OBI) were also implemented.

> Mr. Siddhartha Kanodia, Executive VP & Head Corporate Service said "ERP Project SMILE was not just a plain vanilla ERP implementation. Besides financials, it involved implementing and planning of CRM tools such as Demantra, Advanced Supply Chain Planning and Siebel CRM. This called for a huge change initiative and I am proud to say that the entire operations team at Bajaj Electricals embraced the changed processes and leveraged the planning tools extremely well. The support from the IT team also was more than commensurate to make this a possibility".

Post deployment

After the ERP roll out, the company has been able to get the investment payback achieved within the first year, and just from the savings coming out from one module called Siebel Dynamic Pricing Module. The company can now make right items available at the right time with Advanced Supply Chain Planning solution, which has reduced the overall inventory in the pipeline and also improved the company's ability to service customer orders. The overall inventory losses have been brought down by 2 per cent due to this.

5.2 Case Studies in Manufacturing, Services and Other Organisations

In this section we will take some case studies where ERP is deployed in manufacturing and service sector and other organisations. To deploy ERP in a manufacturing organisation is very challenging and takes longer time. This is because in the shop-floor, the existing processes are not defined, and usually it is left to the department manager's experience. ERP streamlines all the activities and links them like a chain. The following examples will help you understand some of the issues, challenges and benefits of ERP.

Fig. 5.4: Finished Goods: Electronic Counters

5.2.1 ERP Case studies for Manufacturing Organisations

In this section some case studies for manufacturing organisations will be discussed. These examples would highlight the typical requirements from an ERP that would be best suited to a manufacturing organisation.

(i) ERP Case Study of Electronic Manufacturing Company Control Instruments

This Electronic manufacturing company is one of the leading manufacturers and exporters of world-class electronic instruments and electromechanical instruments in Pune. The brand is well known in India as well as in the global market because of its superior quality, technical superiority, precision electronic instruments, precision electromechanical instruments, performance, and durability.

They manufacture a variety of Electronic Instruments and Electromechanical Instruments that include Electronic Sensors, Indicators and Electromechanical Controllers for sensing Position, Oscillation, Rotational Speed, Linear speed, Displacement, Direction, Level, Weight, Humidity, Temperature, Pressure and Vibration. They also offer complete turnkey automation solutions. They design, install and commission complex data acquisition and control and automation package specially designed for their clients.

The company has gained expertise in electronic instruments manufacturing, electromechanical instruments, Instrumentation, Electronic Drives, SCADA, EMS, PLC based and software based automation projects. They work for automation of forging, automobile, cement, Power Generation, Chemical and Steel Industry.

Necessary manufacturing, testing facilities, and quality control procedures are developed in-house. They undertake turnkey projects in process automation and instrumentation. About 3000 high quality products are offered to customers from the steel industry, cement industry, automotive, etc.

ERP user feedback: Director of this electronic manufacturing company shares his experience; he says after ERP implementation, "I can go home at six o'clock. My sales department can answer customer calls more confidently and reply within sixty seconds."

Issues and Challenges: Prior to implementation of ERP in this Company, issues and challenges of inefficiency existed the following areas:

- Users working hard - late hours
- Smoother and faster process flow
- Efficient distribution of information
- Decentralisation of task and decision
- Increased transparency and better control
- Protection/ Security of data
- Wastage, scrap, rejection
- Integration of all departments

- Cost control
- Productivity through elimination of duplication
- Inventory of raw materials
- Delivery performance
- Customer satisfaction

The Company manufactured many sophisticated items. One such item is shown below to provide an idea of the final product of the Company:

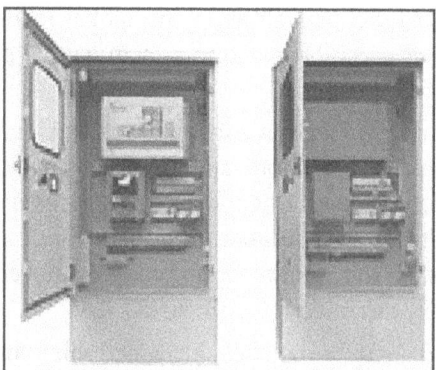

Fig. 5.5: Finished Product: Electrical Panels

Product: Electrical Panels as shown in the figure above, Variable Frequency Drives and panels, Logic and Automation Panels.

Key Benefits: Through the implementation of ERP, the following key benefits were accrued:

- The customer master captures information such as 'which sales engineer will coordinate with which customer. When ERP was not installed, who was responsible for tacking the technical queries arising from the customer and others was not known. By storing the name of the sales engineer along with the customer name in ERP, it is now possible to pin-point the accountable and responsible employee for each customer.

- The work order (job card) link with material issue from stores and the production ensures high level of material management. This is a great benefit because the stores cannot issue wrong material to the production department. Work order will clearly give quantity of all child items required to produce a father item. For example, for producing one switch, the assembler requires four nuts and four bolts. Now let us say the work order is for five switches, because material issue is linked to work order, the stores keeper will issue twenty bolts and twenty nuts only and no more and no less. This will ensure high level of inventory management and accuracy.

- Top management involvement and necessary ERP training made the project a success. ERP modules are deployed in various functions such as Marketing, Production, R & D and Finance. Without top executives' involvement, especially in a small and medium organisation, ERP fails. Here in this company because top management was involved, ERP could be deployed and went live in six months period.

(ii) ERP in 'Process instruments' Manufacturing Industry

ERP Case Study: This case study refers to a company specialising in manufacturing electromagnetic flow meters and orifice based flow metering systems. Its product comprises process instruments an example of which is shown below:

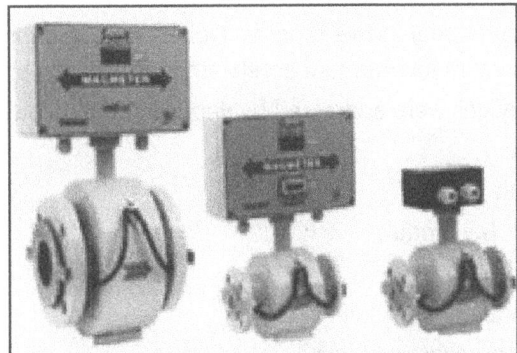

Fig. 5.6: Product for Process Flow Measurement and Control

Background

This an ISO 9001:2000 company situated in the MIDC area in India. Its customer base is industrial sectors like Steel, Aluminium, ETP's, STP's, Sugar and Distilleries, Chemical / Pharmaceutical, Petrochemical / Fertilisers.

ERP that is deployed is a scalable and fully secured IT solution for managing manufacturing business.

Issues and Challenges: The issues and challenges faced by this company are enumerated below:

- Continued brisk business growth and slowdown, was placing immense strain on existing business systems at this medium size factory. Committed to the JIT (Just-in-time) delivery model – made to order – it was necessary to improve efficiency in the legacy system. ERP offered a cost effective software to meet the challenges.
- Middle level managers and other users tended to postpone the work or bypass the system. This was resulting in delays and intangible losses.

- Customer satisfaction was always an issue that needed to be addressed carefully. Customer's purchase orders and the sales invoice needed to be linked to avoid miscommunication between sales and production and shipping.
- Management needed latest and accurate information to sell and service customers.
- Users spent large amount of time in manual transactions to gather and update information due to islands of information.

Salient Points and Issues addressed by the ERP
- The company has now deployed ERP software for business management.
- Tightly integrated business processes enforce discipline and bring accountability in key departments like purchase, stores, production, and sales.
- Real-time and secured system empowers management with status reports to take timely decisions.
- ERP became operational in five months. Quick and proven implementation method and top management involvement accelerated installations of all modules.

The issues and challenges were addressed by deploying the following ERP modules:
1. Security module
2. Accounts module –
   (a) VAT / Sales Tax module
   (b) Excise module
3. Inventory Management module
4. Purchase & Pre-purchase module
5. Payroll system
6. BOM – Bill of Materials module
7. Production module
8. Sales accounting module
9. Cost sheet / estimation
10. Subcontractor OUT. Outsourcing.
11. Pre-sales and sales module

A significant milestone for this company was its capability of maintaining competitive advantage in today's time by using cutting-edge business management solutions. Key benefits that the company accrued through introduction of ERP are as follows:
- Robust MIS (Management Information System).
- Availability of real-time data helps in strategic and tactical decision making.
- Integration of financial and business operations resulted in improving efficiency.
- Greater control of Production, Inventory, and Sales Processes.
- Better visibility and transparency.
- Business agility helps the enterprise to compete with other large corporates and win over prestigious contracts.

(iii) ERP Case Study: Mother's Recipe makes Pickle and Spices a Processed Food Industry

Fig. 5.7: Finished Goods: Mango Pickle

Mother's Recipe used ERP called ERP SYSTEM, designed and developed by the author of this book, Mr. Zaveri.

Background

Mother's Recipe makes pickles, Masala, and Papad, for the Indian market as well as export. Their strong business acumen added to their overall growth enabling them to expand their range of offerings that included a wide variety of Indian mango pickle, mixed vegetable pickle, ginger pickles, spices and Papad.

At Mother's Recipe, Supply chain management of the following items for making pickle was carried out using the ERP software.

- Pickle Items – 17 varieties of pickles
- Mango Pieces
- Sesame Oil
- Red chilli powder
- Mixed Spices
- Acetic Acid
- Mustard
- Asafoetida

- Amla, Lime
- Garlic, Ginger
- Jaggery
- Papad

Issues and Challenges

The Issues and Challenges faced by this company were:
1. Perishable food items with an expiry date. This is the biggest issue that ERP should address in the case of such an industry because shelf time to store food item is limited.
2. Smoother and faster process flow.
3. Efficient distribution of information.
4. Decentralisation of task and decision.
5. Increased transparency and better control.
6. Protection/ Security of data.
7. Wastage, scrap, rejection.
8. Lack of quality awareness.
9. Cost control.
10. Productivity through elimination of duplication.
11. Inventory of raw materials, packing material, fruit and vegetables.
12. Delivery performance.
13. Sales and distribution through branches.

How ERP Can Address These Issues
- Protect the business information such as secret recipes of pickle, etc.
- Improve team performance through enhanced collaboration.
- **Multi-location:** Information Technology, such as two Servers were installed, one at the head office and another at the factory about 50 km apart.

ERP Modules that were deployed are as follows:
1. Security module.
2. Accounts module – General Ledger Accounts.
3. VAT / Sales Tax module.
4. Multi-location: Send and receive data on net.
5. Inventory Management module.
6. Purchase and Pre-purchase module.
7. MRP - Material Requirement Planning module / Supply Chain Management (SCM).
8. ISO 9000 – Quality check module.
9. BOM – Bill of Materials module.
10. Production module (Assembly Production and Process Production) CRM module (Customer relationship management) and pre-sales module.
11. Automatic email alerts module.

12. Payroll and HR module.
13. Cost sheet module – preparing estimate.
14. Order Fulfilment module – Sales Accounting - (Shipping).
15. Sub-contractor OUT module to manage outsourcing.

Key Benefits: Implementation of ERP resulted in the following benefits:

- Created a positive environment to inspire individuals/teams towards increased productivity for greater results. Individuals and teams were energetic with an impressive work ethic and were at ease in high stress, fast-paced situations with multiple responsibilities.
- Customer's order is linked with the Indent and Sales invoice. Chances of mistakes / miscommunication are reduced with this kind of tight integration. The work order (job card) link with material issue from stores ensures high level of material management.
- Top management involvement, especially at the factory, and necessary ERP training made the project a success.

(iv) Case study: ERP Software for the Pulp and Paper Industry

Fig. 5.8: Raw material is waste paper for this paper mill

Fig. 5.9: Finished Goods: Paper
Paper Mills Ltd., Aurangabad

Multiple locations: This company is using ERP in their factory which is located about 100 Km from the office in the main city of Aurangabad, India.

Background

- Manufactures paper for the corrugated industry.
- Locally procured, imported waste paper or used paper and board is used as raw material (recycled).
- 'Finished Goods' are sold through dealers or directly to other manufactures where paper is the main raw material.
- ERP software integrates business processes automatically and gives real-time information to the authorised users.

Issues and Challenges

- Pulp and paper manufacturers face challenges stemming from continued industry decentralisation and overcapacity of plants.
- Like all industries, pulp and paper producers must balance operational activities against customer service levels to achieve optimal margins. This reduces inventories without compromising delivery performance by accurately depicting real-time inventory levels, so you can adjust forecasts and inventory restocking points, to ensure adequate waste-paper supplies.
- The plant is situated far away from the head office in Aurangabad. The challenge is to provide affordable data exchange technique to synchronise both computer servers to get real time MIS. Dialup internet connection was the only connectivity solution viable for the management under current situation.
- ERP should take care of excise rules, sales tax, VAT computation, TDS and such statutory requirements and the Government of India compliance. Purchase Order (PO) is raised in the head office and material is received at the plant (multi-location scenario).

How ERP Can Address These Issues

- ERP is specialised enterprise resource planning for paper manufacturers.
- ERP creates a competitive advantage by seamlessly integrating sales, purchase, stores, production, and accounts modules.
- ERP for paper manufacturers streamlines production operations to meet actual demand because it is linked with the order receipt information (ORI) or Sales Order. The SO link to dispatch also ensures accuracy in GSM and size of the Finished Goods that is paper.
- ERP supports the Make-to-stock, Make-to-order and Mixed Mode Environments.

Fig. 5.10: The Paper Mill

By deploying ERP modules the following issues are addressed:
1. Security module
2. Accounts module –
   (i) VAT / Sales Tax module
   (ii) Excise module
3. Inventory Management module
4. Purchase and Pre-purchase module
5. MRP - Material Requirement Planning Automatic email alerts module
6. Order Fulfilment module – Sales Accounting.
7. Send/ Receive data
8. Pre-sales and sales module.

Key Benefits

- ERP is suitable for process Industries such as pulp and paper industries, because it helps determine the optimum inventory. Not only can it help optimise mill operations, ERP for paper manufacturers provides the visibility needed to better understand relationships among sales orders, production, inventory and sales agent's excise invoice.

- Features such as instant reports for any period, reel number requirements, production statistics reporting, specification management and change management provide the control and predictability you need to gain exact control over all materials; track complete histories and audit trails; and have diligent yield optimisation and specification management.

(v) Case study for ERP in an Industrial Process Equipment Manufacturing Company

Fig. 5.11: Drying Plant

Background

This company is a well-known name in the 'drying industry'. A recognised name for industrial process equipment, equipped with a state-of-the-art product development facility. They specialise in large turnkey projects.

Their products are used in diverse range of industries like Ceramics & Minerals, Chemical industry, Food & Dairy industry, Pharma Industry, Detergent industry, Herbal Industry, Fine Chemicals etc.

It is a TUV certified ISO 9001: 2000 organisation. The company manufactures Industrial Dryers and Spray Dryers, evaporators, detergent Plants, as per specific requirements of the customer.

This company also takes turnkey projects such as erecting Dairy Plants. Milk Powder Plant consists of a multiple effect evaporator with or without pasteurizer and a spray dryer.

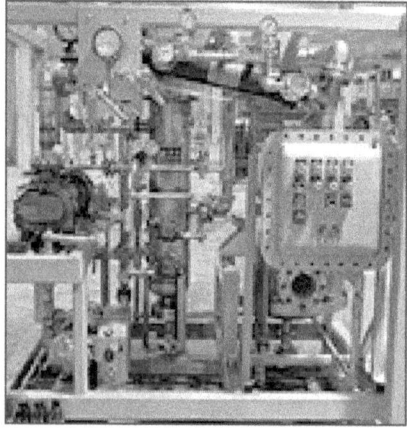

Fig. 5.12: Spray Dryer

The above given picture shows a product called, Spray Dryer.

Issues and challenges: The issues and challenges identified by the ERP team were as follows:
- Project wise activities need to be tracked.
- Project code needs to be linked to the Bills of materials (BOM), and Drawing number.
- Work order (production order) and project code integrations is required.
- Efficient collaboration of information.
- Increased transparency and better control.
- Protection / Security of data.
- Payroll accounting and wages to be integrated with financials.
- Purchase indent and Purchase order processing is required to be streamline with the stock in hand.
- Head office and the manufacturing is situated at a distance of ~ 30 K. M. (Multiple locations).

Fig. 5.13: The finished goods shown in the picture of a chemical plant

HOW ERP CAN ADDRESS THESE ISSUES

ERP is deployed with the following modules to integrate various functions. ERP provided a module that synchronizes the data of both ERP servers. Since a fast broadband was not practical, the solution to update database in batch mode was used successfully. By using the following ERP modules above challenges were met:

1. Security module
2. Accounts module – General Ledger Accounts
3. VAT / Sales Tax module
4. Excise module
5. Inventory Management module
6. Purchase and Pre-purchase module
7. MRP - Material Requirement Planning module.
8. ISO 9000 – Quality check module
9. BOM module

10. Production module
11. CRM module
12. Automatic email alerts module
13. Payroll and HR module
14. Cost sheet module – preparing estimate
15. Sales Accounting.
16. Send / receive data – multiple locations.

Multi-locations:
Head office in Kothrud, Pune city
Factory in Pirangut industrial area

Key Benefits: The benefits resulting from ERP are as follows:

The purchase order is raised in head office, whereas the material is received in the factory. The invoice is made in the plant whereas the accountant is seated in the office.

Top management at both locations are aware about status of various business processes. Great amount of time and money is saved due to availability of information.

Project wise work bench gives details of each project. Integration of project code in the Bills of Material (BOM) ensures that there is no communication gap between marketing and design and production, purchase, and so on.

5.2.2 Case Study: Service Industry

In this section, some examples of ERP employment in the services industry are provided. These highlight the typical requirements from ERP packages suitable to a services industry.

(i) ERP For Tours and Travel Service Business

A tour and travels business would normally require the following master database as part of ERP.

Master database
- Vehicle Master
- Driver Master

- Item Master
- Supplier Master
- Account Master

For efficient management of the bus hire or car hire business it was considered important to automate the business.

Background

Contrary to popular belief, even small and medium size organisation can get benefit tremendously from ERP software and that too at an affordable price. Tour operators typically have to work in very dynamic environment on a day to day basis. Being a service industry, timely provision of the service is very crucial. Tour operators run on very tight budgets, have extremely limited and well dispersed resources and the norm of operations is cash and carry. In such an environment, very efficient exploitation of available resources assumes paramount importance. This can be ensured through use of ERP. Following are some salient points for this type of ERP:

- ERP for tour operators is an initiative to replace traditional management software with a new tightly linked system.
- Consider example of a company providing bus service to pick up boys and girls from home, drop at the school and pickup from school and drop them home safely.
- ERP solutions can be applied for established as well as start up companies.

Highlights of ERP software system

- **Security module:** Multi user / multi location solution. Access rights as per role and responsibility matrix.
- Accounts integration with sales – Bank master, overheads master. Monthly fees receipt data entry, payment voucher. Income – expense register, Cash book, bank book, etc. Department master, designation master. Region – suburb master, building master.
- **CRM module:** Customer master – student master – capturing pickup time and drop time. Email integration. MIS – Student master list showing school name. Printing accurate sales bill.
- **Payroll module:** Employee master information e.g. driver's licenses number. Printing salary slips automatically.
- **Trips module:** Trip master, Monthly trips records, petrol – diesel slip entry. Local as well as out-station trips data entry screen to capture details in a user friendly way.
- MIS: Driver wise student pick-up report. Fuel consumption records. Trip status register. Vendor payment register.

ERP in Services Industry benefits a large number of agencies. Following are the stakeholders in a Tour Operations ERP.

Stakeholders

Who will benefit?

- Students
- Parents

- Corporate (Placements)
- Faculty
- Top Management
- Staff – Middle level managers
- Alumni

Issues and Challenges: In a tour operations service ERP would normally be used to address the following issues and challenges.

- Vehicle management for efficient use of this resource.
- Managing fuel consumption to improve operational efficiency.
- Maintaining trip- wise records for monitoring, account and decision making.

How ERP Can Address These Issues?

ERP is deployed with the following modules to integrate various functions. ERP has given the module that synchronizes the data of both ERP servers. Since fast broadband was not practical, the solution to update database in batch mode is used successfully. By using the following ERP modules above challenges are met:

1. Security module
2. Accounts module – General Ledger Accounts
3. Assets management
4. VAT / Sales Tax module
5. Purchase module
6. Inventory management
7. Attendance
8. Examination
9. Subject master
10. Faculty master
11. Automatic email alerts module
12. SMS alerts integration
13. Payroll and HR module
14. Sales Accounting
15. Send / receive data – multiple locations

Key benefits applied to tour operators using ERP

- No limit on number of users. As your organisation grows you can add more users, more locations, use internet for networking your ERP server with booking agents.
- Requires minimum training. Your existing staff can start using ERP software.
- ERP gives 'smart view' of the organisation.
- Authorised user can view reports that are relevant and export instantly to MS Excel worksheet instantly.
- MIS (Management Information System) that helps top management to take critical decisions, monitor expenses and increase efficiency.
- Low TCO – Total cost of ownership.

5.2.3 ERP Case Studies for Other Organisations

Campus ERP

Enterprise Resource Planning for educational institutes and colleges. The goal is to capture entire business process from admission to placement.

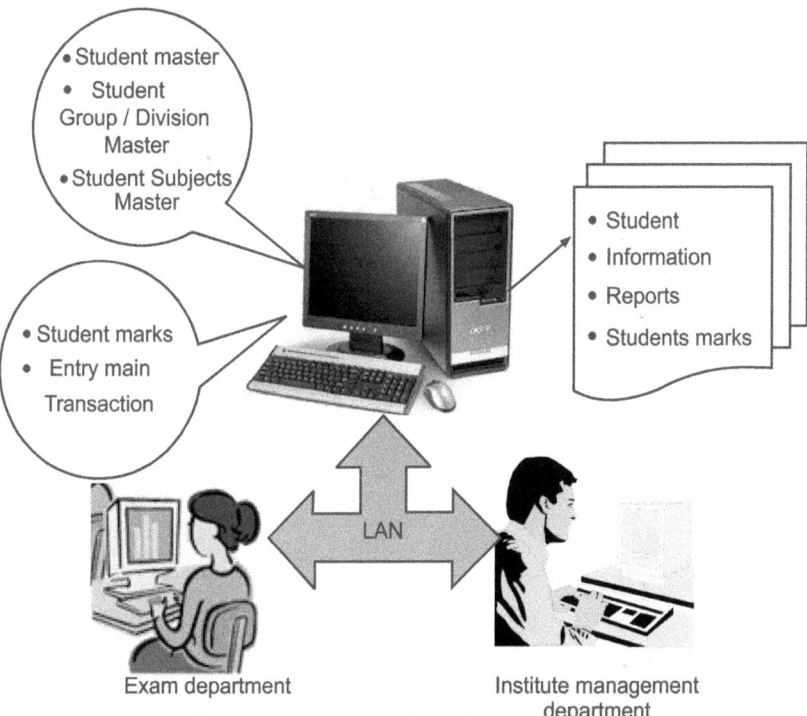

Fig. 5.14: Concept Diagram for the Campus Management ERP System

(i) Institute Management Master

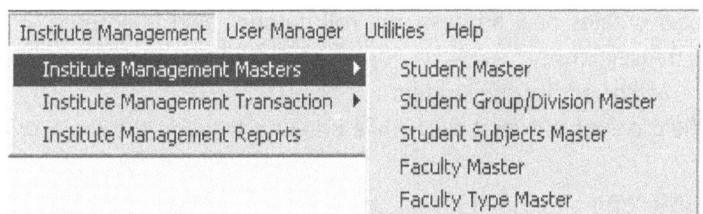

Fig. 5.15: A Typical Menu for Entering Master, Transaction and Reports

In the above screen, there is a submenu under master, to select student master, student group or division master, subjects, faculty, etc.

In the Campus ERP database there are five different masters:
1. Student Master
2. Student Group /Division Master
3. Student Subjects Master
4. Faculty Type Master
5. Faculty Master

(ii) Student Master
Student's details are entered in student master database.
General Information

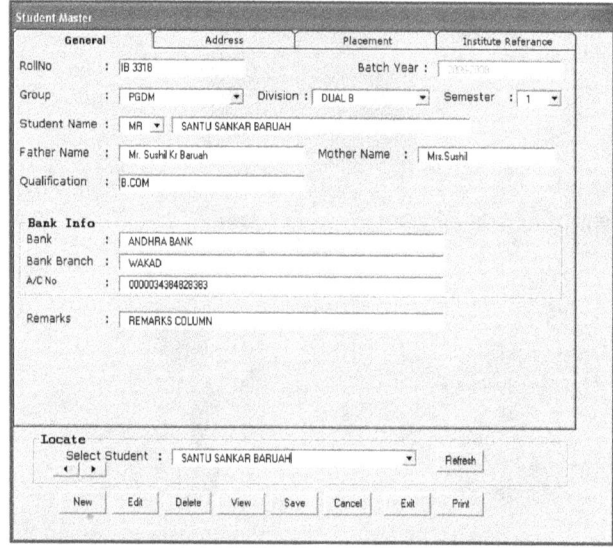

Fig. 5.16: A Data Entry Screen for Entering Student Information in ERP

A unique Roll number is generated to identify student while entering the student master information. Some of the key fields that are required while creating master are given below:

1. **Student Roll Number** – Roll Number for the Student.
   User will enter the specified roll number of particular person as provided by the institute.
   When the user creates new address, the roll number field is entered in his record and used for further transactions.
2. **Batch Year** – Batch year for the student.
   Batch year field comes automatically while entering through the login screen of the ERP System.
3. **Group** – Course type.
   List selection field.
   User has to select the course type from the given list.
4. **Division** – Division type
   List selection field.
   User has to select the Division type from the given list.

5. **Semester** – Semester type
   List selection field.
   User has to select the semester type from the list.
6. **Initial for the Name** – Initial before the Name of the Student.
   Can select from the drop down list either Mr or Ms.
   User has to enter the initials before name of the student.
7. **Student Name** – Name of the Student
   Manual entry field.
   User has to enter the full name of the student.
8. **Father's Name** – Name of the student's father.
   Manual entry field.
   User has to input the name of the student's father.
9. **Mother's Name** – Name of the student's mother.
   Manual entry field.
   User has to input the name of the student's mother.
10. **Qualification** – Enter the Student's qualification
11. **Bank Information** – Manual entry field.
    User has to enter the Bank name, Branch and Account number of the student.
12. **Remarks** – User can enter any remarks if needed for any particular person. For example, if a student has left in between the academic year, the user can enter in the remarks field as left.

Address

It is necessary to capture address of all students at the time of admission stage itself. Some students may migrate from their home town, therefore there are two addresses as explained below.

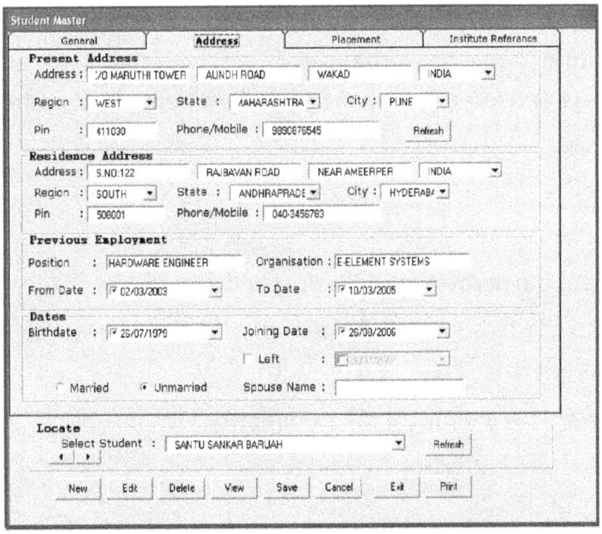

Fig. 5.17: A Master Data Entry Screen

The previous screen shot shows a master data entry screen to enter both address of student, current and permanent address, birth date, etc.

(1) Present Address

1. **Address** – Address of the Student

    Manual entry field.

    User has to input the detail address.

2. **Country** – Country in which student resides

    List selection field.

    User has to select the country.

3. **Region** – Region in which it exists

    List selection field.

    User has to select the region from the given list.

4. **State** – State in which the student exists.

    List selection field.

    User has to select the state from the given list.

5. **City** – City in which it exists

    List selection field.

    User has to select the city from the given list.

6. **Pin** – Pin code.

    Manual entry field.

    User has to input the pin code of the area.

7. **Permanent address same as address** – If it is selected then address is copied to permanent address. Otherwise, user has to input the permanent address separately.

(2) Residence Address

1. **Address** – Residence Address of the Student.

    Manual entry field.

    User has to input the permanent or Residence address of the student.

2. **Country** – Country in which student resides

    List selection field.

    User has to select the country of the student from the given list.

3. **Region** – Region in which it exists

    List selection field.

    User has to select the region from the given list.

4. **State –** State in which the student exists.

    List selection field.

    User has to select the state from the given list.

5. **City –** City in which it exists

    List selection field.

    User has to select the city from the given list.

6. **Pin –** Pin code.

    Manual entry field.

    User has to input the pin code of the area.

In case of some of the colleges / institutes, the placement plays an important role for students. In ERP student master, details of student is captured who have worked somewhere before. This will help the placement department to arrange for interview with the HR manager of a company likely to recruit the student.

⇒ Previous Employment – User can enter the details of the student's previous employment who has worked previously.

⇒ Dates – User can enter the dates like student's birth date, joining date, left date and also can enter the spouse name if married and can enter the spouse name only when one selects the option as married.

Placement

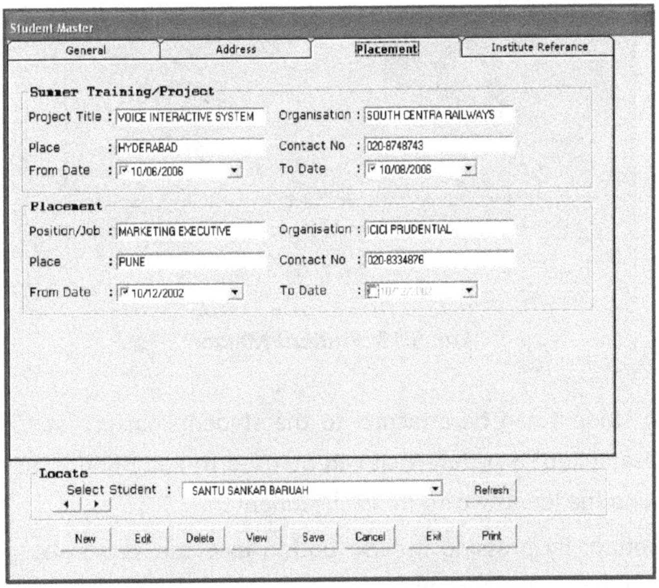

Fig. 5.18: A Master Data Entry Screen

The previous screen shows the master data entry screen to capture the students details pertaining to the placement department of the institute.

Placement Details of the Student

1. Summer Training/Project – Project Title.

   User can enter the Project Title

   Manual Entry field.

   User has to input the Organisation name, Place, Contact number, From Date and To Date of the Training he has done

   Placement – This is to enter the information of the student's last placement.

   User can enter the data like Position / Job, Organisation, Place, Contact number, From Date and To Date of the organisation in which he was placed.

   Institute Reference

   User can attach picture → Click on Browse button and enter folder / file name.

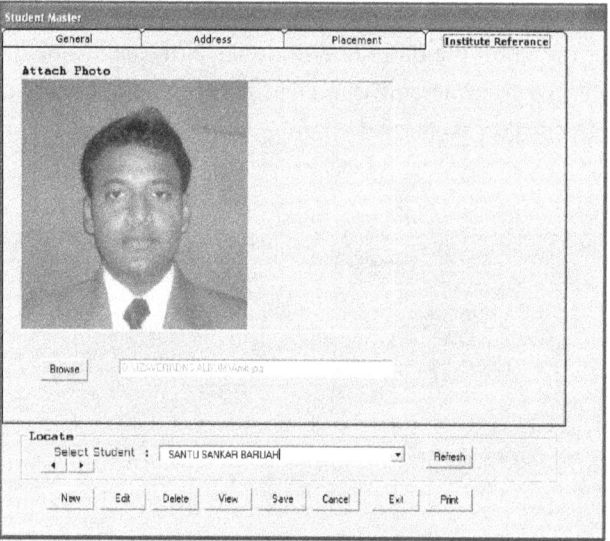

Fig. 5.19: Student Master

Photo of each student can be attached to the student master data. The above screen dump shows an example of a picture that can be used to identify the person easily. This is important for making the Identity card for each student.

1. Browse Button: By pressing browse button user can select the .jpg image of the student which is present in the system by selecting the path of the photo and can view the photo whenever necessary. It also shows the path from where the photo is selected.

(iii) Student Group / Division Master

Fig. 5.20: The Master Data Entry Screen to Enter the Student Division or a Group

This entry screen is in the table form. There are two fields.

(i) Student Group Code – Manual entry field.

User has to input the students group code.

(ii) Student Group Description – Manual entry field.

User has to input the description for the student group code.

This is to enter any group newly commenced and can default these groups in all the transactions of the system. It can also print the excel sheet by pressing on the excel symbol button.

In **Student Group / Division master** form, another table of student division master is provided.

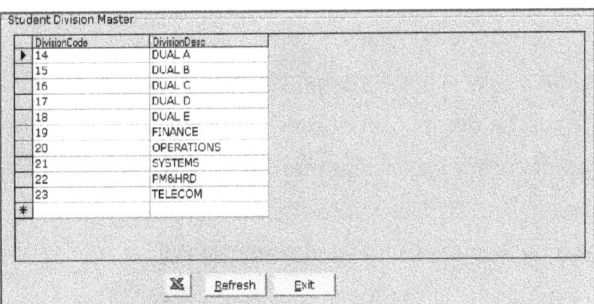

One institute may have many divisions. For example, in a B-School students may opt for single specialisation, say, Finance, or dual specialisation, say Finance and Marketing. The above example of master data entry screen shows an example of division master.

(a) Division Code – Manual entry field.

User has to input the division code.

(b) Division Description – Manual entry field.

User has to input the description for the division code.

These divisions are defaulted in all the transactions of ERP wherever the division drop down box is provided and user can select the division accordingly as required. To export list to MS excel sheet click on Excel icon.

(iv) Student Subjects Master

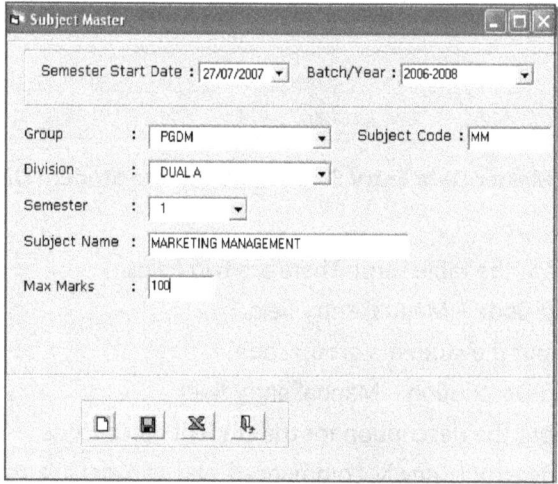

The previous screen shows example of storing the subjects that are taught in the institute. User who is authorised can only create or update this important master. Marks for each subject is stored, which will be used in the exam system to print the marksheet.

- **(i) Date:** Date input is done manually.
- **(ii) Batch Year:** Batch year is generated automatically.

    User has to input the description of batch year while entering the ERP System.
- **(iii) Group:** Group of course has to be entered from the list.
- **(iv) Division:** Division is to be filled from the list manually.
- **(v) Semester:** The semester is to be filled from the list.
- **(vi) Subject:** User has to input the name of the subjects per semester manually.
- **(vii) Max Marks:** This is to enter the maximum marks for which the exam of that particular subject is conducted and is used for the calculation of the student's average or percentage in the marksheet automatically.
- **(viii) Subject Code:** This field is to enter the code of the subject. For example, PPM code for Principles and Practices of Management.

This transaction is mainly to view the subjects present in each semester dual wise and also can enter a new subject in any dual or semester.

The subject information can be seen in the excel sheet dual wise and semester wise.

(v) Faculty Type Master

This is to enter the types of faculty present in the Institute like permanent or visiting etc. and also use the excel report if necessary.

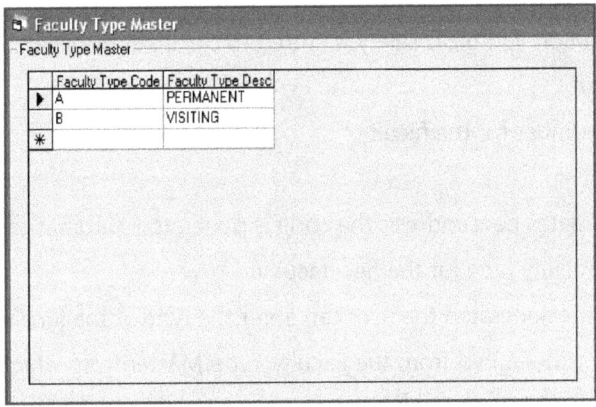

Fig. 5.21: The Screen to Store the Type of Faculty

The above screen shows the screen to store the type of faculty. There are two types of teachers / faculty – permanent employee or temporary / visiting or guest faculty.

(vi) Faculty Master

Faculty's details are entered in master database.

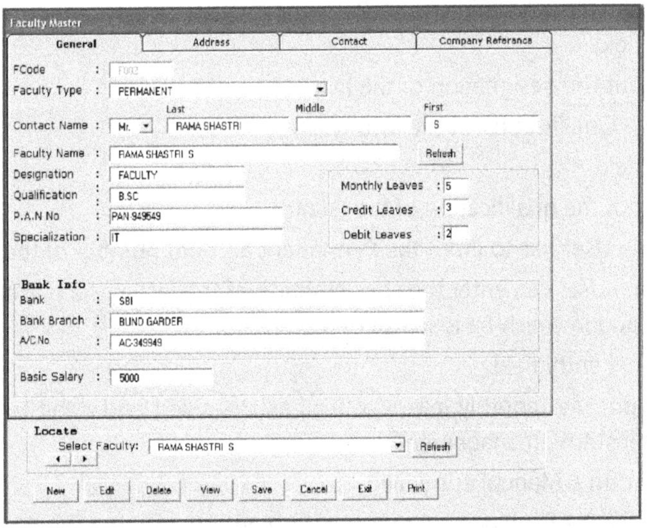

Fig. 5.22: Master Database for Faculty Information

The previous screen shows screen dump to capture faculty information. This will be used further to schedule timetable for each faculty / teacher by ERP. For permanent employee (faculty) the leave information can also be stored, which is useful for leave management by the HR department.

The bank information and basic salary is stored to calculate the salary.

General Information

1. **F Code** – Code number for the faculty.

   Auto generated field.

   When the user creates new address, the code is generated automatically by the system.

2. **Faculty Type** – Faculty type for the new faculty.

   When the F code is generated the user can enter the type of the faculty

   This faculty type is defaulted from the Faculty Type Master from which the user can enter the faculty types in the given fields.

3. **Initial For The Name** – Initial for the name of the faculty.

   Manual entry field.

   User has to input the initial before the name of the faculty

4. **Contact Name** – Name of the Faculty.

   Manual entry field.

   User has to input the name of the faculty, like his first name, middle name, and last name as the fields provided and this will be defaulted in the Faculty Name field

5. **Designation** - Designation of the faculty.

   Manual entry field.

   User has to input the designation of the faculty.

6. **Qualification** – Qualification of the faculty.

   Manual entry field.

   User has to input the qualification of the faculty.

7. **PAN Number** – User has to input the Permanent account number of the faculty.

8. **Specialisation** – User can enter the specialisation of the faculty such as the subjects taken by the faculty and in which he is specialised.

9. **Leaves** – Manual entry field.

   User has to input the monthly leaves as well as the credit and debit leaves provided for the faculty by the institute management.

10. **Bank Information** – Manual entry filed.

    User has to enter the Bank name, Branch and account number of the faculty.

11. **Basic Salary** – Manual entry field.

    User has to enter basic salary of the faculty

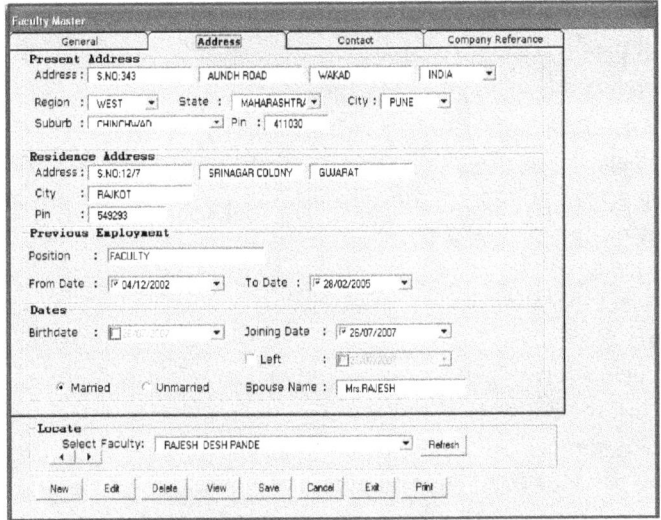

Fig. 5.23: Faculty Master Data Entry Screen

ADDRESS
1. **Address** – Address of the Faculty.
   Manual entry field.
   User has to input the detail address.
2. **Country** – Country in which it exists
   List selection field.
   User has to select the Country.
3. **Region** – Region in which it exists
   List selection field.
   User has to select the region from the given list.
4. **State** – State in which the student exists.
   List selection field.
   User has to select the state from the given list.
5. **City** – City in which it exists
   List selection field.
   User has to select the city from the given list.
6. **Pin** – Pin code.
   Manual entry field.
   User has to input the pin code of the area.

Residence Address
1. **Address** – Residence address of the faculty.
   Manual entry field.
   User has to input the residence or permanent address of the faculty.
2. **Country** – Country in which it exists
   List selection field.
   User has to select the country of the faculty from the given list.

3. **Region** – Region in which it exists
   List selection field.
   User has to select the region from the given list.
4. **State** – Residence state of the faculty.
   List selection field.
   User has to select the state from the given list.
5. **City** – Residence city of the faculty
   List selection field.
   User has to select the city from the given list.
6. **Pin** – Pin code
   Manual entry field.
   User has to input the pin code of the area.
7. **Previous Employment**
   Position in the previous company and period of work.
8. **Date**
   Select filter is provided for stating the period of from and to date of the employment.
9. **Dates**
   Birth date, joining date, etc.
   Leaving date, if the user clicks on the left combo then the field gets enabled and the user can only enter the Faculty left date if left the college or company. Date picker is provided.
   Marital status as married or unmarried has to be ticked and accordingly the spouse name field and marriage date fields get enabled.
   Then user has to enter the spouse name.
   Then select the date from the date picker.

Contact data

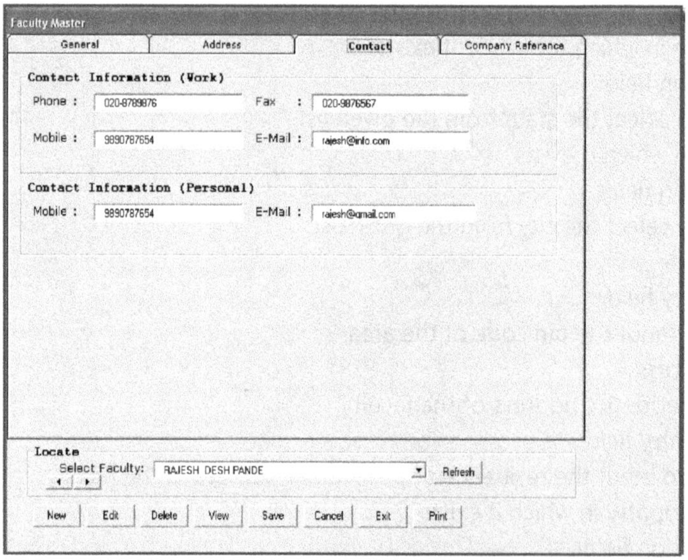

Fig. 5.24: Faculty Contact Information Screen

The previous screen is used to store the contact information of all faculty.

Contact Information (Work)
1. **Phone** – Telephone number of the contact person.
   Manual Entry field.
   User has to input the phone number of the faculty.
2. **Fax** – Fax number
   Manual Entry field.
   User has to input the fax number of the faculty.
3. **Mobile number** – Mobile number of the faculty.
   Manual Entry field.
   User has to input the mobile number of the faculty.
4. **E-Mail** – E-mail address of the faculty.
   Manual Entry field.
   User has to input the e-mail address of the faculty.

Contact Information (Personal)
1. Mobile number – Personal mobile number of the faculty
   Manual Entry field.
   User has to input the mobile number of the faculty.
2. E-Mail – Personal e-mail address of the faculty
   Manual Entry field.
   User has to input the e-mail address of the faculty.

Reference / Photo

In this tab we can browse and insert the photo of a faculty in faculty master form. It also shows the path from where the photo is copied.

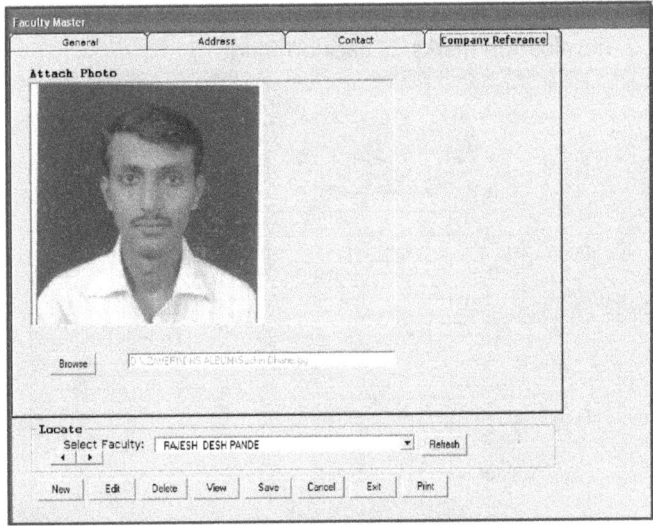

Fig. 5.25: Faculty Picture is stored

Similar to student master in the faculty master also there is a provision to store the picture of the faculty as shown above.

2. Exam System Module

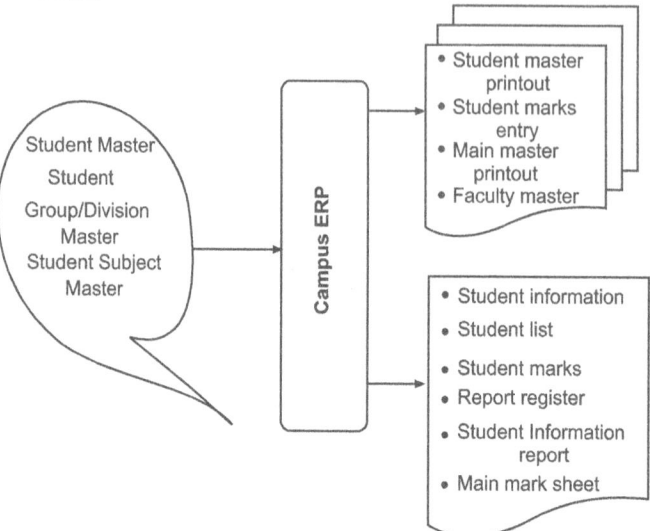

Fig. 5.26: An exam module of a ERP system for an educational establishment

Note that there are a number of master data that needs to be prepared first, such as student master, subject master, and so on.

2.1 INSTITUTE MANAGEMENT TRANSACTION
2.1.1 Student Marks Entry
2.1.2 Student Marks Entry Main

There are three data entry screens to enter marks of students:
1. Main marks, 2. Revaluation marks, 3. Backlog marks.

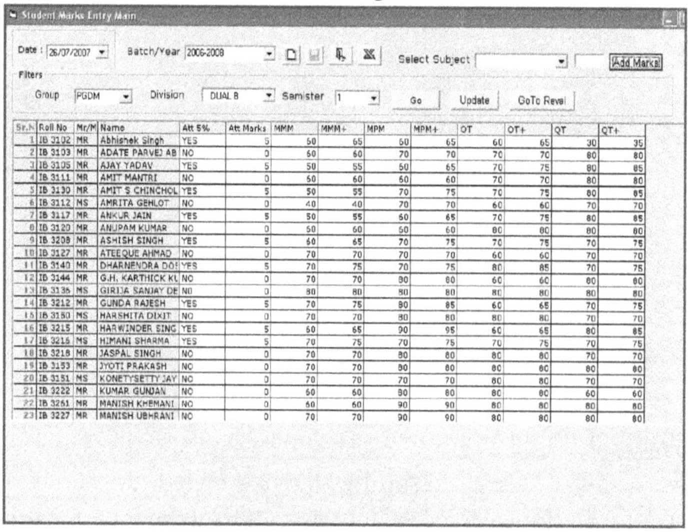

Fig. 5.27: Screen for marks entry

Previous screen is used by the exam department to enter the marks of each student. The roll number and the name defaults automatically from the student master. To encourage attendance, in many colleges some marks are added as bonus mark as shown above. Once the marks data is added for each subject, marksheet is generated by ERP.

1. Marks Entry form for Main Exam – Manual entry field.

User has to input the marks of the student manually.

After selecting Group, Division and Semester field, press Go button.

The marks detail of the students for the selected group will be displayed and can be updated further.

There is a button in this form i.e. **Go To Reval**. On clicking this button the marks from the main entry form goes to Revaluation table and is saved there and can be further changed in the Marks Entry Reval form.

Student Marks Entry Reval – Revaluation.

In this form the marks details of the students comes from the marks main table and can be changed during the Reval results.

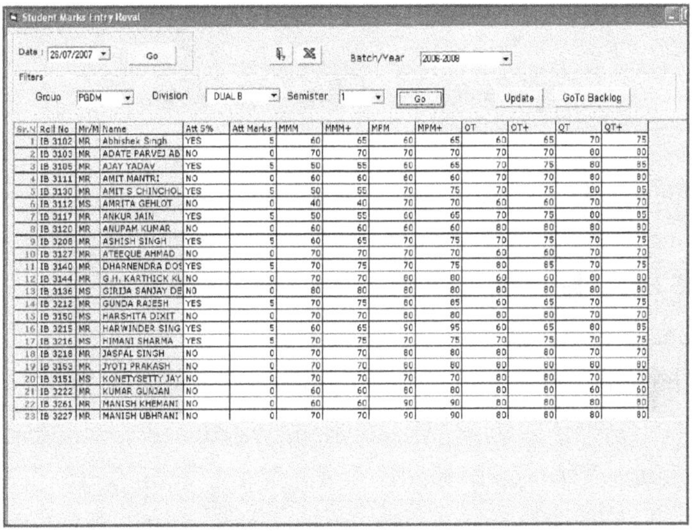

Sr.N	Roll No	Mr/M	Name	Att 5%	Att Marks	MMM	MMM+	MPM	MPM+	OT	OT+	QT	QT+
1	IB 3102	MR	Abhishek Singh	YES	5	60	65	60	65	60	65	70	75
2	IB 3103	MR	ADATE PARVEJ AB	NO	0	70	70	70	70	70	70	80	80
3	IB 3105	MR	AJAY YADAV	YES	5	50	55	60	65	70	75	80	85
4	IB 3111	MR	AMIT MANTRI	NO	0	60	60	60	60	70	70	80	80
5	IB 3130	MR	AMIT S CHINCHOL	YES	5	50	55	70	75	70	75	80	85
6	IB 3112	MS	AMRITA GEHLOT	NO	0	40	40	70	70	60	60	70	70
7	IB 3117	MR	ANKUR JAIN	YES	5	50	55	60	65	70	75	80	85
8	IB 3120	MR	ANUPAM KUMAR	NO	0	60	60	60	60	80	80	80	80
9	IB 3208	MR	ASHISH SINGH	YES	5	60	65	70	75	70	75	70	75
10	IB 3127	MR	ATEEQUE AHMAD	NO	0	70	70	70	70	60	60	70	70
11	IB 3140	MR	DHARNENDRA DOS	YES	5	70	75	70	75	80	85	70	75
12	IB 3144	MR	G.H. KARTHICK KL	NO	0	70	70	80	80	60	60	80	80
13	IB 3136	MS	GIRIJA SANJAY DE	NO	0	80	80	80	80	80	80	80	80
14	IB 3212	MR	GUNDA RAJESH	YES	5	70	75	80	85	60	65	70	75
15	IB 3150	MS	HARSHITA DIXIT	NO	0	70	70	80	80	80	80	70	70
16	IB 3215	MR	HARWINDER SING	YES	5	60	65	90	95	60	65	80	85
17	IB 3216	MS	HIMANI SHARMA	YES	5	70	75	70	75	70	75	70	75
18	IB 3218	MR	JASPAL SINGH	NO	0	70	70	80	80	80	80	70	70
19	IB 3153	MR	JYOTI PRAKASH	NO	0	70	70	80	80	80	80	80	80
20	IB 3151	MS	KONETYSETTY JAY	NO	0	70	70	70	70	80	80	70	70
21	IB 3222	MR	KUMAR GUNJAN	NO	0	60	60	80	80	80	80	60	60
22	IB 3261	MR	MANISH KHEMANI	NO	0	60	60	90	90	80	80	80	80
23	IB 3227	MR	MANISH UBHRANI	NO	0	70	70	90	90	80	80	80	80

Fig. 5.28: Screen for Student Marks Entry Reval

As shown in the above screen, in this form the user can update the marks of the student according to the marks of the revaluation examination, after rechecking the paper

In this form there is a button i.e. **Go To Backlog:** This is used to insert the marks details of the student's from the Reval table and can be further changed accordingly in the backlog form.

All these marks details from Main, Reval and Backlog can be viewed in Excel sheet

Student Marks Entry Backlog

This form is used to enter the backlog exam marks of the student and the same can be viewed in the Excel sheet.

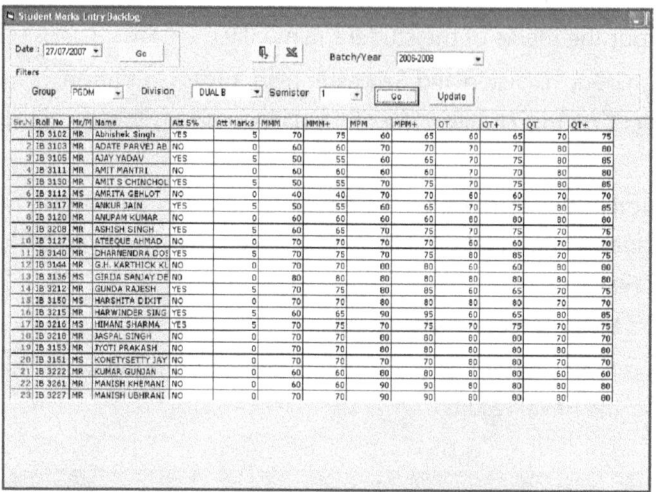

Fig. 5.29: Student Marks Entry Backlog

The above screen is for the backlog exam marks entry i.e. for students reappearing for a subject that was not cleared in the first attempt.

5.2.4 Key MIS Module

(i) Institute Management Reports

This is the form where the user can see the types of reports the existing system gives.

It consists of reports for every transaction in the system and can see the details and can also take a print out.

In this system the reports like:

1. Student Information
2. Faculty Information
3. Student Marks Entry Report Main
5. Student Marks Entry Report Reval
6. Student Marks Entry Report Backlog and
7. Student Labels are present

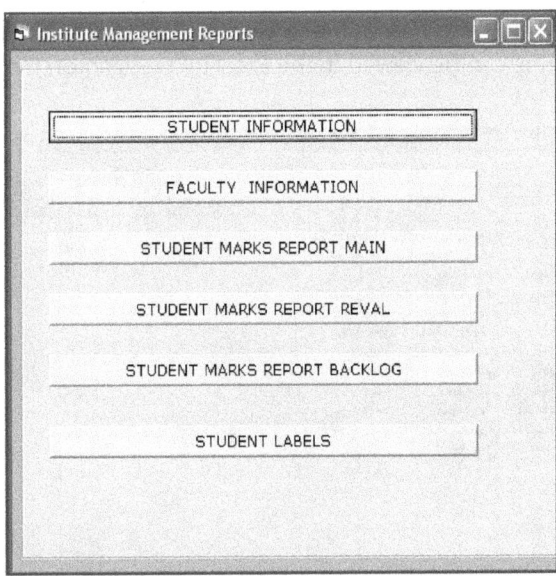

Fig. 5.30: The main menu to create required reports from the Institute ERP

Only the user who has the correct login id and password can create and print outputs, such as, faculty information, student marks report, or address labels.

(ii) Student Information Report

In this report, the user can view all the student information like roll number, group, and address etc.

This report can be viewed group wise to give the information of all the students of that particular group.

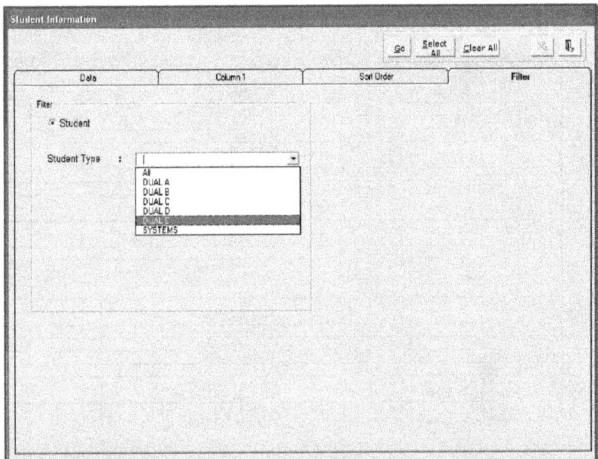

Fig. 5.31: Student Type Drop Down Menu

User can also select the fields he wants to view in the column 1 tab and view the details accordingly and the same can be viewed in the Excel by pressing on the Excel button.

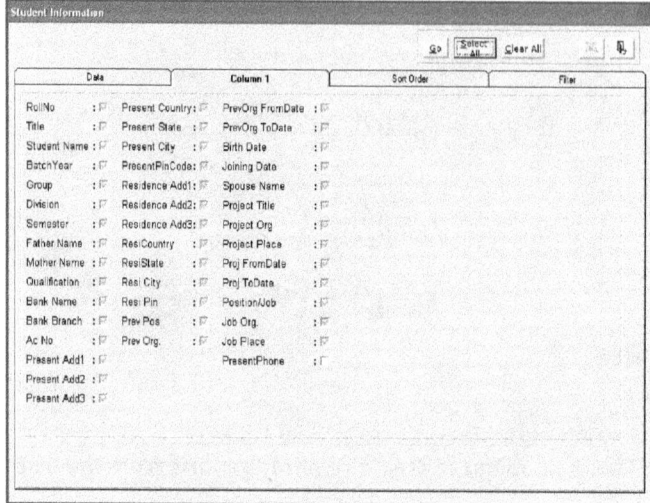

Fig. 5.32: Student Master

In the above tab user can select the fields he want to view and can get the information as he requires.

All the selective fields information is displayed as below in the tabular format and also can be taken print through the Excel button.

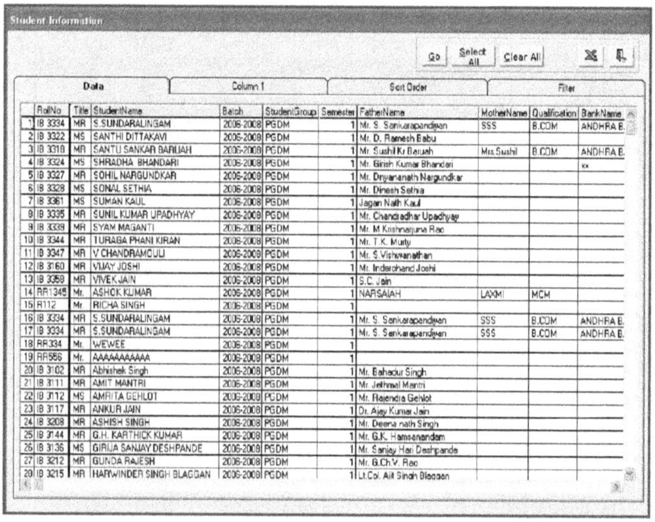

Fig. 5.33: Screen shows online information for any student instantly

(iii) Faculty Information Report

In this form the user can view the faculty information same like the Student Information Report.

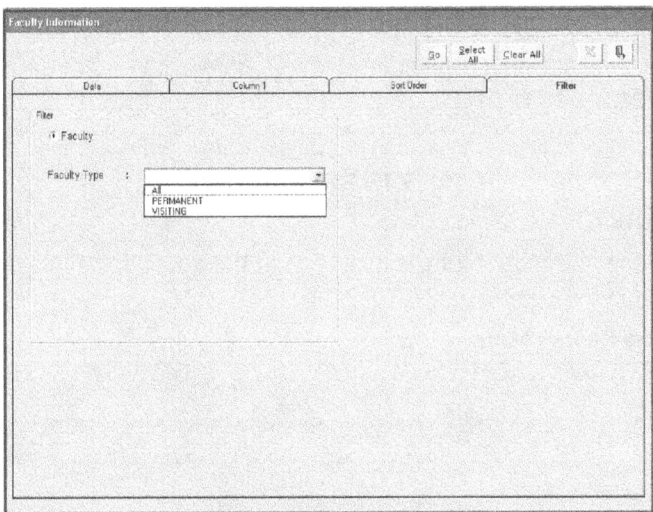

Fig. 5.34: Faculty Type

In the above tab user can select the faculty type and view the information accordingly.

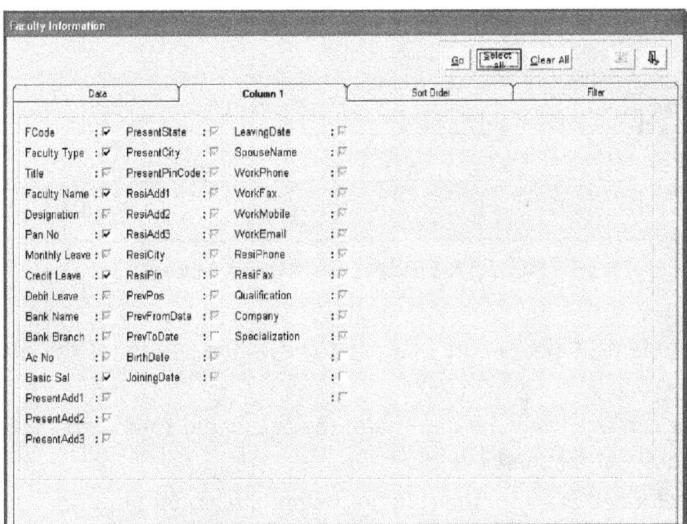

Fig. 5.35: User selects the column for Report

In the above Column 1 tab user can select the required fields and can view the information as selected.

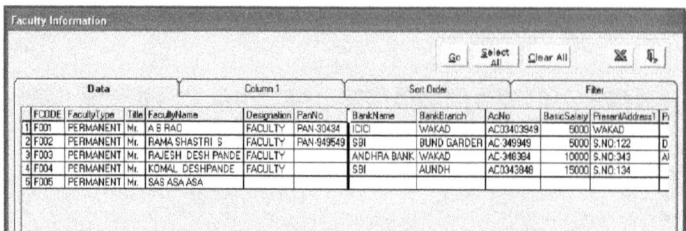

Fig. 5.36: Faculty Report

Faculty information is displayed online.

User can view the information of the faculty as in the above form in a tabular format and can also be viewed in the Excel sheet.

(iv) Student Marks Report Main

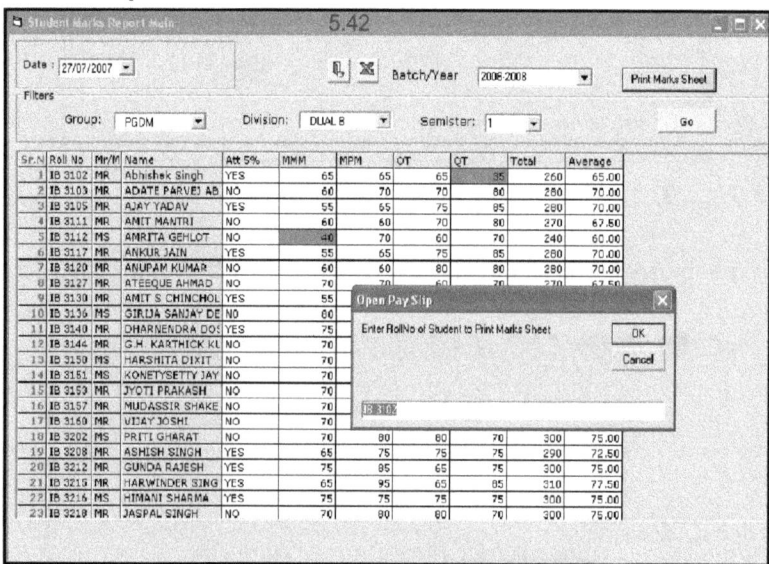

Fig. 5.37: Student Marksheet Report

This is the Student Marks Report Main and shows the results of the main exam of the students.

Here the user can only view the marks and the calculated total marks and average of the student and cannot edit the marks in this form.

Here green colour appears for the columns where the student has got less than 50 marks, which is termed as fail or backlog.

In this form there is a button called Print Marks Sheet. By pressing this button user can print the mark sheet of a student according to the selected roll number of the student of that particular division as shown below.

In the above form when user clicks on the Print Marks Sheet button a window appears to select the roll number of a particular student to print the mark sheet.

In this dialog box the user can select the roll number of the student and can print the mark sheet of that student by pressing on OK button.

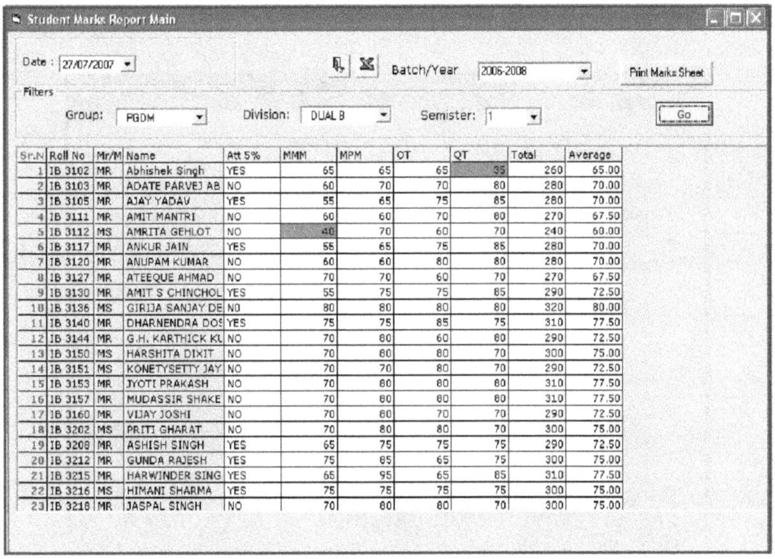

Sr.N	Roll No	Mr/M	Name	Att 5%	MMM	MPM	OT	QT	Total	Average
1	IB 3102	MR	Abhishek Singh	YES	65	65	65	35	260	65.00
2	IB 3103	MR	ADATE PARVEJ AB	NO	60	70	70	80	280	70.00
3	IB 3105	MR	AJAY YADAV	YES	55	65	75	85	280	70.00
4	IB 3111	MR	AMIT MANTRI	NO	60	60	70	80	270	67.50
5	IB 3112	MS	AMRITA GEHLOT	NO	40	70	60	70	240	60.00
6	IB 3117	MR	ANKUR JAIN	YES	55	65	75	85	280	70.00
7	IB 3120	MR	ANUPAM KUMAR	NO	60	60	80	80	280	70.00
8	IB 3127	MR	ATEEQUE AHMAD	NO	70	70	60	70	270	67.50
9	IB 3130	MR	AMIT S CHINCHOL	YES	55	75	75	85	290	72.50
10	IB 3136	MS	GIRIJA SANJAY DE	NO	80	80	80	80	320	80.00
11	IB 3140	MR	DHARNENDRA DOS	YES	75	75	85	75	310	77.50
12	IB 3144	MR	G.H. KARTHICK KL	NO	70	80	60	80	290	72.50
13	IB 3150	MS	HARSHITA DIXIT	NO	70	80	80	70	300	75.00
14	IB 3151	MS	KONETYSETTY JAY	NO	70	70	80	70	290	72.50
15	IB 3153	MR	JYOTI PRAKASH	NO	70	80	80	80	310	77.50
16	IB 3157	MR	MUDASSIR SHAKE	NO	70	80	80	80	310	77.50
17	IB 3160	MR	VIJAY JOSHI	NO	70	80	70	70	290	72.50
18	IB 3202	MS	PRITI GHARAT	NO	70	80	80	70	300	75.00
19	IB 3208	MR	ASHISH SINGH	YES	65	75	75	75	290	72.50
20	IB 3212	MR	GUNDA RAJESH	YES	75	85	65	75	300	75.00
21	IB 3215	MR	HARWINDER SING	YES	65	95	65	85	310	77.50
22	IB 3216	MS	HIMANI SHARMA	YES	75	75	75	75	300	75.00
23	IB 3218	MR	JASPAL SINGH	NO	70	80	80	70	300	75.00

Fig. 5.38: Student Master Data Report

POST GRADUATE DIPLOMA IN MANAGEMENT (PGDM)

EXAMINATION HELD:

MARK SHEET

NAME: ADATE PARVEJ ABDUL RAHIM

REGISTRATION NO. IB 3103 BATCH OF 2006-2008

SEMESTER I

SUBJECTS	**MARKS**	
	MAXIMUM	**OBTAINED**
MMM	100	60
MPM	100	70
OT	100	70
QT	100	80
Total	**400**	**280**

Date: 27-Jul-07

Prof. Suresh Chandra Padhy
Director (Academics)

Fig. 5.39: Marksheet Example

Likewise the user can view the student total and average marks along reval and backlog report.

(v) Student Labels

This form is used to print the labels of the student like Student roll number, name, address, contact number, and e-mail etc.

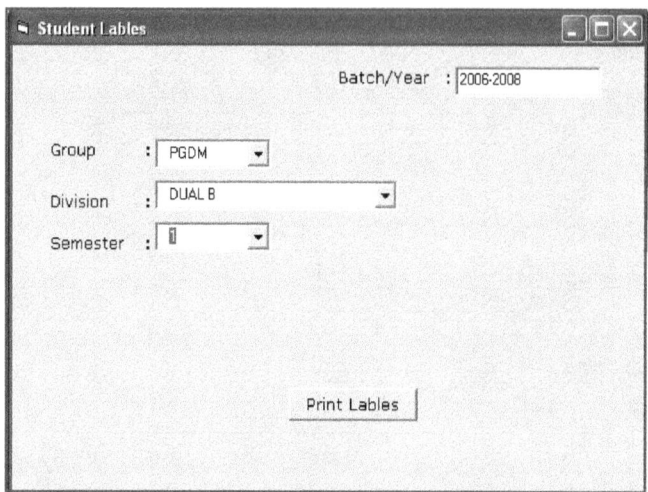

Fig. 5.40: Example of Students Labels

Screen shows example of the menu to print address labels for post. Provision is also made to send emails.

Security Module - User Manage
Define Group Permissions.
Define Individual Permissions.
User Manager
User Groups Master

Security Module: Access rights are decided by giving login-id and secret password by the administrator only. This will decide who will be able to access which area (menu / sub-menu) of ERP system. Confidentiality can be maintained by carefully assigning the 'Rights'.

Password: Traditionally, we used to keep physical files in a cupboard with a lock and the key or duplicate key is given to a responsible manager in the office. How do you protect electronic files? Password is the solution. The ERP system access rights module allows access or denies access to various menu and submenus. You can help to protect database confidentiality by following these simple precautions.

1. Keep your ERP system User ID and Password secret and difficult to guess.
2. Change secret password regularly.
3. Make sure your computer is protected with latest Anti-Virus software.

4. Make sure you close ERP system (Exit) by clicking on the "Close" button – right hand top corner marked' X '.
5. In addition, you may also use the windows screensaver password protection, which can lock your keyboard automatically if you do not use for a pre-set time.
6. Remember your login id and password is secret and do not share this with others.
7. On ERP system transactions and reports, the name of the person who has login is captured automatically.

5.3 Customisation of ERP for Different Types of Industries

Introduction: ERP requirements for different types of industries are bound to be different. To provide the student an idea of these differences, some examples of ERP typical to certain common industry types are covered as follows to clarify the ERP concept to the reader.

5.3.1 ERP for OEM

OEM industry implies manufacturing as per contract of original equipment manufacturer or in simple terms - Make to order.

Fig. 5.41: Electric Motor

Background

Original Equipment Manufacturer (OEM) are those manufacturers whose production is directly linked to their customers production. They undertake supply or "Making as per the customer order (make to order)" which is totally linked to customers requirements.

Unlike FMCG products, all activities such as production, purchase, sales is linked to the customer's purchase order (sales order). ERP is deployed successfully in many such engineering companies. This case study is of a company that is a leader in manufacturing high quality motors and alternators for electrical industry.

At the same time, ERP software can take both kinds of automation – standard products as well as customised products manufacturing company.

Issues and Challenges

1. Smoother and faster process flow.
2. Decentralisation of task and decision.
3. Increased transparency and better control.
4. Protection/ Security of data.
5. Wastage, scrap, rejection.
6. Integration of all departments.
7. Cost control.
8. Productivity through elimination of duplication.
9. Inventory of raw materials.

How ERP can address these issues after some customisation?

ERP pre-sales and sales module helps managing marketing activities by capturing sales enquiry, preparing quotation, sales order, sales schedule, sales invoice, etc.

These challenges are mitigated through the use of following ERP modules:

1. Security module
2. Accounts module – General Ledger Accounts
3. VAT / Sales Tax module
4. Excise module
5. Inventory Management module
6. Purchase and Pre-purchase module
7. MRP - Material Requirement Planning module / Supply Chain Management (SCM)
8. ISO 9000 – Quality check module
9. BOM – Bill of Materials module
10. Production module (Assembly Production and Process Production)
11. Automatic email alerts module
12. Sub-contractor IN module.
13. Cost sheet module – preparing estimate
14. Order Fulfilment module – Sales Accounting - (Shipping)
15. CRM module (Customer relationship management) and pre-sales module

Key Benefits

1. Machine Master and Process Master are linked to Work order. The Production Planning module is linked to sales order and Bill of Material master. With these the user is able to track stage-wise production.
2. When the work order is prepared, the user (from production section) will do the daily planning keeping in mind machines that are available to him and according to work order quantity and the process that has to be done.
3. The user is able to select the work order number for which the planning is to be done. When the user selects the work order number, item code and work order quantity is defaulted automatically. The user can then select the machine name for the respective process that has to be done.
4. In the process drop down the process defined in the work order which are required will get defaulted. The user has to select the process one by one and then define its plan quantity and shift and click on add button.

In Production entry, user can enter the time required for manufacturing a given item i.e. start time and end time.

5.3.2 ERP for a Typical Special Purpose Machines (SPM) Manufacturer

In this case, we will take a look at how ERP can be useful for a manufacturer of standard products and hi-tech engineering products.

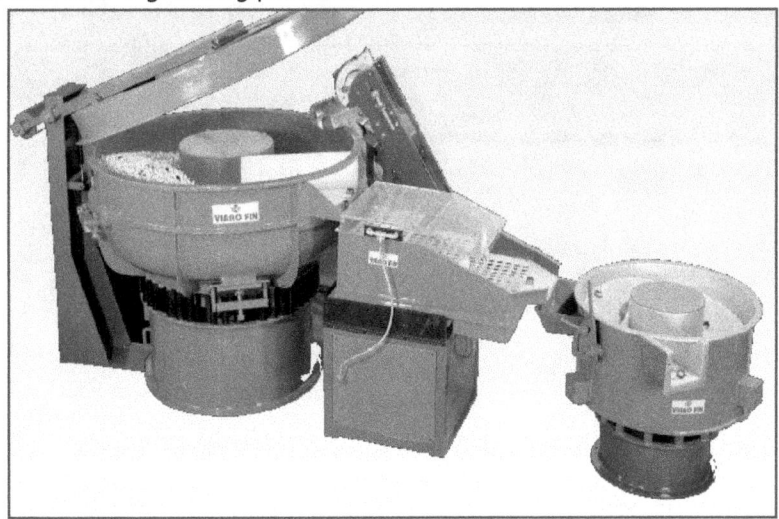

Fig. 5.42: SPM

Special Purpose Machines made by this company uses ERP System to manage business.

(i) Background

This company specialises in metal finishing machines. The company is engaged in manufacturing of Vibratory Finishing Machines and Centrifugal Finishing Machines. It also makes relevant Accessories and Consumables. This company enjoys unchallenged leadership in the market.

(ii) About Products (FG)

Product finishing is no longer an optional process. It has now become a compulsory and vital process. With mass production, the industry needs to operate with minimum manual skill and labour involvement to remain competitive. Rich dividends can be reaped with implementation of ERP.

Typically, any mass finishing system will comprise of a combination the following operations:

- Loading
- Pre Treatment
- Roughing
- Polishing
- Drying
- Post Treatment

A simple system can be a Vibrator in tandem with Dryer and fully auto control panel.

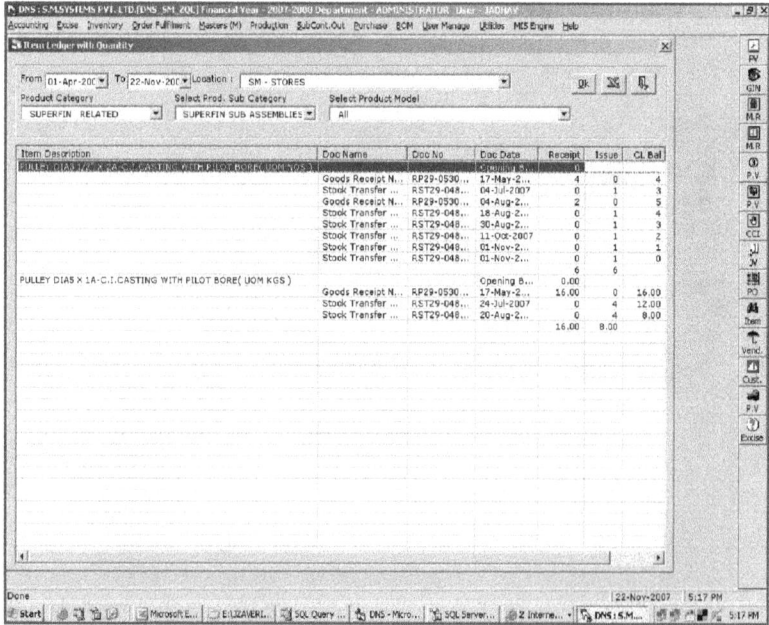

Fig. 5.43: The screen shot shows typical item ledger with quantity

In the previous screen shot, user can select from date and to date to specify period of the report. User can also select inventory location for which the item ledger is required. Filter is used to select specific item or specific category of items.

(iii) Issues and Challenges faced by this medium size Manufacturing Enterprise
1. Smoother and faster process flow.
2. Efficient distribution of information.
3. Decentralisation of task and decision.
4. Increased transparency and better control.
5. Protection/ Security of data.
6. Wastage, scrap, rejection.
7. Integration of all departments.
8. Cost control.
9. Productivity through elimination of duplication.
10. Inventory of raw materials.
11. Delivery performance.
12. Business Process Reengineering (change management).
13. Training to shop floor users.
14. Government compliance

Purchase Module: This is the Purchase Voucher created under ERP.

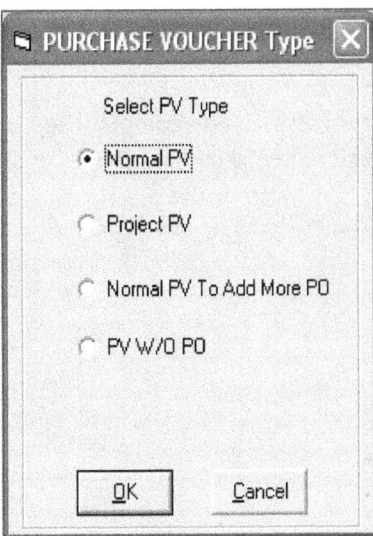

Fig. 5.44: Purchase Voucher Menu

Above screen shot shows radio buttons that user can select the type of purchase voucher: Normal PV, Project PV, Normal PV to add more Purchase Orders or Purchase voucher without Purchase order.

To integrate various processes and provide timely information for decision making the details of every purchase were made comprehensive. The data entry screen where user can select types of purchase order is shown below.

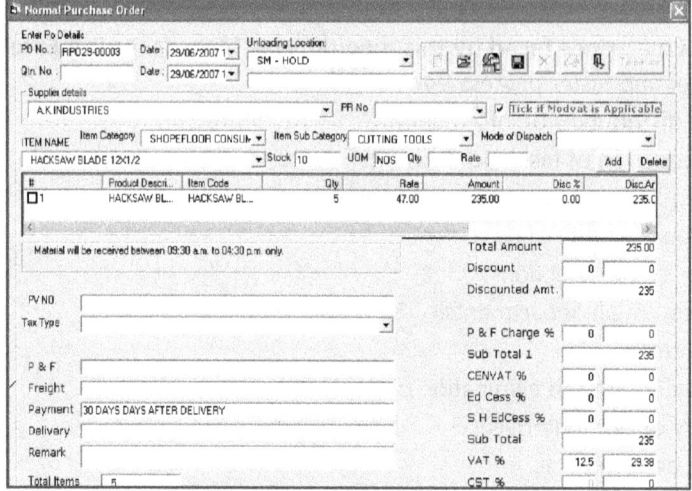

Fig. 5.45: Purchase Order Data Entry Screen

The PO number and PO date is automatically generated by ERP. User will select the supplier from the dropdown, the item and enter quantity to order. Finally the save button will commit this transaction.

(iv) Supply Chain Management

The entire supply chain processes were computerised based on various filters. This assisted in proper Material Requirement Planning (MRP). A screen shot of MRP for Just in Time (JIT) inventory management is given below.

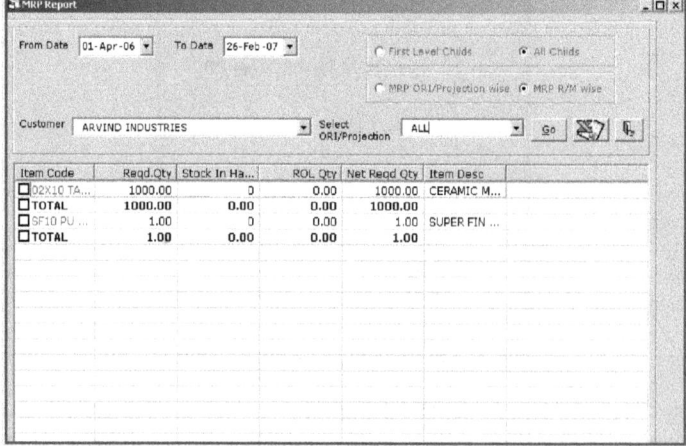

Fig. 5.46: Material Requirement Planning Report

Above screen shot shows the MRP (material requirement planning) report. User can select the period and name of customer from the dropdown, to get the required stock quantity, stock in hand, reorder quantity, net required quantity of the items.

Above figure shows the Material Requirement Planning (MRP) report for Just-in-Time (JIT) inventory management.

Inventory of raw material and bought out items, WIP (Work in Progress) inventory and Finished Goods is also created.

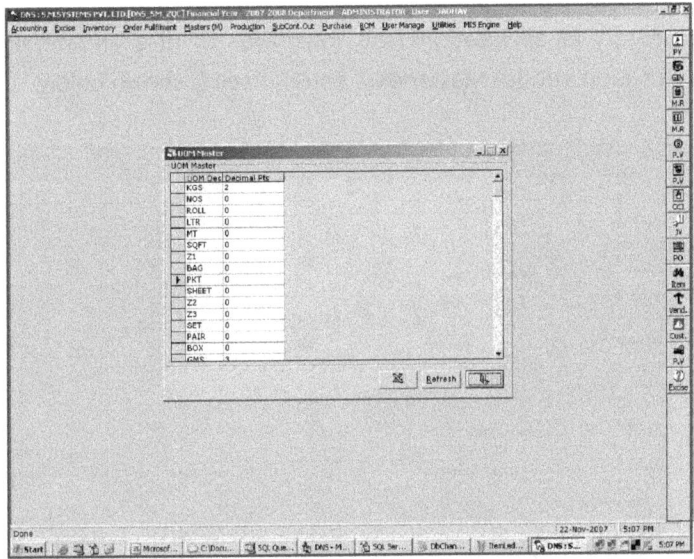

Fig. 5.47: A screen shot showing the UOM or the unit of measurement master

User can define level of accuracy by entering the decimal point for each UOM. For example, user wants to measure kilogram with two decimal accuracy. This is useful when in some cases high accuracy level is required, say in case of items like gold, user may need four decimal level of accuracy. E.g. 0.0005 gram.

This inventory included the following items:

A. Mechanical items
1. Nut, Plate
2. Paint
3. Pipe, Rod
4. Rivet, Screw ,Washer
5. Section
6. Sheet
7. Spring

B. Electrical items
1. Indicator, Relay
2. Insulation Material
3. Junction Box
4. Lighting Lamps
5. Meter, Motor
6. Panel Meter, Lug

The entire inventory at all locations was integrated to give an overall picture to the decision makers. A typical Vendor Master data entry screen is shown below.

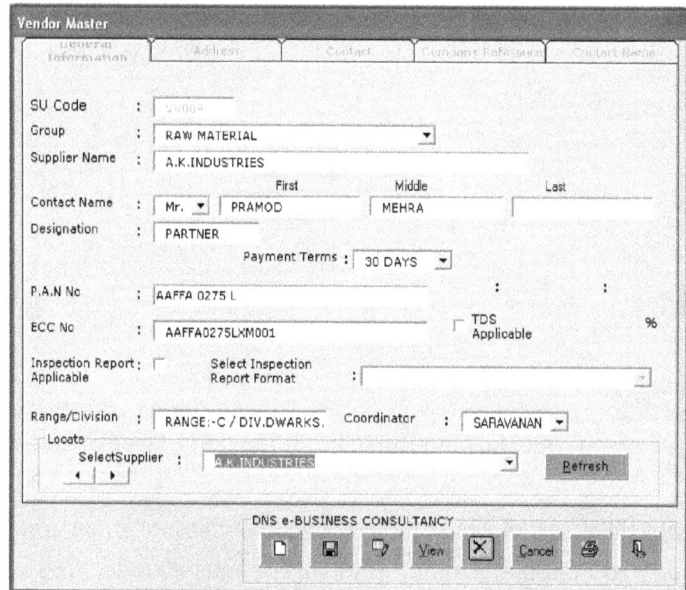

Fig. 5.48: Vendor Master Data Entry Screen

Above screen shot is used to create the new vendor information or update existing information, such as name of supplier, contact person's name, range/ division related to excise department, payment terms. Note that there are number of tabs to enter more information pertaining to address, contact details, etc.

(v) Sub Location Master ONLINE

Example

A Sub-contractor is also defined as inventory location. This is because some stocks were to be sent for processing to the third-party as shown in the figure below:

LocationCode	subLocationDesc	ServerDesc	Company
SM	STORES	HARI	S.M.SYSTEMS
SM	SHOP FLOOR	HARI	S.M.SYSTEMS
SM	FG	HARI	S.M.SYSTEMS
SM	REJECTION	HARI	S.M.SYSTEMS
SM	HOLD	HARI	S.M.SYSTEMS
THIRD PARTY	ROCKWELL HEAT	HARI	S.M.SYSTEMS
THIRD PARTY	SPECIALITY URE	HARI	S.M.SYSTEMS
THIRD PARTY	EMKAY RUBBER V	HARI	S.M.SYSTEMS
THIRD PARTY	RAJINDRA ENGIN	HARI	S.M.SYSTEMS
LABOUR BILL	OM FABRICATOR	HARI	S.M.SYSTEMS
LABOUR BILL	S.N.ENGINEERIN(	HARI	S.M.SYSTEMS
LABOUR BILL	SHRI AYYAPPA E	HARI	S.M.SYSTEMS
LABOUR BILL	RAJINDRA MECH	HARI	S.M.SYSTEMS

Fig. 5.49: Sub-location master

Note that the third party means the sub-contractor location is also considered as a sub-location, where the stock is found.

(vi) ERP has helped this company in the following way

The manufacturing industries have witnessed significant changes that include process improvements, environmental conscious manufacturing, reducing time to manufacture and constant need to launch new products with innovation.

Due to these dynamics the sector has been an early adapter of ERP, such as this company making special purpose machines with standard configuration, yet customised as per customer specific requirements.

ERP has been able to get many projects in these domains due to combination of affordable price, delivery, and well defined implementation methodology.

ERP Modules implemented in the SPS Systems Pvt. Ltd., Mumbai, India which is a special purpose machines manufacturer are listed below for example.

1. Security module
2. Accounts module –
   (i) VAT / Sales Tax module
   (ii) Excise module

3. Inventory Management module
   (i) Purchase and Pre-purchase module
   (ii) MRP - Material Requirement Planning module / Supply Chain Management (SCM)
4. ISO 9000 – Quality check module
5. BOM – Bill of Materials module
6. Production module (Assembly Production and Process Production) CRM module (Customer relationship management) and pre-sales module.
7. Sub-contractor OUT – outsourcing
8. Cost sheet module – preparing estimate
9. Order Fulfilment module – Sales Accounting - (Shipping)

Fig. 5.50: Special Purpose Machine

Finished Goods is a Special Purpose Machine as shown in above figure.

(vii) Key Benefits

The key benefits that could be accrued from introduction of ERP are as follows:
1. ERP Software provided a fully integrated Business Management.
2. It provided solutions for 'machine' manufacturing.
3. It ensured automated work flow and document flow.
4. It assisted in bringing about an engineering change management in BOM.
5. Well-versed with excise procedures with reports like RG1, RG23, PLA as per government compliance. This facilitated government approvals
6. 'Project workbench' report gives project wise (sales order wise) details of each project. This assisted in efficient and educated management decisions.

The following article was published in a recent newspaper in India.

Infosys develops software for Japanese firms

IT bellwether Infosys has developed an enterprise resource planning (ERP) software solution that enabled its Japanese clients to set up their IT infrastructure in India in eight weeks.

"The pre-packaged solution is tailor-made for the Indian market as it addresses issues such as local taxation and accounting," the company said in a statement here on Monday.

Based on the industry-standard, Microsoft platform for ERP functions, the 'India in a Box' solution supports the international accounting standards committee and complies with Indian GAAP (generally accepted accounting principles), facilitates supply chain management, monitor production, planning, processing and scheduling and keeps track of employees and customers.

"The all-in-one business solution has been customised for Japanese firms looking to grow their business in the complex Indian market place," the statement noted.

According to the company's Japan operations head V. Sriram, the product will enable executives in Tokyo to manage sales and production of their Indian operations on a daily basis without a hitch.

"The software solution improves real time decision-making and governance," Sriram asserted.

The global software major has set up its Japan operations in 1997 with development centres in Tokyo and Nagoya.

[**Source:** *DNS Newspaper site dnaindia.com dated 19 November 2012*]

Practice Questions

1. List points to prevent ERP implementation failure.
2. Give guidelines for a successful ERP Project implementation.
3. Which areas are ignored during ERP implementation?
4. Besides ERP software what are the other things required for a successful ERP use?

Activity

1. Visit two medium or large Manufacturing Company (Factory) that you know.
   (a) Find out if Server is installed or not, find out what kind of ERP they are using, find out how much time it took to implement ERP, and a make a note and share with the class.
2.  Additional online study material:
   (a) Study PowerPoint presentations about ERP published on site http://www.slideshare.net/jzaveri
   (b) Click on Follow button to get automatic updates about ERP.

gramcontent.com/pod-product-compliance
g Source LLC
burg PA
1301170426
300017B/2870